Networking Fundamentals Using Novell NetWare® (4.11)

Ann Beheler

Richland College

Prentice Hall

Upper Saddle River, New Jersey   Columbus, Ohio

Library of Congress Cataloging-in-Publication Data

Beheler, Ann.
    Networking fundamentals using Novell NetWare® (4.11) / Ann Beheler.
      p.   cm.
    Includes index.
    ISBN 0-13-409806-4 (alk. paper)
    1. NetWare (Computer file)   2. Local area networks (Computer networks)   I. Title.
TK5105.8.N65B446   1999
005.7'1369—dc21   98-29725
                                   CIP

Editor: Charles E. Stewart, Jr.
Production Editor: Alexandrina Benedicto Wolf
Design Coordinator: Karrie M. Converse
Cover photo: Photo Researchers, Inc.
Cover Designer: Rod Harris
Production Manager: Deidra M. Schwartz
Marketing Manager: Ben Leonard

This book was set in Arial by Carlisle Communications, Ltd. and was printed and bound by The Banta Company. The cover was printed by Phoenix Color Corp.

©1999 by Prentice-Hall, Inc.
Simon & Schuster/A Viacom Company
Upper Saddle River, New Jersey 07458

All rights reserved. No part of this book may be reproduced, in any form or by any means, without permission in writing from the publisher.

Printed in the United States of America

10 9 8 7 6 5 4 3 2 1

ISBN: 0-13-409806-4

Prentice-Hall International (UK) Limited, *London*
Prentice-Hall of Australia Pty. Limited, *Sydney*
Prentice-Hall of Canada, Inc., *Toronto*
Prentice-Hall Hispanoamericana, S. A., *Mexico*
Prentice-Hall of India Private Limited, *New Delhi*
Prentice-Hall of Japan, Inc., *Tokyo*
Simon & Schuster Asia Pte. Ltd., *Singapore*
Editora Prentice-Hall do Brasil, Ltda., *Rio de Janeiro*

Preface

Since the introduction of the personal computer in the early 1980s, data communication and computer networking usage have grown exponentially. Today's computer information sciences students must have a solid understanding of data communications and networking to form a framework for any specialized study that they may pursue. Communications is no longer just voice; computers and their users no longer operate singly. Truly, the world is connected via a world-wide network. This course forms the foundation in networking.

The range of topics in the field of data communications and networking is very broad. The novice student can easily get lost. The purpose of this book is to present a survey of networking fundamentals, utilizing Novell NetWare 4.11 as a representative system.

Objectives of the Text

1. To teach the basic terminology of networking.
2. To explain the characteristics of NetWare 4.11.
3. To explain the administrative utilities of NetWare 4.11.
4. To describe file system and NDS trustee assignments and their ramifications in NetWare 4.11.
5. To explore various types of clients used with NetWare 4.11, including DOS and Windows 95.
6. To show the student how to install and operate both the client and server portions of NetWare 4.11.
7. To present a troubleshooting methodology and give students practice scenarios to diagnose.

Organization of the Text

The book consists of nine chapters which provide the essential terminology and concepts for an introductory course in computer networking. It presents a discussion of Novell NetWare 4.11 topics, ranging from overview, through user creation, login script creation, printing, file system rights, Novell Directory Services rights, and troubleshooting.

The book assumes a basic level of computer literacy usually attained in a college-level introduction to computer science course or an equivalent continuing education course. The book provides the foundation for both concepts and terminology of networking needed to pursue advanced networking courses.

Exercises at the end of each chapter focus on helping the students grasp the concepts presented in the chapter. Optional projects are also provided to help the student further solidify and apply his or her knowledge. It is highly recommended that every attempt be made to complete all or most of the projects to provide a stronger learning experience for the student.

The appendix contains information on how to obtain products and technical support information from a variety of computer-related vendors, and a glossary of commonly used terms.

Supplements

For the instructor, there is a comprehensive instructor's guide that includes;

1. Suggestions on how to organize the course, depending on the desired emphasis and focus.
2. Answers to all end of chapter questions.
3. Solutions to projects.
4. Transparency masters of the art in the book.
5. Test bank of questions for use in quizzes and examinations.

Acknowledgments

I am indebted to my students and fellow colleagues for their input during the creation of this book. I also appreciate the contributions of each of the following reviewers: Alan Rowland, Ivy State Technical College, Indianapolis, Indiana; Mike Awaad and William Lin, DeVry Institute, North Brunswick, New Jersey; Renee Curtis, Computer Learning Center, Philadelphia, Pennsylvania; and Carl Beheler, Satellite Communications Engineer, Rockwell International, Richardson, Texas.

I am also indebted to my family for their support and encouragement. Without their willingness to be without Mom during this project, this book would never have been completed.

Finally, I would like to thank all the people at Prentice Hall who are really the people who made this book happen. Specifically, I would personally like to thank Charles Stewart, my editor and Kim Yehle, his assistant, for their patience and support throughout the development of this book.

To my mother, Ardath Ferry, whose goals for me did not really include my having a career, but who did her best to support me in my endeavors.

Contents

Chapter 1. Introduction to Novell NetWare 4 1
Objectives 1
Key Terms 1
Introduction 2
Overview of NetWare 3
    Novell Client Software 4
    IPX.COM and NETX.COM 5
    Open Data-Link Interface 5
    NetWare DOS Requester 6
    Client 32 7
The User Environment 7
    Network Volumes and Network Drives 7
        DOS Directories 8
        Drive Mappings 9
        Paths and Search Drives 10
        File System Trustee Rights 11
        Novell Directory Services Trustee Rights 13
Novell Network Example 14
Summary 16
Questions 18
Project 19

Chapter 2. NetWare 4 Installation 21
Objectives 21
Key Terms 21
Introduction 22
    Installing NetWare 4 on the File Server 22
        Installation Preparation 23
        Hardware Required 23
        Software Required 23
4.11 Installation 24
    Installation Overview 24
    Creating the Bootable DOS partition 24
    Background Information Needed Before Proceeding
       with Server Installation 25
        File Server Name 26
        IPX Internal Network Number 26
        External Network Number 26
        SERVER.EXE 26
        AUTOEXEC.BAT 26
        STARTUP.NCF 27
        AUTOEXEC.NCF 27
        Disk Drivers 27

LAN Drivers	28
Interrupt Number	28
Memory Address	28
Port Address	28
Choices for Server Installation	28
Hands-On Simple Installation	29
Creating Workstation Installation Diskette Sets for NetWare 4.11 Clients	30
Installing the Workstation Boot Disk Using NetWare DOS Requester	38
Introduction to the NetWare DOS Requester	38
Installing the NetWare DOS Requester	38
Testing the New Boot Process	39
Installing Client32	40
Installing the Client 32 for DOS/Windows 3.1	40
Testing the New Boot Process with Client 32 for Windows 3.1	41
Installing the Client 32 for Windows 95	42
Testing the New Boot Process with Client 32 for Windows 95	45
Summary	45
Questions	45
Project	46

Chapter 3. Novell Directory Services 49

Objectives	49
Key Terms	49
Introduction	50
Overview of NDS	50
NDS Architecture Overview	51
(ROOT)	52
Container Objects	52
Country Object	52
Organization	53
Organizational Unit	53
Leaf Objects	53
Putting the Objects Together	53
Naming Conventions	54
Context	54
Current Context	55
Common Name	56
Distinguished Name	56
Relative Distinguished Name	56
Utilities for Managing and Manipulating NDS	58
NetWare Administrator	59
Hands-On Creating an Icon for NetWare Administrator in Windows 3.1	59
Hands-On Creating an Icon for NetWare Administrator on the Desktop in Win95	60
Summary	60
Questions	61
Project	62

Chapter 4. Creating the User Account, Mappings, and Login Scripts 65
Objectives 65
Key Terms 65
Introduction 66
NetWare Administrator 66
   Introduction 68
     Creation of a User Account 68
       Identification 70
       Environment 70
       Login Restrictions 73
       Password Restrictions 73
       Login Tiime Restrictions 73
       Network Address Restrictions 75
       Print Job Configuration 75
       Login Script 75
       Intruder Lockout 77
       Rights to Files and Directories 77
       Group Membership 77
       Security Equal To 77
       Postal Address 79
       Login Scripts 79
Login Scripts 79
   Container Login Script 79
   Profile Login Script 80
   User Login Script 81
   Default Login Script 81
   Commands 82
Hands-on NetWare 93
   Preparing the Network for Operation 94
   Logging In 94
   Starting the NetWare Administrator Utility 95
   Creating a User 95
   Making the New User Admin Equivalent 97
   Logging in as the Admin Equivalent New User and Creating Another User . . .99
   Creating a User Login Script for USERXXX 101
Summary 105
Questions 105
Projects 107

Chapter 5. File System Security and Organization 109
Objectives 109
Key Terms 109
Introduction 109
Levels of Security 110
   Passwords 110
   Allowing the User to Change the Password .111
   Minimum Password Length 112

    Force Periodic Password Changes 112
  Directory and File Trustee Rights 112
    Directory Inherited Rights Filter 115
    File Attributes 117
    Directory Attributes 118
  Organization 120
    Types of Users 120
      Groups 121
        Group Hierarchy 121
    Data Organization 121
    Types of Data 122
  Hands-on NetWare 124
    Levels of Security 124
    Passwords 124
      Changing the Password and Minimum Password Length 125
      Force Periodic Password Changes 126
    Trustee Rights 127
    Directory Attributes 131
    File Attributes 131
    Effective Rights 133
  Groups 137
  Summary 139
  Questions 140
  Projects 141

Chapter 6. Network Printing 145
Objectives 145
Key Terms 145
Introduction 146
Print Queue 146
Print Server 149
Printer 150
Tying the Print Queue, Print Server, and Printer Together 150
  Assigning the Printer to the Print Server 152
  Assigning a Print Queue to a Printer 152
  Configuring the Printer 153
  Checking the Print Queue Assignments 157
  Print Queue Operators and Users 157
  Print Queue Jobs 160
  Print Server Operators and Users 162
  Activating the Print Server 163
  Redirecting Print Output to a Print Queue 164
    Redirecting Print Output Using the CAPTURE command 164
Hands-on NetWare 168
  Configuring the Print Server and Print Queue 168
  Running PSERVER 170
  Sending Output to the Print Server 171

Summary 172
Questions 173
Projects 173

Chapter 7. NDS Security 175
Objectives 175
Key Terms 175
Introduction 175
NDS Object and Property Rights 176
  A Broad Overview of NDS Trustee Rights 176
  NDS Object Rights 177
  NDS Property Rights 177
  Default NDS Object and Property Trustee Assignments 178
  Inheritance and Effective Rights 180
  Considerations for Proper Assignment of NDS Object and Property Rights .. 182
    (PUBLIC) 182
    Container Rights 182
    Groups 182
    Organizational Role Rights 183
    Security Equivalence 184
    Pitfalls to Avoid 184
Hands-On NetWare 185
  Assigning Object Rights 185
  Exercising the NDS Rights Assigned 189
  Giving USERXXX File System Rights 190
  Reattempt the Hands-On Activity: Exercising NDS Object Rights Assigned .. 191
  Setting an Inherited Rights Filter and Determining Its Effect .. 195
Summary 197
Questions 197
Projects 199

Chapter 8. Backing Up NetWare 4.11 201
Objectives 201
Key Terms 201
Introduction 201
Why Take the Time To Perform Backups 202
Common Backup Methodologies 202
The Backup Tape Archival Approach 204
SBACKUP 206
Practical Considerations for Backups and Restores 207
Backup Responsibility 207
How to Determine Whether or Not a Backup Is Good 207
What to Back Up 208
Summary 208
Questions 209
Projects 209

Chapter 9. Troubleshooting Methodology and Tidbits 211
Objectives 211
Key Terms 211
Introduction 211
A Solid Troubleshooting Model 212
   Begin to Document the Problem 213
   Verify That the Problem Exists 214
   Gather Information About the Problem 215
   Formulate and Prioritize Possible Solutions 216
   Apply Possible "Quick Fixes" 216
   Apply Other Possible Solutions 216
   Resolve and Document the Problem 217
Troubleshooting Resources 217
   Hardware and Software Documentation 217
   NetWire on Novell's Internet Site 218
   Novell Support Connection 218
   Other Troubleshooting Resources 219
Troubleshooting Scenarios 219
Hands-On with NetWare 222
Summary 223
Questions 224
Projects 224

Appendix. Where to Get Product Information and Technical Support 229
Glossary 239
Index 251

Networking Fundamentals Using Novell NetWare® (4.11)

1
Introduction to Novell NetWare 4

Objectives

After completing this chapter you will

1. Understand the history of Novell NetWare and the important features of NetWare 4.
2. Understand the basic hardware components required to install NetWare 4.
3. Obtain an overview of the software components of NetWare 4.
4. Understand the concepts of volumes and drive mappings.
5. Understand the concept of trustee and trustee rights for both the file system and Novell Directory Services.

Key Terms

Novell NetWare

Server Computer

Client Computer

Network Interface Card

Volume

Drive Mapping

Search Drive

Trustee

File System Rights

Novell Directory Services Rights

Introduction

This chapter introduces a network operating system known as **Novell NetWare** and begins to explain the importance of Novell NetWare version 4, specifically version 4.11. It will introduce concepts that will be more thoroughly discussed in later chapters.

Originally designed for computers running the CP/M operating system, NetWare was quickly adapted by Novell for use on the IBM PC when the PC was introduced in the early 1980s. This adaptation was a key strategic move that helps account for the large market share currently enjoyed by Novell in the local area network arena.

NetWare's software and hardware components are:

1. Software:

    a. Novell NetWare 4.11 Operating System running on shared computers called **servers.**

    b. The Novell NetWare client software that runs on the **client computer** which is alternately referred to as a node or workstation.

    c. The software, known as drivers, that controls the network card for both the server and the client workstation and the hard disk of the file server.

2. Hardware

    a. 386 or faster Intel-based PC with at least 20 MB RAM and at least 115 MB of hard disk space to hold the DOS partition (15 MB) and for the SYS volume (100 MB minimum) for the server.

    b. 386 or faster workstation.

    c. Network interface card in all nodes and in the file server.

    d. Cable (and hubs if needed) to connect these network interface cards.

The NetWare 4.11 Operating System is installed on the servers. The servers under NetWare 4.11 are connected by Novell Directory Services (NDS), which allows multiple servers to be linked in an enterprise network. NetWare 4.11 allows the servers to act as "traffic cops" which manage access by clients to the files stored on the servers' hard disks and the printers controlled by the servers.

The NetWare client software, called the NetWare DOS Requester or Client 32, allows the user to treat the servers as though they were disk drives attached to the user's client computer. Ordinary activities on the client computer can access disk drives on the servers just as though the servers' disks were on the local client computer. Additionally, the data and programs on the servers can be protected by assigning the proper file system trustee rights to users on the network. Client software is introduced later in this chapter, and its installation is discussed in Chapter 9. File system trustee assignments are discussed in Chapter 12, and Novell Directory Services trustee assignments are discussed in Chapter 14.

Overview of NetWare

Little remains constant in the world of networking. Network operating systems, hardware components, and topologies have changed rapidly over the last several years to keep pace with advancing technology and consumer demand. Novell, Inc. has performed better than most at maintaining a salable product and a share of the market. Novell's original network product, however, did not do well. The system was a file server and network operating system software, with serial cables to connect to client computers running the CP/M operating system. The product line was expanded somewhat, but the company went bankrupt. Novell's reorganization, however, took place at an opportune point in history. The introduction of the IBM PC gave Novell an entirely new market. Novell's operating system was eventually rewritten to allow the IBM PC to be used as both the file server and the client. Novell has introduced many software and hardware products since then. It now controls the largest single share of the local area networking market with Novell NetWare. "NetWare" refers to all of Novell's network operating system products. The term IntranetWare refers to Novell's latest release of NetWare, version 4.11, bundled with the Novell Web Server, the FTP Server, the Multi Protocol Router, and the IPX/IP gateway products.

Novell NetWare was originally designed around hardware using a star topology to communicate with a single file server. The file server simply allowed client computers to store and share files. This structure has influenced all of Novell's products to date although NetWare 4.11 is not strictly server-centric. NetWare has become largely hardware independent, allowing many topologies and file servers to be used simultaneously, but communication on the network is still handled almost entirely through a primary file server. Two client computers may be connected directly to each other by a network cable, but for a file to be transferred from one to the other, that file must first be sent to a file server, then to the target client computer. Of course, the network provides many other functions, but they are generally centered around the idea of a client computer connected to one or more file servers.

NetWare 4, as an enterprise network operating system, goes beyond the strictly server-centric model. It can represent a whole company in a single location or a whole global company with multiple file servers and thousands of users. This concept is supported by Novell Directory Services, a topic which will be discussed in Chapter 10. However, even though NetWare 4 has a more global focus, many operations are still server-centric. These functions will be pointed out when we come to them in later chapters.

Novell Client Software

By far, the most common client on a Novell network is an IBM PC or PC-compatible computer running DOS or Windows 95. Macintosh, OS/2, and Windows NT clients are also now used, but their numbers are not yet large. DOS or Windows 95 handles all of the low-level functions of the computer such as reading and writing to the disk drives, loading and executing application programs, and handling input from the keyboard. When running an application program such as a word processor, DOS or Windows 95 allocates memory, reads the program from the disk drive and then allows the program to begin. The application program can then use the resources of the computer through what are known as DOS or Windows 95 function calls.

For instance, there are many different types of printers and dozens of companies manufacturing them. To the application program, this is irrelevant. It will simply make a DOS or Windows 95 function call to write data to the printer, and DOS or Windows 95 will handle the output to the device. Since even DOS can't "know" the details of every peripheral device one might attach to a computer, including a network, programs known as drivers are often used to help the local operating system provide a common environment for application programs to work in.

Attaching a Novell network to a computer is a good example of this. It essentially involves two components: the **network interface card** or NIC and the network driver programs. Novell offers a variety of programs that serve as the drivers depending on the configuration of the workstation. The NIC is the hardware that is physically connected to the network, much as a telephone is the piece of hardware that is physically connected to the telephone network. It generates the proper electrical signal to communicate on the particular type of network being used. It may use pulses of light or radio waves to send signals across the network. The network drivers used on a particular workstation must consist of an appropriate combination of the programs needed to perform three functions: provide a hardware dependent driver for the network card, provide the appropriate communications protocol to be used on the network, and provide an interface for the user.

IPX.COM and NETX.COM

Historically, Novell's long-used system of providing the hardware-dependent driver and the communications protocol was to use a program called IPX.COM. It was generated at the time NetWare was installed because it is actually built out of two components. One component is the hardware-dependent NIC driver and the other is the IPX protocol driver. (IPX stands for Internetwork Packet eXchange.) The resulting IPX.COM program was then unique to the type of NIC it ran on.

IPX.COM together with NET#.COM formed an early version of the NetWare client shell program which allowed the client to connect to a server. Note that the # in NET# represents the version of DOS running on the client workstation when the NET# is executed. NET# was later replaced by NETX which runs with all versions of DOS. This basic NetWare shell supported only one communications protocol, IPX.

Open Data-Link Interface

Later, Novell changed the focus of its efforts to a standard called Open Data-Link Interface. The purpose was to create client software that would support multiple communications protocols, such as IPX and TCPIP, running simultaneously over the same network interface card. ODI also provided a modular approach to client software creation. The two functions of the NIC driver and IPX protocol driver were spread out over three programs:

LSL.COM

MLID (LAN driver)

IPXODI

The first program is called LSL.COM (LSL stands for Link Support Layer). It allows multiple communications protocols, which are loaded later, to be run on the same NIC.

The second program is strictly an ODI-compliant NIC driver program called the Multiple Link Interface Driver (MLID) and is given a name that indicates which brand of NIC it supports. Intel EtherExpress 16 cards, for instance, use a program called EXP16ODI.COM. A network card called the SMC EtherCard PLUS Elite10T/A uses a program called SMCPLUS.COM. These driver programs are packaged with the NIC, and Novell also provides them on their distribution media for major brands of network interface cards.

The third program is the communications protocol driver, IPXODI.COM. As its name indicates, it is an Internetwork Packet Exchange protocol driver that conforms to the Open Data-Link Interface standard and is specific to Novell. Other communications protocols such as TCPIP may also be loaded so that a given workstation can communicate simultaneously with a TCPIP network and with a Novell IPX network.

Note that LSL, the MLID, and IPXODI do not have to be compiled together; they are complete programs on their own. They obtain the configuration parameters for the network interface card from a file called NET.CFG. NET.CFG will be discussed further in a later chapter.

Prior to the introduction of NetWare 3.12 and NetWare 4, the fourth function, that of a user interface, was provided by one of three different versions of essentially the same program: NETX.COM, XMSNETX.EXE, or EMSNETX.EXE. The three different versions of this program were needed to take advantage of different memory configurations of the workstation. NETX.COM uses conventional memory, XMSNETX.EXE uses extended memory, and EMSNETX.EXE uses expanded memory. The letter "X" appears before the extension (.EXE or .COM) in each of these names to indicate that they can be used with any DOS version. Prior to the release of DOS version 5.0, Novell supplied the rather cumbersome collection of NET2, NET3, NET4, XMSNET2, XMSNET3, XMSNET4, EMSNET2, EMSNET3, and EMSNET4 for use with DOS 2.x, DOS 3.x, and DOS 4.x respectively. Using the ODI approach for IPX, one must merely include the following in one's AUTOEXEC.BAT:

    LSL

    NIC driver such as SMCPLUS

    IPXODI

    NETX (or XMSNETX or EMSNETX)

NetWare DOS Requester

Although the NETX version of workstation software will still allow the user to connect to a NetWare 3.12 network, NetWare 3.12 and NetWare version 4.0 and later have provided a new version of workstation software called the NetWare DOS Requester. The NetWare DOS Requester version of workstation software is ODI-compliant and still requires the use of LSL, the NIC driver, and IPXODI. However, NETX has been replaced with the workstation VLM (Virtual Loadable Module) manager which coexists with DOS and uses DOS tables. VLMs will be addressed further in Chapter 2.

Client 32

With NetWare 4.11 came an even newer and more efficient type of client software setup called Client 32. Client 32 together with the network drivers make up the NetWare client software which provides a complete interface between DOS/Windows 3.1, Windows 95, or Windows NT and NetWare. The NetWare client software provides an interface that allows users to interact with the computer in a transparent or natural manner. This shields users from the complex low-level operations of the computer and the network. Therefore, the NetWare client software protects the user from having to know how to interact directly with the network.

The User Environment

Network Volumes and Network Drives

The highest level in the NetWare directory structure is the NetWare **volume**. All file servers must have a volume called SYS:, and a NetWare file server may have a total of up to 64 volumes. A single NetWare file server can support up to 32 physical disk drives and 32 TB (terabytes, or trillion bytes) of physical hard disk space. Volumes may span physical disk drives, or they may divide a physical disk drive. In either case, volumes are specified during installation.

Volumes are divided into directories. The NetWare client software allows DOS or Windows 95 and the user to treat the file server as a disk drive attached to the client computer. DOS assigns a drive letter to each of the disk drives physically attached to the computer. In general, A and B designate floppy disk drives while C, D, and E usually represent hard disk drives local to the user. On a typical system, with two floppy disk drives and a hard disk drive, DOS would assign A, B, and C to the those disk drives.

When the NetWare client software programs are loaded, another drive letter is made available to the user. Typically, F is used to designate the first network drive and is often used to designate the SYS: volume. In this textbook, all references to the F: drive assume that F designates the entire SYS: volume. Ordinary DOS commands like DIR (which displays a list of the files on the disk) and CHDIR (which moves access to a different area of the disk) can be used on the network drive F. In addition, application programs can make ordinary DOS function calls to carry out their functions on the network drive as if it were a hard disk attached to the computer. The network drive is the hard disk on the file server, the same hard disk accessed by every other user on the network. Figure 1-1 shows three computers, a file server and two client computers. The first client has local disk drives A, B, and C. It also has access to drive F, which is actually on the file server. The second client has only one local disk drive, but can also access drive F.

DOS Directories

In DOS you can create directories to organize the data on a disk. A directory contains files grouped together on the disk. Every disk has what is called the root directory even though it is not referred to as "root" in any DOS command. Since a "\" (a backslash) is used to separate directory names, a backslash with no name is considered the root directory.

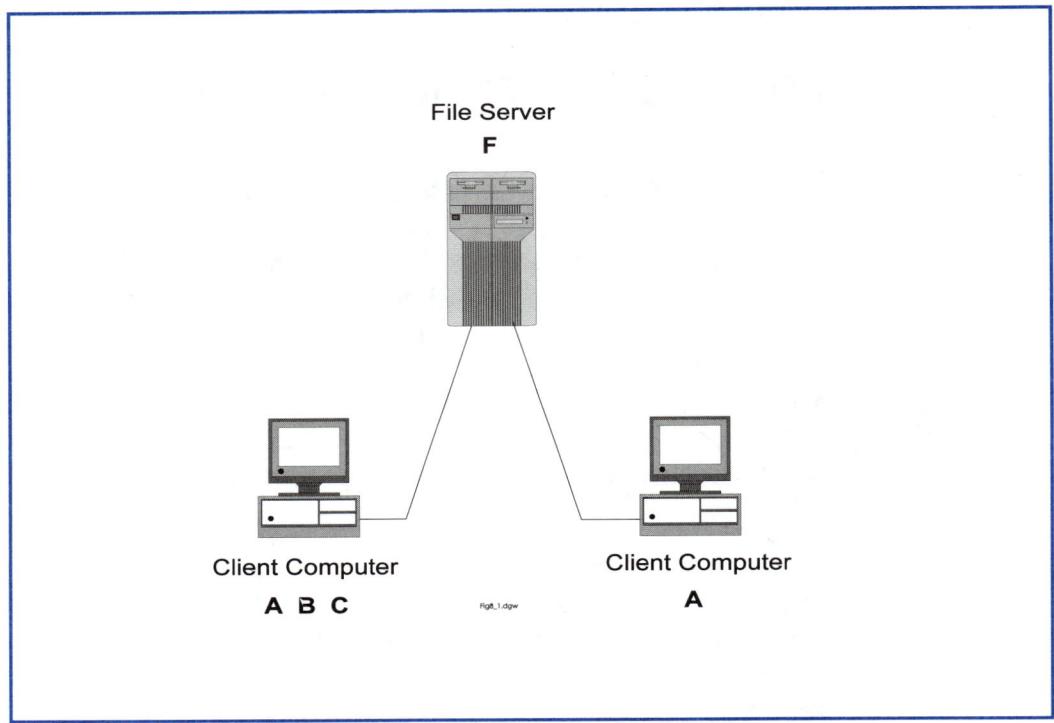

Figure 1-1. Client computers networked to a server.

Figure 1-2 shows how a hard disk might be organized. The files in the root directory could be listed by typing the DIR command. The DIR command lists the files in the current directory. In this case DIR C: would list the files COMMAND.COM, LSL.COM, SMCPLUS.COM, IPXODI.COM, VLM.EXE and a directory called WORD. The files in the directory WORD could be displayed by typing DIR C:\WORD and pressing the ENTER key. WORD.EXE and LETTER.DOC would be listed. Another way to view the list of files in the WORD directory would be to use the CHDIR command. CHDIR stands for change directory and can be abbreviated further by using only CD. If you were to type CD C:\WORD, the current directory would be changed to the WORD directory and DIR C: would list the files WORD.EXE and LETTER.DOC. In this way the drive letter C moves around the disk drive pointing to

Introduction to Novell Netware 4

different areas. Just as the root directory contains a directory called WORD, the WORD directory could contain another directory and so on. The same commands can be used on the network drive F.

In Figure 1-1 the first computer could create a directory called F:\HISFILES by using the MKDIR command. MKDIR stands for make directory and can be abbreviated further by using only MD. By typing the command MD F:\HISFILES, the first user can create a place to store files on the file server. The user at the second computer could type MD F:\HERFILES. Now, if either computer user typed DIR F:, both directory names would be listed.

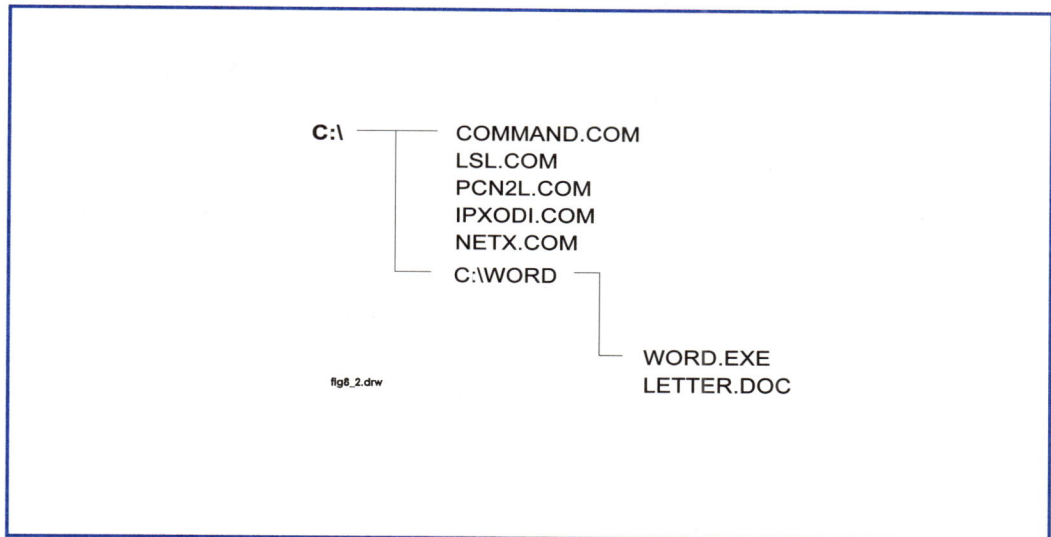

Figure 1-2. Possible hard disk organization.

Drive Mappings

With directories containing directories and every user on the network creating directories, the directory structure can become quite complex. Suppose a user on the network needed quick and easy access to files in both the F:\HISFILES directory and the F:\HERFILES directory. Rather than constantly using the CHDIR command to move drive F to the other area, he could use the NetWare MAP command to create a drive letter for one of the directories. Figure 1-3 shows the result of the first user typing MAP G:=F:\HERFILES. This creates drive letter G, which points to the HERFILES directory on the same physical drive as F:\HISFILES. This arrangement does not affect the second user. **Drive mappings** pertain only to the client computer where the MAP command was issued. Each user still has access to the HERFILES directory through drive letter F. The first user simply has the choice of using drive letter F or drive letter G.

Paths and Search Drives

Drive mappings allow users to access data easily without worrying about the directory names. The DOS PATH statement allows the user to completely ignore the current directory when running programs. NetWare combines these functions in the **search drive**. Ordinarily, to execute a program, it must reside in the current directory or the full path must be used when referring to the program. The "path" is the complete directory name where the program resides. Referring to Figure 1-3, the first user may have a program in the HISFILES directory called WORD.EXE. If the current directory is F:\HERFILES, he would have to type F:\HISFILES\WORD to execute the WORD program. DOS provides a way to eliminate the need to precede a command with the directory location. The PATH command tells the computer where to look for a program if it can't be found in the current directory. If the first user types PATH F:\HISFILES he can use all the programs in the HISFILES directory without typing the entire path. He could simply type WORD and the computer would look in the current directory first, then look in the HISFILES directory and find, and then execute, the program. Multiple directories can be included in the PATH command to instruct the computer to search several areas for the program.

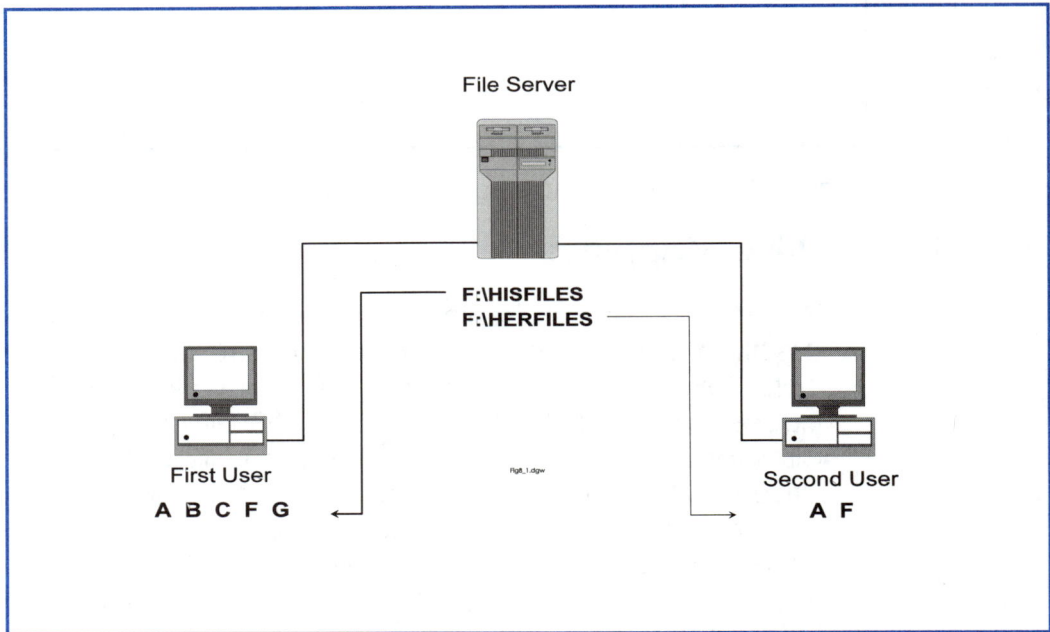

Figure 1-3. Paths for different network users.

The command PATH F:\HERFILES;F:\HISFILES would tell the computer to search the current directory first (as it always does), then the F:\HERFILES directory, and lastly the F:\HISFILES directory. A NetWare search drive is a drive mapping that is automatically inserted in the PATH. In Figure 1-4, the second user has typed the command MAP

S1:=F:\HISFILES. This NetWare command automatically chooses a drive letter starting from the end of the alphabet and maps it to the directory indicated. But the drive letter is more than the pointer used in the other drive letters, it is also a PATH to the directory. The second user can use drive letter Z as she would any other drive letter, but if she is using drive A, for instance, she needs only to type WORD to run the program contained in the F:\HISFILES directory. A user may have up to 16 search drives mapped at a given time.

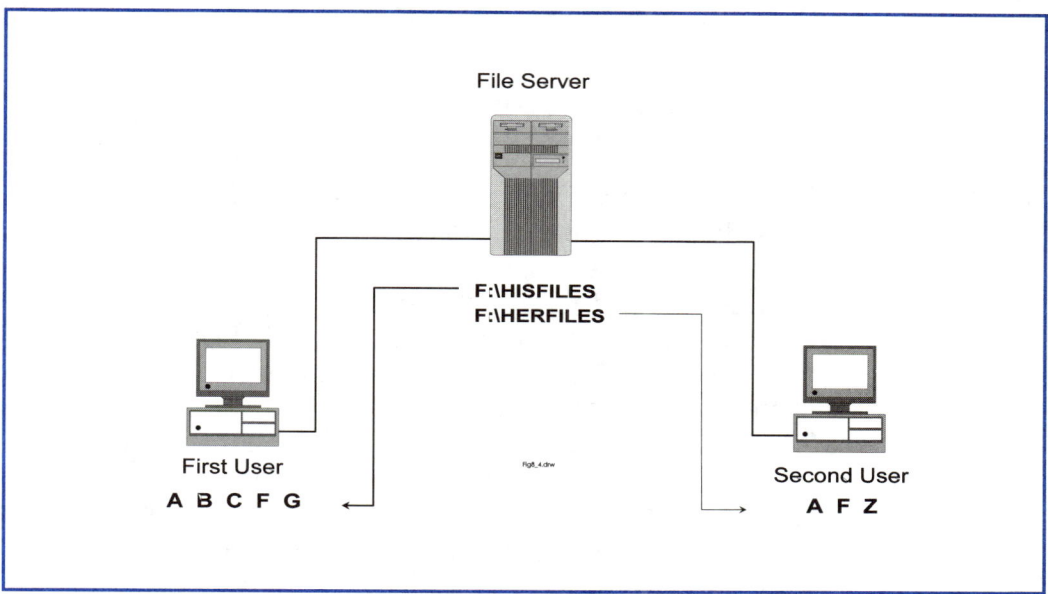

Figure 1-4. New paths of users after MAP command.

File System Trustee Rights

NetWare allows users to share data or to restrict access to data. **Trustee rights** allow access to specific directories on the file server. Without trustee rights to a certain directory, a user cannot access the data in that directory. Trustee rights are composed of several permissions a user may have to a specific directory or file. These permissions include Supervisory, Read, Write, Create, Erase, Modify, File Scan and Access Control. Each of these permissions may be granted or denied to a user. The meanings of these permissions or rights with respect to a directory are listed below:

1. **Supervisory**. The user has all other rights in the directory even if the directory does not allow certain rights.

2. **Read**. The user can open and read files in the directory. The File Scan right is usually also given with the Read right so that the user can see the directory's directory listing.

3. **Write**. The user can write to existing files in the directory.

4. **Create**. The user can create new files in the directory.

5. **Erase**. The user can erase files in the directory.

6. **Modify**. The user can modify the attribute flags of the files in the directory. The attribute of a file indicates what access all users have to a file.

7. **File Scan**. The user can see what files and subdirectories are listed in the directory.

8. **Access Control**. The user can grant rights to other users in the directory.

Figure 1-5 shows the trustee rights each of the users has to the file server using the first letter of the above listed rights. The first user has all rights except Supervisory and Access Control to the F:\HISFILES directory. He can use all of the files there any way he wants, but he cannot grant those rights to any other users. He only has Read and File Scan rights in the F:\HERFILES directory. This means he can only read from the data there, not change it or add to it. The second user has all rights to the F:\HERFILES directory. She could even grant additional rights in that directory to the first user. Her access to the F:\HISFILES directory is restricted to Create and File Scan. This allows her to create new files in the directory but not to read or change the files already there.

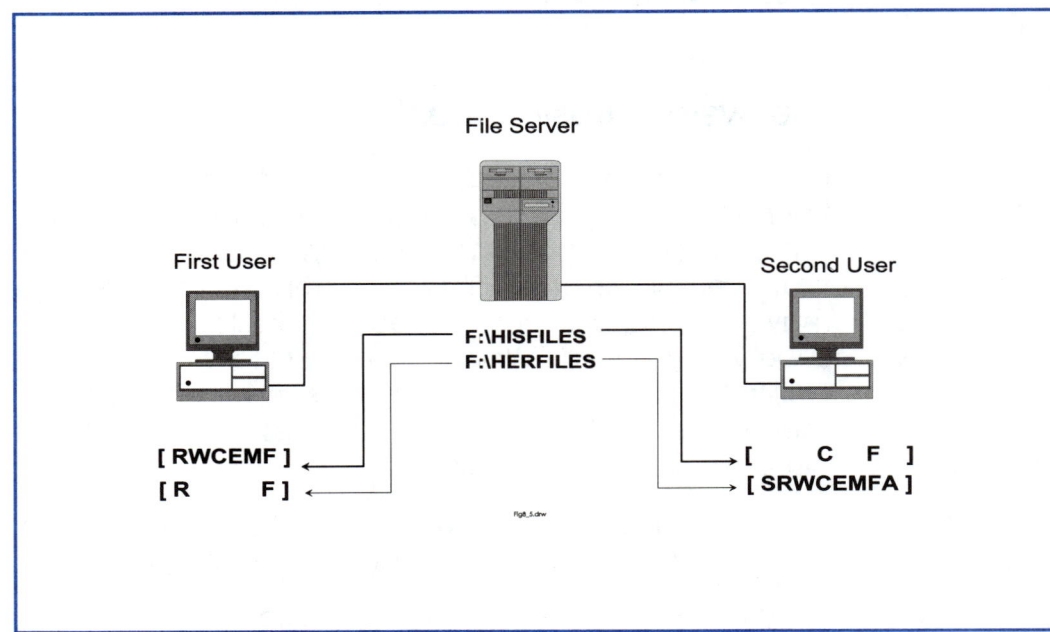

Figure 1-5. Trustee rights for users.

Novell Directory Services Trustee Rights

NetWare 4.11 allows a user to have a single login ID and obtain access to multiple servers and resources within the enterprise network system. Novell NetWare 4.11 utilizes Novell Directory Services to link servers, users, and resources such as printer and print queues into an enterprise network system. Access to resources in the enterprise network system is controlled by **NDS** object and property **rights**. Every resource in the enterprise network is an object. Users, printers, print queues, etc. are all objects, and each object has characteristics called properties. NDS object rights determine what level of access a user has to an NDS object, while NDS property rights control the ability to manipulate the specific properties or characteristics of an NDS object. The NDS object and property trustee rights are listed below and discussed further in Chapter 14.

NDS Object Trustee Rights

Supervisor: The trustee with this right has all object privileges and has access to all properties.

Browse: The trustee with this right has visibility of all objects in an NDS tree.

Create: The trustee with this right can create a new object beneath this object in the NDS tree. Only available on container objects.

Delete: The trustee with this right can delete this object from the NDS tree.

Rename: The trustee with this right can change the name of the object.

NDS Property Rights

Supervisor: The trustee with this right has all rights to the property.

Compare: The trustee with this right can compare a value of the property to any other value.

Read: The trustee with this right can read the values of the property, and this right implies that the trustee also has the compare right.

Write: The trustee with this right can add, change, or delete any of the values of the property, and this right implies that the trustee also has the Add Self property right.

Add Self: The trustee with this right can add or delete itself as a value of the property.

Chapter 1

Novell Network Example

As outlined before, a local area network links two or more computers and other peripherals together for the purpose of sharing data and equipment. A Novell NetWare 4.11-based local area network normally consists of multiple file servers linked together to form an enterprise network. Each of these file servers is considered to be a dedicated file server. In its simplest configuration, a NetWare 4.11 network can be composed of a single NetWare 4.11 file server. Novell networks can consist of one or more file servers, each with dozens of workstations, multiple shared printers, and other devices that can be attached to the file server or workstations. A small office network or a teaching laboratory can be established easily by creating one for the first time or by using existing networks.

The basic components of a LAN are as follows:

1. A file server (an IBM PC or compatible computer with a 80836 or faster processor) with at least 20 megabytes of RAM and a hard disk (with a minimum of 115 megabytes of free storage).

2. Network interface cards (NICs), at least one for the server and one for each of the workstations.

3. Transmission media (twisted pair, coaxial, or other type according to the type of NICs used).

4. Novell NetWare 4.11.

5. A printer should also be added to the network (preferably more than one).

If a Novell NetWare-based network is not already available, the process for installing one is outlined in Chapter 9. The following list provides a general review of the process.

1. Find a location for the server.

2. Find locations for the workstations.

3. Configure each NIC to contain a unique node address if not already preconfigured from the factory.

4. Install the NIC in each of the workstations and servers that will make up the nodes of the network.

5. Connect each node with the medium chosen.

6. Document all the hardware used as well as the specific configuration settings for all hardware that makes up the network.

7. Install the NetWare network operating system and use the data from item 6 to answer NetWare's requests.

8. Install workstation software.

Figure 1-6 displays a possible configuration for such a laboratory or work environment. If the network is used to provide instructions on the use of commands and network management, a program called LANSKOOL from Intel, Inc. may be a good addition to the system. This program allows the instructor to project his or her workstation screen on the screen of other users for the purpose of answering questions or for instructional needs.

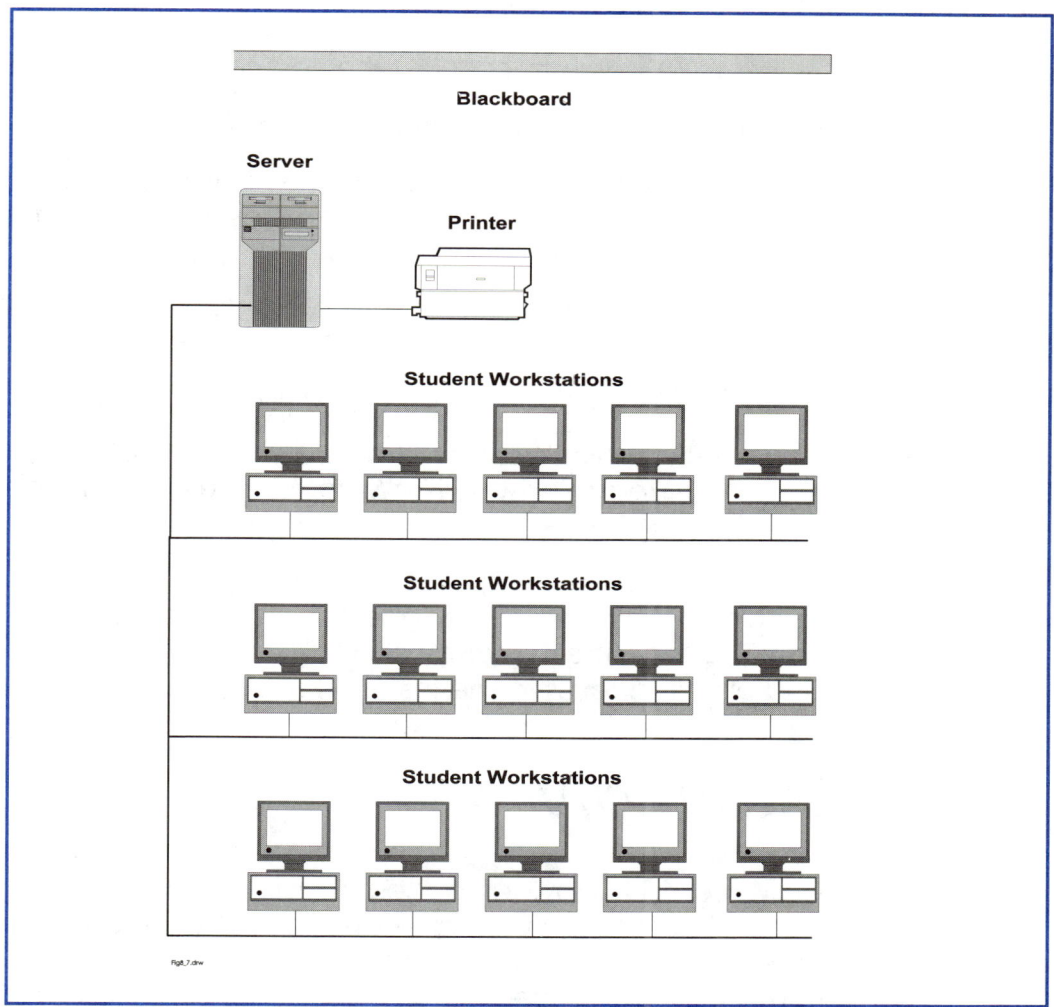

Figure 1-6. Possible network configuration for training users.

The other scenario consists of a Novell network that already exists. It is costly to purchase additional workstations, materials, and space if all that is required is a laboratory or room for providing training to users. If a current network is in place with users' workstations available, all that is needed is an additional server that can function as a training server for the users. This server can be connected to the existing wiring and, after NetWare is installed in it, training can be conducted using existing workstations. Figure 1-7 depicts this type of network.

The equipment required for this situation is as follows:

1. A file server (an IBM-PC or compatible computer with an 80386 or faster processor) with at least 20 megabytes of RAM and a hard disk (with a minimum of 115 megabytes of free storage).

2. A network interface card (NIC) for the server.

3. Novell NetWare 4.11.

4. A cable to connect the new server to existing network cable.

The process for installing the server is as follows:

1. Find a location for the server. If it is going to be used for training, then probably the classroom or a secluded area near the classroom is a good place.

2. Install the NIC in the server and, if required, provide a unique node address for the board.

3. Connect the server to existing network transmission media.

4. Install NetWare on the server, installing this new server into the already existing NetWare 4.11 tree which was created for the first file server.

The process of installing NetWare 4.11 is provided in the next chapter in this book. After the server goes on line, users who need training will simply attach their workstation to the tree which contains both servers and obtain access to the files and directories of either server based on rights assigned by the network administrator.

Summary

NetWare 4.11 provides access to multiple file servers by many client computers through the hardware and software on each computer. The hardware consists of a network interface card, or NIC. Under DOS, using the ODI concept, the NIC is controlled by LSL.COM, a program named to represent the brand of NIC being used, and a program called IPXODI.COM. Another program, NETX or the newer VLM.EXE VLM manager, provides the interface to DOS and to the file server.

Introduction to Novell Netware 4

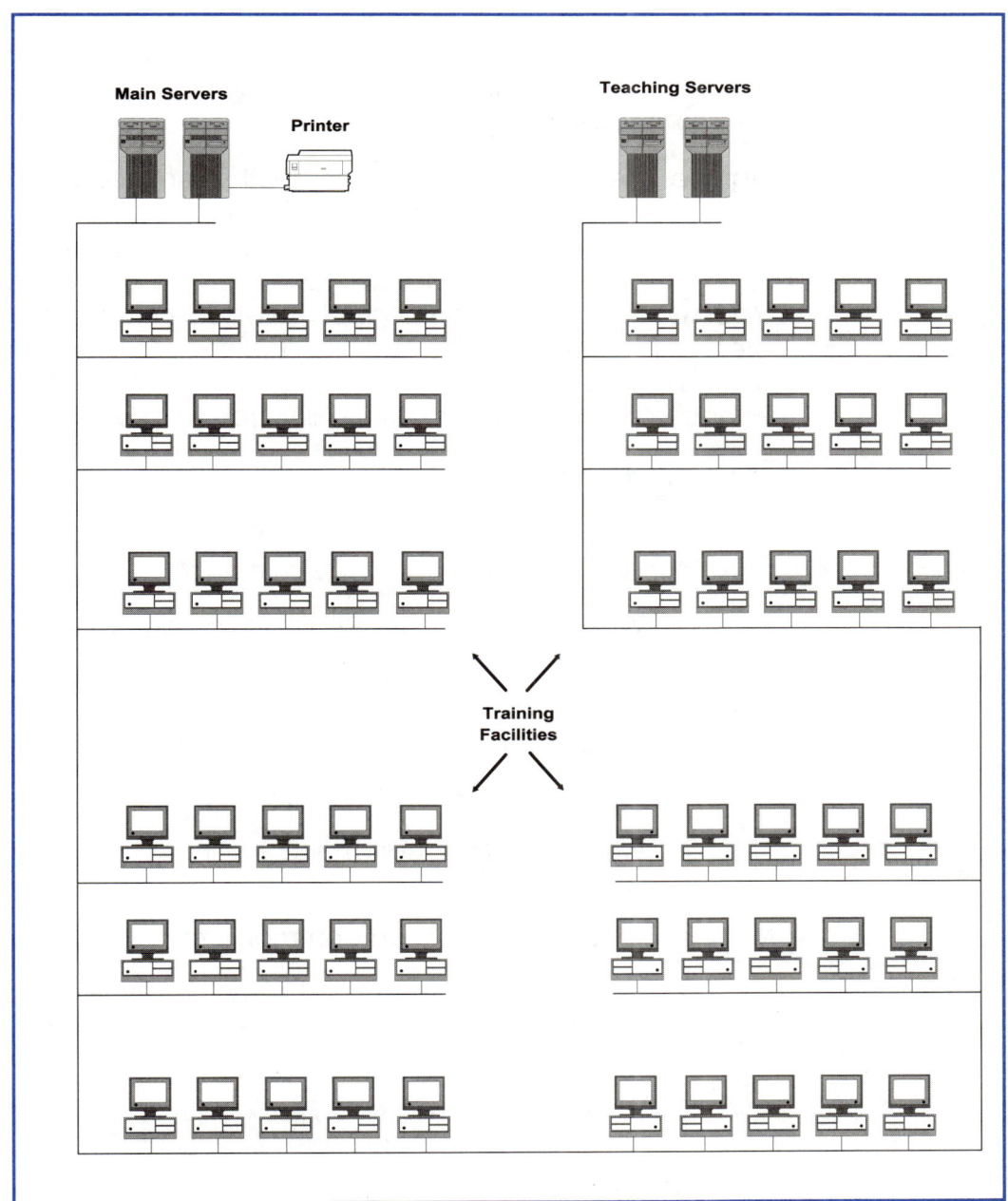

Figure 1-7. Additional configuration for setting up a network to train users.

With these programs loaded, the file servers of the NetWare 4.11 network appear to the client computer as a disk drive attached to the client computer. DOS commands can be used to create and access directories on the file server.

The four programs make up the NetWare VLM version client software that serves as the interface between the computer operating system and the network operating system. Alternatively, the newer Client 32 workstation software can be used. The NetWare client software allows

DOS and the user to treat file servers as a disk drive attached to the client computer. This protects the user from having to learn new commands and makes using the network a natural extension of the user's workstation.

With the use of drive mappings, paths, and search drives, a user's environment can be customized without affecting other network users. In addition, security of the network and user files are enhanced by the use of login IDs and passwords and trustee rights. The login ID/password combination controls physical access to the network. File system trustee rights determine file and directory access privileges that each user possesses. NDS trustee rights determine what a user can do with the various elements of the NDS tree, explained in Chapter 14.

Questions

1. What function does DOS perform?
2. What functions does Windows 95 perform on the client workstation?
3. Under DOS and Windows 95, files may be stored in different areas on the same disk. What are these areas called?
4. What does CHDIR stand for?
5. What NetWare command changes the assignment of drive letters?
6. What does the PATH command tell the computer?
7. A user on a Novell network must have a set of permissions to use a directory on the file server. What are these permissions called?
8. If a user has Read and File Scan rights in a directory, can the user store data there? Why or why not?
9. What does Novell Directory Services provide for the NetWare 4.11 network?
10. What is controlled by NDS object trustee rights?
11. What is controlled by NDS property trustee rights?
12. What is an enterprise network system, and how does NetWare 4.11 support this concept?

Project

Objective

Before NetWare 4.11 can be installed on a system, a listing of hardware, prospective users, and other resources must be recorded. Also, all steps taken during the installation process must be recorded in case something goes wrong and the process has to be repeated.

Additionally, knowing the applications, directories, users, and workstations on the network will help in maintaining the network and in performing future upgrades or expansions that may be required.

Creating a Novell NetWare Log Book

A typical log book contains the information outlined below. One should be created for each server that is part of a NetWare 4 tree. Additionally, information about the overall tree should also be documented.

- Name of the server.
- Type of hardware.
- Date of installation.
- Name of installer.
- Name and version of the operating system in use.
- Installation date of the operating system.
- Name of the operating system installer.
- Server name.
- Purchase date of the server.
- Server's network address(es).
- Location of the server.
- Volume name(s) in the server.
- Volume disk number.
- Volume size(s).
- Users' workstations.
- Users' names.
- Users' locations.

Users' network addresses.

Users' workstation types.

Users' workstation RAM.

Users' workstation disk options.

Users' workstation graphics boards and monitors.

Users' workstation hardware options and configuration.

Applications:

For each application in use:

Name of the applications in use.

Application's vendor.

Application's purchase date.

Application's version number.

Serial number.

Type of license (single user/network).

Number of simultaneous user licenses purchased.

Application's memory requirements.

Application's disk space requirements.

Additional log information. Using a word processor and the preceding list as a guide, create an application log book and fill in the information requested for the network that you will be installing during the hands-on portion of this class. Make sure that all information is correct because once the network is set up, it is difficult and time consuming to correct major errors or omissions in the setup process.

2
NetWare 4 Installation

Objectives

After completing this chapter you will

1. Understand the hardware and software requirements for installing NetWare 4.11.

2. Know the steps to install NetWare 4.11 on a file server.

3. Be able to install appropriate NetWare client software on a DOS/Windows 3.1 client computer.

4. Be able to install appropriate NetWare client software on a Windows 95 client computer.

5. Understand the difference between upgrading a 3.12 NetWare server to a 4.11 and performing a NetWare 4.11 new installation.

6. Have installed a NetWare 4.11 server.

7. Have installed Client 32 for Windows 3.1 and/or Windows 95.

Key Terms

Client 32

Client computer

Server Computer

Bootable partition

DOS

CD-ROM

Drivers

File Server

IPX Internal Network Number

Network Number

AUTOEXEC.BAT

STARTUP.NCF

AUTOEXEC.NCF

Disk Drivers

LAN Drivers

Interrupt

Memory Address

Port Address

CD-ROM drivers

Introduction

As NetWare 4 has matured, the installation process for both server and client software has been simplified. As an enterprise system, the installation of earlier versions of NetWare 4 were cryptic at best and often seemingly impossible. NetWare 4.11, however, is a major improvement and even has a version once again dedicated to the small business owner.

This chapter will compare and contrast various methods for installing the NetWare 4.11 file server and will provide hands-on practice in performing a simple NetWare 4.11 installation. Additionally, the chapter will explore various choices for client software ranging from a historical perspective on how client software has been done up to a detailed discussion and hands-on practice for installing Novell's latest client software, **Client 32**.

At the end of this section, you will get the opportunity to install a NetWare 4.11 server and a NetWare 4.11 client. You will then test the installation by a simple login process. Details about login and other functions will be discussed in later chapters.

Installing NetWare 4 on the File Server

Traditionally, NetWare has focused on a server-centric architecture for its network operating systems. **Clients** share resources by first attaching and then logging into a central **server**. NetWare 4.11 goes beyond the strictly server-centric design to combine multiple servers into an enterprise network tree which contains and organizes the users, file servers, printing resources, etc. of the overall network. But, although version 4.11 goes beyond the single server, each file server must itself be installed into the network tree.

NetWare 4 Installation

The first server to be installed for a given tree actually defines the tree during its installation. Succeeding servers are installed into an existing tree. With respect to the server, the focus of this chapter is to detail the steps needed to prepare for and to install the first NetWare 4.11 server in a given tree. The chapter will then give an overview of design considerations that must be weighed when installing successive servers into the tree.

Installation Preparation

If you were installing a complicated home appliance that you had never installed before, you would want to pay special attention to the installation instructions, making sure that you had all the required materials and equipment to accomplish the installation. In addition, you would want to make sure that you fully understood the steps needed for installation. Installing the first NetWare 4.11 server is a similar process. It is a process that functions very well when required materials and equipment are obtained and when a complete understanding of the installation steps is obtained prior to beginning the installation process. If installation preparation is shortchanged, the installation process can become unnecessarily complicated. This section details the steps needed for proper installation preparation.

The high-level requirements for installation are detailed in Figure 2-1.

Hardware Required:

- 386 (faster is highly recommended) PC or PC compatible with
    - 20 MB RAM memory
    - 115 MB minimum hard disk
    - VGA monitor (color optional)
    - ODI-compliant network interface card and cable
    - CD-ROM preferred but not absolutely required

Software Required:

- NetWare 4.11 Original Operating System CD-ROM disk or access to same over a network connection
- DOS 3 or higher for creating the bootable DOS partition
- DOS drivers for the CD-ROM on the machine which will become the new file server
- Drivers for the hard disk drives in the computer which will become the file server (obtained on the NetWare 4.11 CD or from the hard disk drive manufacturer)
- Drivers for the network interface card(s) in the computer which will become the file server (obtained on the NetWare 4.11 CD or from the NIC manufacturer with the latter preferred).

Figure 2-1. Hardware, software, and equipment required for a NetWare File Server Installation

4.11 Installation

Installation Overview

A NetWare 4.11 server must have a **bootable** DOS **partition** with server boot files to be able to bring up the file server. The server boot files directory is created by using the NetWare 4.11 Operating System installation CD either directly on a CD-ROM attached to the file server or by connecting to the installation files over the network. After the server boot files are copied to the DOS partition, the installation can then proceed to create and configure the NetWare partition on the first and succeeding hard drives.

Creating the Bootable DOS partition

As mentioned, the first step in installing a Novell server is to create a bootable DOS partition on the first drive of the NetWare server. This generally requires the computer to be booted with a previously created DOS diskette with the **DOS** operating system on it.

The simplest method for creating a bootable DOS diskette is to utilize an already existing DOS machine and

> Bring up the already existing DOS machine to the C:> prompt
>
> Put a blank formatted diskette in the diskette drive
>
> Enter
>
> **FORMAT A:/S**

By formatting the diskette with the /S parameter, the diskette becomes a system diskette, able to boot a computer on its own.

Before leaving the already existing DOS machine, some additional DOS system files must be copied to the diskette. These files are

> **FDISK.COM**
>
> **FORMAT.COM**

The FDISK command will be used to create the DOS partition on the first hard drive on the server, and the FORMAT command will be used to make that blank partition into a bootable DOS partition.

Note that if the new file server has a **CD-ROM**, the **drivers** for the CD-ROM must be copied to the boot diskette as well so that they can be copied to the DOS partition of the new server. Refer to CD-ROM documentation for instructions for these drivers or copy them from a

DOS machine already running the same type of CD-ROM drive as is in the new file server.

Once the bootable DOS diskette has been made, it is used to boot the new server. Once the server has been booted, the FDISK command from the diskette is used to create a DOS partition of at least 15 MB on the new hard drive. If space is not at a premium, it is a good idea to create a larger DOS partition to store client boot files, etc.

Once the primary DOS partition has been created on the new hard drive, the system reboots, still with the DOS diskette in the diskette drive. Then, the DOS partition is formatted using

    FORMAT C:/S

This operation formats the DOS partition and transfers the system files necessary for the new hard drive to boot to the DOS operating system itself.

At this point, the DOS diskette must be removed, and the new file server must be booted on its own to verify that the new DOS system partition functions. Before moving on, the CD-ROM drivers must be copied from the DOS diskette to the DOS partition on the new server so that the new CD-ROM can be "seen" from DOS. Once these drivers have been installed, it is imperative that they be tested by booting the new server without the DOS diskette and then accessing files on the CD-ROM by doing a simple directory listing. If the CD-ROM drive cannot be accessed, these problems must be resolved before proceeding with a CD-ROM installation.

Background Information Needed Before Proceeding with Server Installation

Before we proceed with the actual installation, several terms and files must be discussed. They are as follows:

    File Server Name

    IPX Internal Network Number

    Network Number (or External IPX Network Number)

    SERVER.EXE

    AUTOEXEC.BAT

    STARTUP.NCF

    AUTOEXEC.NCF

    Disk Drivers

>   **LAN Drivers**
>
>   **Interrupt**
>
>   **Memory Address**
>
>   **Port or I/O Address**

File Server Name

The name of the **file server** is one of the first pieces of information required in setting up a new file server. It must uniquely identify the server among other servers connected over the same cabling system. It must be 2 to 47 characters in length and can contain letters, numbers, and the underscore character. It should be descriptive of the server while not being unnecessarily long.

IPX Internal Network Number

This is a hexadecimal number of up to 8 hexadecimal numbers, not 00000000 and not FFFFFFFF. This number uniquely identifies the server from a systems viewpoint. The number cannot be the same as any other server's internal IPX network number, and it cannot be the same as another network number on a connected network. An example of a legal **IPX Internal Network Number** is 3D2AA153.

External Network Number

This is a hexadecimal number of up to 8 hexadecimal numbers, not 00000000 and not FFFFFFFF. This number uniquely identifies the cable segment to which it is assigned. It cannot be the same as any other **network number** on the connected network, and it cannot be the same as any other server's internal IPX network number. It is often called the "wire" number even though the cabling system may contain wireless segments. It must be the same for all servers on a segment.

SERVER.EXE

SERVER.EXE is the core portion of the network operating system. It is stored in a directory on the DOS partition of the server and is the program which, when executed, utilizes multiple configuration files to bring up the server.

AUTOEXEC.BAT

AUTOEXEC.BAT on the DOS partition usually contains only the SERVER.EXE command so that the server can automatically boot itself when it is turned on. If the AUTOEXEC.BAT is not present, one would have to actually enter SERVER on the console to get the server to boot.

STARTUP.NCF

The **STARTUP.NCF** file is a startup configuration file which is stored on the DOS partition on the file server. It is used by SERVER.EXE to, at minimum, provide hard disk drives so that SERVER.EXE can recognize the hard disk of the server. STARTUP.NCF then calls AUTOEXEC.NCF, explained below. A sample STARTUP.NCF file is shown in Figure 2-2.

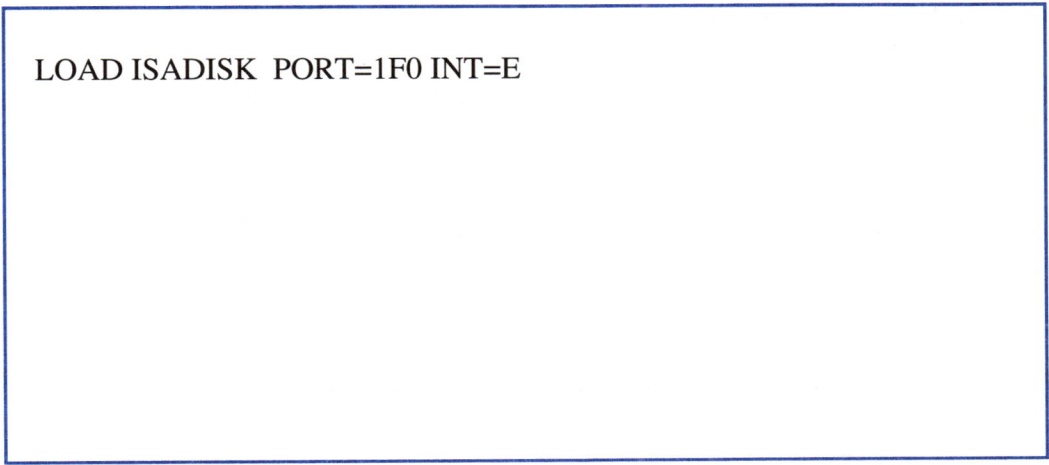

LOAD ISADISK PORT=1F0 INT=E

Figure 2-2. A sample STARTUP.NCF file.

AUTOEXEC.NCF

The **AUTOEXEC.NCF** file is to NetWare 4.11 much as the AUTOEXEC.BAT file is to DOS. It provides environment and configuration information for bringing up the server. Just like the AUTOEXEC.BAT file, it could technically be omitted. But, if it is omitted, the person bringing up the file server must know the file server's name, the IPX Internal Network Number, the drivers for the network interface cards and the hardware specifications for these cards, etc. In other words, omission of the AUTOEXEC.NCF file is not a practical option. A sample AUTOEXEC.NCF file is shown in Figure 2-3.

Disk Drivers

The hard disk(s) of a file server are not recognizable without the use of a software program, which is a NetWare 4.11-compliant **disk driver**. The hard disk driver is loaded in the STARTUP.NCF file so that the server can recognize its hard disk. The disk driver is a NetWare Loadable Module (NLM), which may itself be a driver that ends in .DSK, .HAM, or .CDM. The disk driver requires that the installer provide the disk drive's

```
SET TIME ZONE = CST8CDT
SET DAYLIGHT SAVINGS TIME OFFSET = 1:00:00
SET START OF DAYLIGHT SAVINGS TIME = (APRIL SUNDAY FIRST 2:00:00 AM)
SET END OF DAYLIGHT SAVINGS TIME = (OCTOBER SUNDAY LAST 2:00:00 AM)
SET DEFAULT TIME SERVER TYPE=SINGLE

SET BINDERY CONTEXT = O=MAINCO
FILE SERVER NAME MAINCO
IPX INTERNAL NET 1011ABD1
LOAD NE2000 INT=3 PORT=300 FRAME=EHTERNET_802.2 NAME=BOARD2
BIND IPX TO BOARD2 NET=80724155
```

Figure 2-3. A sample AUTOEXEC.NCF file.

interrupt number and other configuration parameters, discussed later in the chapter. The disk driver is activated by loading it in the STARTUP.NCF file as shown in Figure 2-2.

LAN Drivers

The network interface card(s) of a file server are recognized through loading a software program, which is a NetWare 4.11-compliant network interface card (NIC) driver. Just like the hard disk, the network interface card is recognized by loading the **LAN driver** NetWare Loadable Module (NLM), which is a driver that ends in .LAN. The LAN driver requires the installer to provide the NIC's interrupt number, memory address, and port (I/O) address. The LAN driver is activated by loading it in the AUTOEXEC.NCF file as shown in Figure 2-3.

Interrupt Number

An IBM PC or PC compatible utilizes **interrupt** numbers for communication with the various devices attached to the PC. In general, only one device can utilize a given interrupt number, 0 to 15, and many of these interrupt numbers are already assigned to such things as the keyboard and mouse. The IDE hard disk generally utilizes interrupt 14, which is represented by the hexadecimal number E, and NICs utilize unused interrupt numbers such as 3, 5, and 10. One must refer to the documentation and usually to the setup diskette that comes with a given NIC to determine how to configure a NIC card to a given interrupt number. This interrupt number must then be entered in the AUTOEXEC.NCF file as shown in Figure 2-3.

Memory Address

Each network interface card utilized in a PC usually uses at least some portion of the RAM memory of the PC itself for normal operation. The **memory address** defined with the NIC in the AUTOEXEC.NCF must correspond to the memory address set on the NIC during setup, and it must not conflict with the memory address for any other device in the PC. Note that some NICs, notably the NE2000 board, do not require a memory address. This can be very important when one is trying to add an NIC to a machine that already has many additional devices installed.

Port Address

The **port address** or I/O address is the location within the RAM of the PC that the board utilizes for communicating with the CPU of the PC. This address also cannot conflict with the memory or I/O addresses of other devices in the PC.

Choices for Server Installation

In general, NetWare 4.11 can be installed using either

> **Simple Installation**
>
>> or
>
> **Custom Installation**.

Simple Installation requires far less effort on the part of the installer and can be used if all of the following conditions are met:

- DOS is already installed on a 15MB DOS partition
- The DOS partition is already bootable
- The remaining free hard disk space is at least 90 MB and is available solely for NetWare to use
- Each hard disk in the system is to contain one and only one volume
- A simple NDS directory with a single container can be used
- Randomly generated internal IPX addresses can be used
- IPX is the only communications protocol to be used
- It will not be necessary to mirror or duplex the hard drives on the system
- The AUTOEXEC.NCF and the STARTUP.NCF files do not have to have custom entries

Custom installation must be used when any of the above conditions is not met, or, at the installer's discretion, custom installation can be used simply so that the installer has an opportunity to view exactly what configuration parameters are being used.

Hands-On Simple Installation

1. Create the bootable DOS partition on the PC that will be the new server following the sets listed earlier in this chapter. Be sure to include the DOS **CD-ROM drivers** so that the CD-ROM can be recognized by DOS.

2. Boot the new server to make sure that the DOS partition is bootable. If it is not, repeat the process of creating the bootable DOS partition before you proceed.

3. Place the NetWare 4.11 Operating System CD in the CD-ROM drive and close it.

4. Assuming that the new CD-ROM's drive letter is D:, enter

    D:

    INSTALL

    This process activates the installation process.

5. Select

    English Language and press <Enter>.

6. Select

    NetWare 4.11 and press <Enter>.

7. Select

    Simple Installation of NetWare 4.11 and press <Enter>.

8. Enter the name of the server, for example, enter the word SERVERXXX where XXX is your three initials. Remember that the server name must be unique among servers on the same cabling system.

    Enter

    SERVERXXX and press <Enter>.

9. Select

    Copy the server boot files to the DOS partition

    (When this operation completes, the server boot files are in the directory C:\NWSERVER on the DOS partition.)

10. **SERVER.EXE** is automatically started once the server boot files have been copied.

11. The installation process will attempt to identify server drivers for the hard disk drive and the network interface card. If the drivers are automatically detected, the drivers selected will be displayed on a Summary Screen. If these drivers are correct, select

    Continue Installation and press <Enter>.

    If the drivers are not automatically detected or if you wish to use different drivers, select the appropriate disk driver and the appropriate network interface card driver for your server following the screen prompts; otherwise skip to step 12.

12. The simple installation process automatically selects a random IPX Internal Network Number.

13. When asked whether or not to continue accessing the CD-ROM from DOS, or to try to mount the CD-ROM as a NetWare volume, select

    Continue accessing the CD-ROM via DOS and press <Enter>.

14. Note that the SYS: volume (the main NetWare volume is automatically mounted at this point during the Simple Installation.

15. Wait while the system files are automatically copied to the hard drive of the server.

16. When the system files have been copied, the server will attempt to locate an existing Novell Directory Services tree. If one or more is found, it will be displayed for you to choose whether or not to install into an existing tree or to select another tree after noting the names of these trees. For purposes of this simple installation, select

    Select another tree and press <Enter>.

    Press <INS>.

    Press <Enter> to confirm that you want to create a new tree.

17. Select

    YES and press <Enter> to create a new tree.

18. Select the **time zone for your server** and press <Enter>.

19. Type in your directory tree name, remembering that it must be unique from all other trees visible on this network (you saw the other tree names displayed in step 16).

Enter

TREEXXX where XXX is your initials and press <Enter>.

20. Enter **the network administrator's password** and press <Enter>.

    (Note: It would be a good idea to use something like PASSWORDXXX where XXX is replaced with your initials. Of course, in a live network, this password would be unacceptable, but in a teaching environment it is more important to have a memorable password than it is to enforce security.)

21. **Confirm the network administrator's password by reentering it** and press <Enter>.

22. When prompted, **insert the license diskette into the A: drive** and press <Enter>.

23. Wait while the **System and Public files are copied to the server**.

24. Select

    Continue the installation and press <Enter>.

25. After reading the closing screen, press <Enter> to return to the server prompt.

26. Bring the server down by entering

    DOWN and press <Enter>.

    EXIT and press <Enter>.

To verify that the server is properly installed:

27. **Reboot the server** by pressing CTRL/ALT/DEL keys simultaneously.

28. Enter

    CD \NWSERVER and press <Enter>.

    SERVER and press <Enter>.

    Wait for the server to "come up"

29. When the server is up, enter

    MODULES to see what Netware Loadable Modules are loaded.

    CONFIG to check that the server's name, IPX Internal Network Number, and network interface card are properly configured.

When the new server is operational

1. From a NetWare 4.11 client station, reboot the workstation using either VLM or Client 32 software.

2. Enter

   F: (or your first network drive as given to you by your instructor).

3. Enter **LOGIN SERVERXXX\.ADMIN.TREEXXX** and press <Enter> if using the VLM client.

4. Enter your password.

5. Wait until the system logs in.

Creating Workstation Installation Diskette Sets for NetWare 4.11 Clients

To ease the need for having CD-ROMs on all machines in a classroom, it is a good idea to create an installation diskette set for each of the clients supported with NetWare 4.11. Instructions for creating diskettes for the VLM client, the DOS/Windows 3.1 Client 32, and for the Windows 95 Client 32 are given here. While Client32 is the client of choice for NetWare 4.11, the VLM client also works and is sometimes needed, especially when there is a need for a small client that can easily fit on a diskette. Creation of the VLM client is presented here for use in these situations, and for use with previous versions of NetWare 4 and NetWare 3.12.

To create an installation diskette set for the VLM client

1. Boot a computer containing a CD-ROM with a DOS diskette with drivers for the CD-ROM.

2. Enter the drive letter of the CD-ROM, D: for example, and press <Enter>.

3. Enter

   INSTALL and press <Enter>.   Figure 2-4 is displayed.

4. Select

   Select this line to install in English and press <Enter>.

5. **Press any key 4 times** after reading each of the 4 license agreement screens.

Chapter 2

6. Select

    Diskette Creation and press <Enter>.

7. Select type of client, **NetWare DOS/WINDOWS Client (VLM)** in this case as shown in Figure 2-5, and press <Enter>.

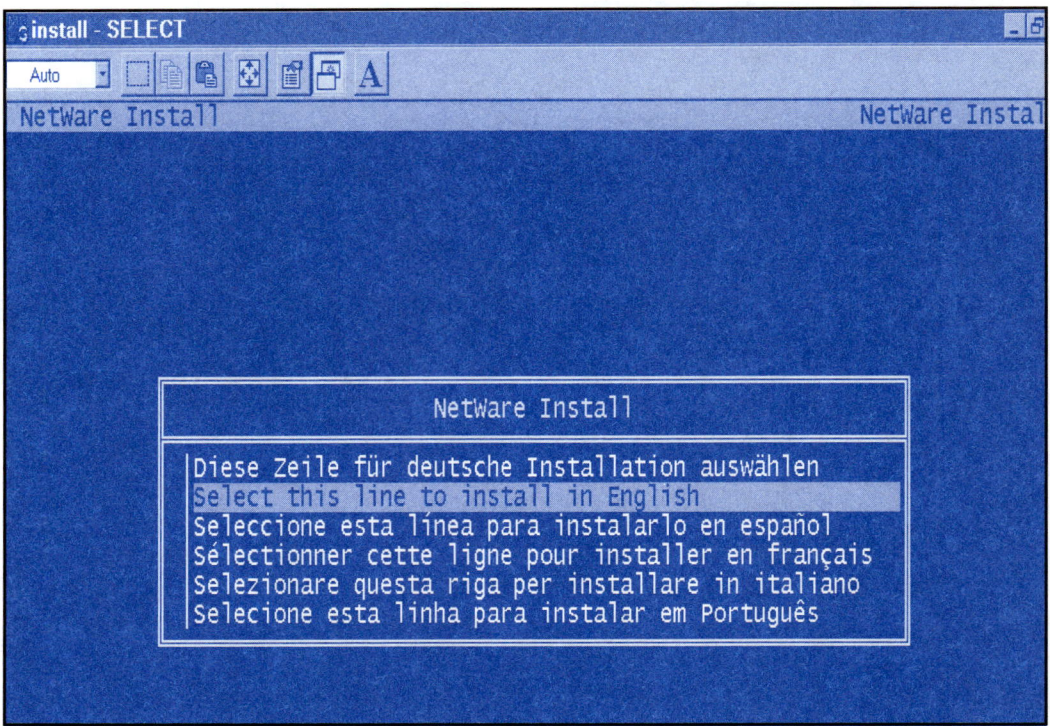

Figure 2-4. An initial server installation screen.

8. Enter the drive letter for the diskette drive as

    A: and press <Enter>.

9. Following the prompt, insert a blank formatted disk into the drive letter you entered and press any key to continue.

10. Wait while the first diskette is created. Label it as prompted as

    NetWare Client for DOS and MS Windows Disk 1

11. Insert a blank formatted disk into the drive letter you entered and press any key to continue.

12. Wait while the second diskette is created. Label it as prompted as

    NetWare Client for DOS and MS Windows Disk 2

13. Insert a blank formatted disk into the drive letter you entered and press any key to continue.

NetWare 4 Installation

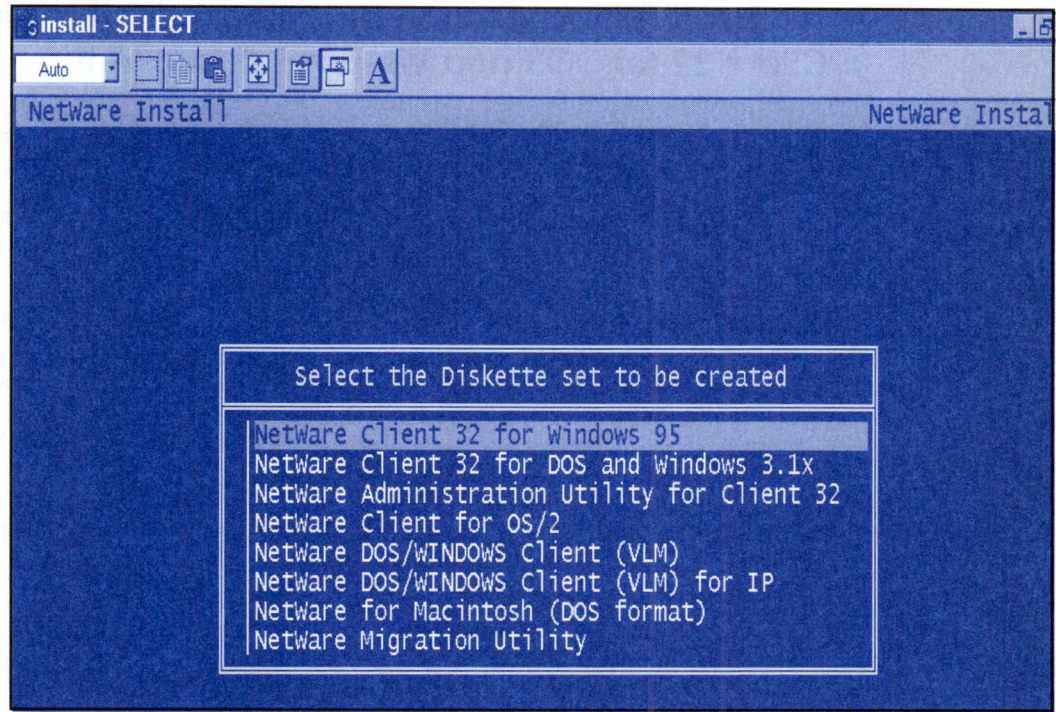

Figure 2-5. NetWare client diskette selection screen

14. Wait while the third diskette is created. Label it as prompted as

    NetWare Client for DOS and MS Windows Disk 3

15. Insert a blank formatted disk into the drive letter you entered and press any key to continue.

16. Wait while the fourth diskette is created. Label it as prompted as

    NetWare Client for DOS and MS Windows Disk 4

17. Insert a blank formatted disk into the drive letter you entered and press any key to continue.

18. Wait while the fifth diskette is created. Label it as prompted as

    NetWare Client for DOS and MS Windows Disk 5

19. Insert a blank formatted disk into the drive letter you entered and press any key to continue.

20. Wait while the sixth diskette is created. Label it as prompted as

    NetWare Client for DOS and MS Windows ODI LAN Drivers

    Press any key to continue.

To create an installation diskette set for the NetWare Client 32 for DOS and Windows 3.1x client

1. Boot a computer with a CD-ROM with a DOS diskette with drivers for the CD-ROM.

2. Enter the drive letter of the CD-ROM, D: for example, and press <Enter>.

3. Enter

    INSTALL and press <Enter>.

    Figure 2-4 is displayed.

4. Select

    Select this line to install in English and press <Enter>.

5. **Press any key 4 times** after reading each of the 4 license agreement screens.

6. Select

    Diskette Creation and press <Enter>.

7. Select

    NetWare Client 32 for DOS and WINDOWS 3.1x and press <Enter>.

8. Select

    English diskettes and press <Enter>.

    Note that you are prompted that you will need 8 diskettes.

9. Enter the drive letter for the diskette drive such as

    A: and press <Enter>.

10. Following the prompt, insert a blank formatted disk into the drive letter you entered and press any key to continue.

11. Wait while the first diskette is created. Label it as prompted as

    NetWare Client 32 for DOS and Windows 3.1x Disk 1 DOS

12. Repeat steps 10 and 11 noting the appropriate diskette label to write on each diskette until all diskettes have been created.

13. Press any key to quit the diskette creation process.

14. Press <Esc> to exit the installation program.

To create an installation diskette set for the NetWare Client 32 for Windows 95 client

1. Boot a computer with a CD-ROM with a DOS diskette with drivers for the CD-ROM.

2. Enter the drive letter of the CD-ROM, D: for example, and press <Enter>.

3. Enter

    INSTALL and press <Enter>.

    Figure 2-4 is displayed.

4. Select

    Select this line to install in English and press <Enter>.

5. **Press any key 4 times** after reading each of the 4 license agreement screens.

6. Select

    Diskette Creation and press <Enter>.

7. Select

    NetWare Client 32 for windows 95 and press <Enter>.

8. Select

    English diskettes and press <Enter>.

    Note that you are prompted that you will need 8 diskettes.

9. Enter the drive letter for the diskette drive such as

    A: and press <Enter>.

10. Following the prompt, insert a blank formatted disk into the drive letter you entered and press any key to continue.

11. Wait while the first diskette is created. Label it as prompted as

    NetWare Client 32 for Windows 95 Disk 1

12. Repeat steps 9 and 10 noting the appropriate diskette label to write on each diskette until all diskettes have been created.

13. Press any key to quit the diskette creation process.

14. Press <Esc> to exit the installation program.

Installing the Workstation Boot Disk Using NetWare DOS Requester

Introduction to the NetWare DOS Requester

The NetWare DOS Requester is usually installed on the hard drive of the workstation rather than on a floppy diskette. NetWare 4.11 utilizes several Windows-based utilities including its on-line documentation, Dynatext, and the NetWare DOS Requester must modify several Windows configuration files to allow Windows to function properly with these utilities. Additionally, the workstation hard drive must be prepared so that it is a bootable DOS device prior to loading the NetWare DOS Requester.

The NetWare DOS Requester utilizes the LSL (Link Support Layer), the ODI-compliant LAN driver, and IPXODI just as the DOS redirector workstation setup did. However, instead of utilizing NETX to connect the user to the network, it uses a VLM manager, often called the DOS requester, to load modular workstation routines much like NLMs that are used on the file server itself. Additionally, instead of keeping two sets of system tables as NETX did, the NetWare DOS Requester utilizes the same tables as DOS. This makes the operation of the client more efficient.

> Note that the command
>
> LASTDRIVE=Z:

must be placed in the CONFIG SYS file of the workstation so that VLMs can recognize all 26 drives and thereby make drives available to NetWare.

Installing the NetWare DOS Requester

Reminder: Before attempting to install the NetWare DOS Requester, it is a good idea to create the diskette set for VLMs from the NetWare 4.11 Operating System Installation CD. Creation of these diskettes from a machine with a CD-ROM alleviates the need for having a CD-ROM drive on all machines in the classroom.

1. On the machine that will become the NetWare client, install DOS (version 3.3 or later) and WINDOWS 3.1. Boot the workstation by pressing Ctrl Alt Del.

2. Insert the diskette labeled Disk 1 into the diskette drive, change to the A: drive, enter INSTALL, and press ENTER.

3. The client installation screen will appear.

NetWare 4 Installation

4. Enter **C:\NWCLIENT** for the directory in which the NetWare Client software is to be installed and **press <ENTER>**.

5. Answer **Yes** to allows for changes to the CONFIG.SYS and AUTOEXEC.BAT files for automatic loading of the workstation software and press ENTER. Note that the previous CONFIG.SYS and AUTOEXEC.BAT files will be stored in files called CONFIG.BNW and AUTOEXEC.BNW respectively so that reclamation of these files will be possible if the client install does not go smoothly.

6. Enter **Yes** and **press <Enter>** to allow for Windows Support.

7. Enter **the name of the directory in which WINDOWS is installed**, usually C:\WINDOWS on the hard drive and press ENTER.

8. Enter **the name of the appropriate LAN driver for the network board** which is installed in the workstation. (Note: You may need to have the driver diskette which was included with the LAN card when it was purchased or an updated driver diskette as part of this process.)

9. If the "Insert the Driver Disk" message appears, put the Disk 2 diskette indicated into the floppy diskette drive.

10. Press **<Enter>** to begin copying files to the workstation hard drive, changing diskettes as prompted.

The installation, when complete, will have inserted the LASTDRIVE=Z: command into the CONFIG.SYS file, and it will have inserted a call to a file called STARTNET.BAT in the NWCLIENT directory. STARTNET.BAT will then set the language for NetWare and load LSL, the LAN driver, IPXODI, and will execute VLM to load the VLMs. Remember that configuration information for the workstation is stored in NET.CFG and may need to be edited for specific equipment configuration information.

Testing the New Boot Process

1. With the workstation cable to the network firmly installed, press the CTRL/ALT/DEL keys simultaneously to boot your workstation. Wait for LSL, the NIC driver, IPXODI, and VLM to run from the default NWCLIENT directory.

2. Type **F:** (or the first network drive) and press <ENTER>.

3. Type **LOGIN SERVERXXX\.ADMIN.TREEXXX** where SERVERXXX is the name of the file server you wish to log in and press <ENTER>.

4. Type the network administrator's password, if one has been assigned.

Note that the boot files copied to the hard disk can be copied to a diskette if desired. If desired, copy the CONFIG.SYS, AUTOEXEC.BAT, and the entire NWCLIENT directory to the diskette for backup purposes.

Installing Client 32

Installing Client 32 for DOS/Windows 3.1

Reminder: Before attempting to install Client 32 for DOS/Windows, it is a good idea to create the diskette set for Client 32 for DOS/Windows from the NetWare 4.11 Operating System Installation CD. Creation of these diskettes from a machine with a CD-ROM alleviates the need for having a CD-ROM drive on all machines in the classroom.

1. On the machine that will become the NetWare client, install DOS (version 3.3 or later) and WINDOWS 3.1. Boot the workstation by pressing Ctrl Alt Del.

2. Activate Windows by entering **WIN** and pressing <Enter>.

3. Insert the diskette labeled Disk 1 into the diskette drive, change to the A: drive, choose **Run A:SETUP** from the File selection on the main Windows menu bar, and click the OK button.

4. Select **English Language** and click OK.

5. Click the **Continue** button on the introductory screen.

6. After reading the license agreement, click the **Yes** button.

7. Click the **Next** button on the Directory locations box.

8. Select the appropriate 32-bit network interface card (LAN) driver for your network board. Note that the board's interrupt number, memory address, and port address must already have been configured using software from the board's manufacturer.

9. Click the **Next** button this time and the next time it is presented.

10. Wait for the installation process to finish and then select

    Restart Computer (Recommended) and click the OK button

NetWare 4 Installation

11. Wait for the station to boot and run Windows by entering **WIN**.

12. Select **NetWare User Tools for Windows**

13. Click the **NetWare Settings** button and click the **Startup tab**

14. Click **Launch at startup**.

15. Click the **Login tab**

16. Click the following selections:

    Display Connection Page

    Display Script Page

    Run login scripts

    Close on exit

    Display Variables Page

    Restore Permanent Connections

17. Click the OK button

18. Click the **Exit Door (upper left button on screen)** to exit NetWare User Tools for Windows

19. Reboot the computer.

Testing the New Boot Process with Client 32 for Windows 3.1

1. With the workstation cable to the network firmly installed, press the CTRL/ALT/DEL keys simultaneously to boot your workstation. Wait for the station to boot and for the client software to run.

2. When prompted, enter .ADMIN.TREEXXX for the user ID on the login tab and the password in the password box. Click on the Connections tab to make sure that the desired server is entered in the connections box as shown in Figure 2-6.

3. Click the OK button to complete the login process. NetWare drives should now be accessible through the File Manager in Windows 3.1.

Chapter 2

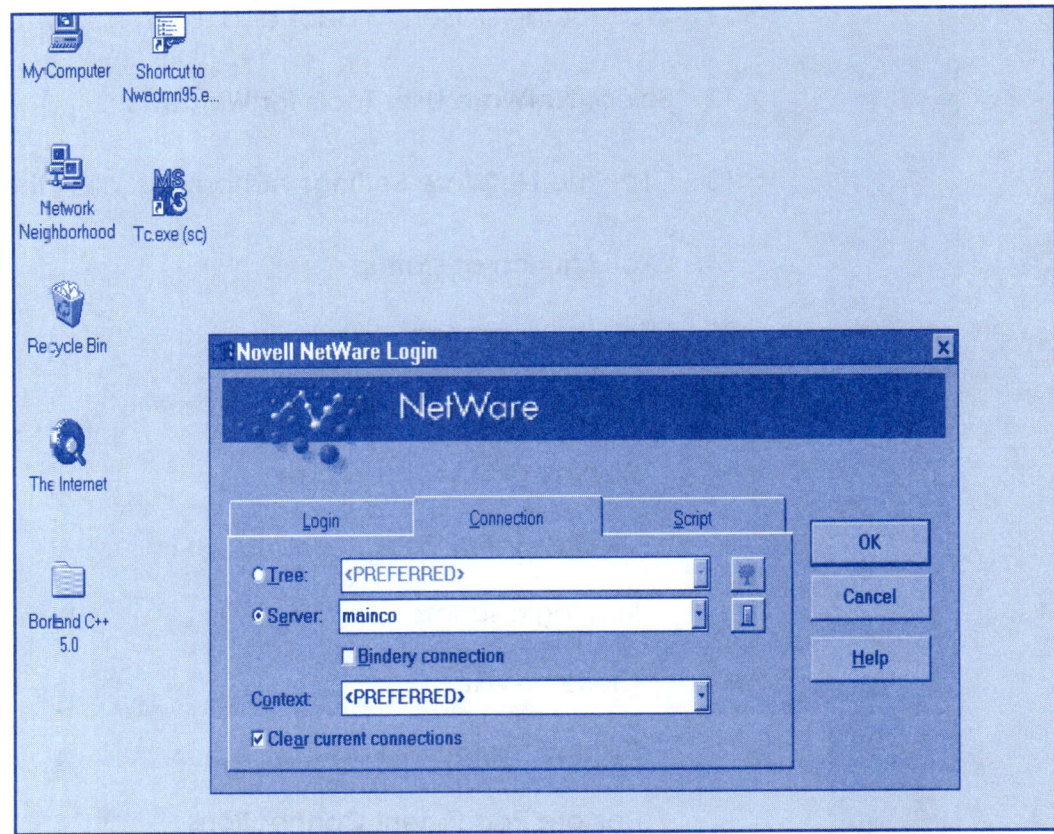

Figure 2-6. Connections tab of login dialog box

Installing the Client 32 for Windows 95

Reminder: Before attempting to install Client 32 for Windows 95, it is a good idea to create the diskette set for Client 32 for Windows 95 from the NetWare 4.11 Operating System Installation CD. Creation of these diskettes from a machine with a CD-ROM alleviates the need for having a CD-ROM drive on all machines in the classroom.

1. On the machine that will become the NetWare client, install Windows 95. Boot the workstation by turning it on or by clicking on Shut Down and then Restart Computer.

2. Insert the diskette labeled Disk 1 into the diskette drive, change to the A: drive, and choose **Run A:SETUP** from the Start Menu Run selection.

3. After reading the license agreement, click the **Yes** button as shown in Figure 2-7.

4. Click **Do not upgrade your NDIS drives to ODI automatically**.

NetWare 4 Installation

5. Click the **Start** button to begin installation as shown in Figure 2-8. Installation will automatically proceed without intervention.

6. When the installation is complete, click on the **Customize** button.

7. Select **Novell NetWare Client 32** and then **Properties**.

8. Enter the name of the preferred server. Set the first network drive to the appropriate letter, probably F:.

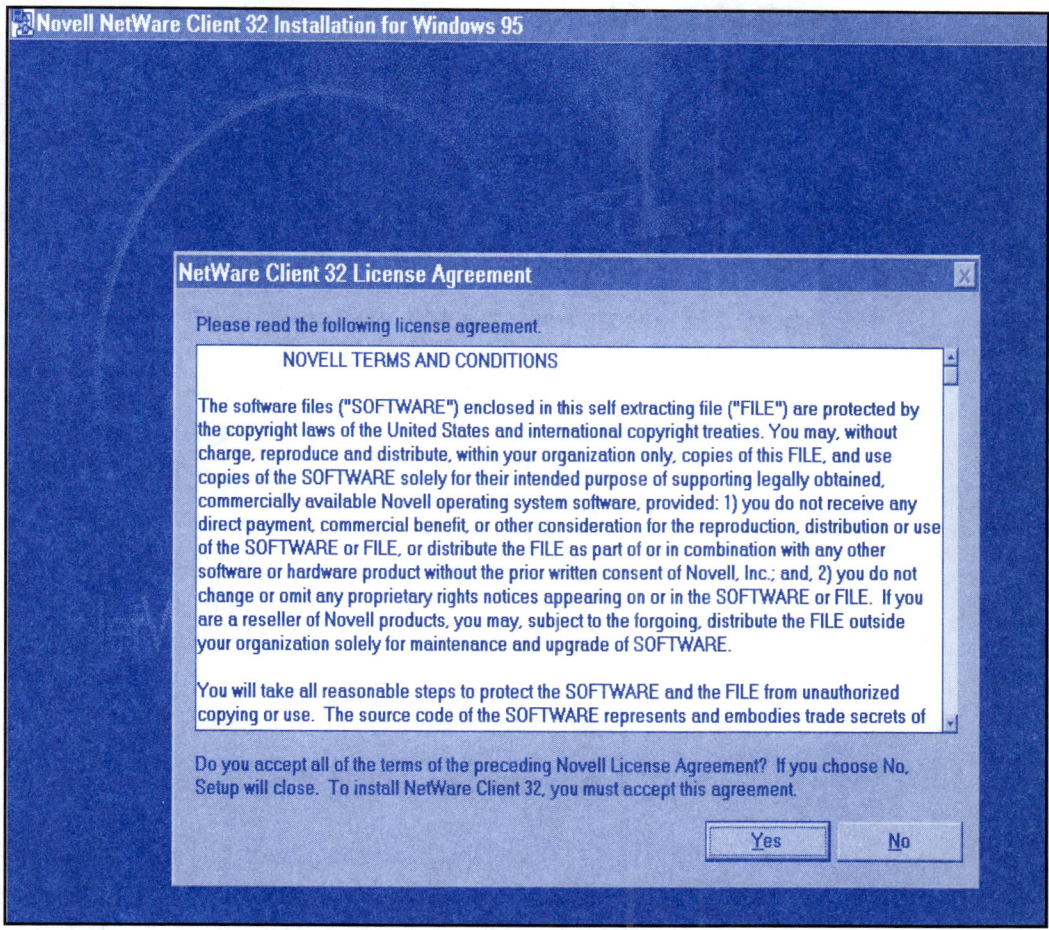

Figure 2-7. Windows 95 Client 32 installation license agreement.

Chapter 2

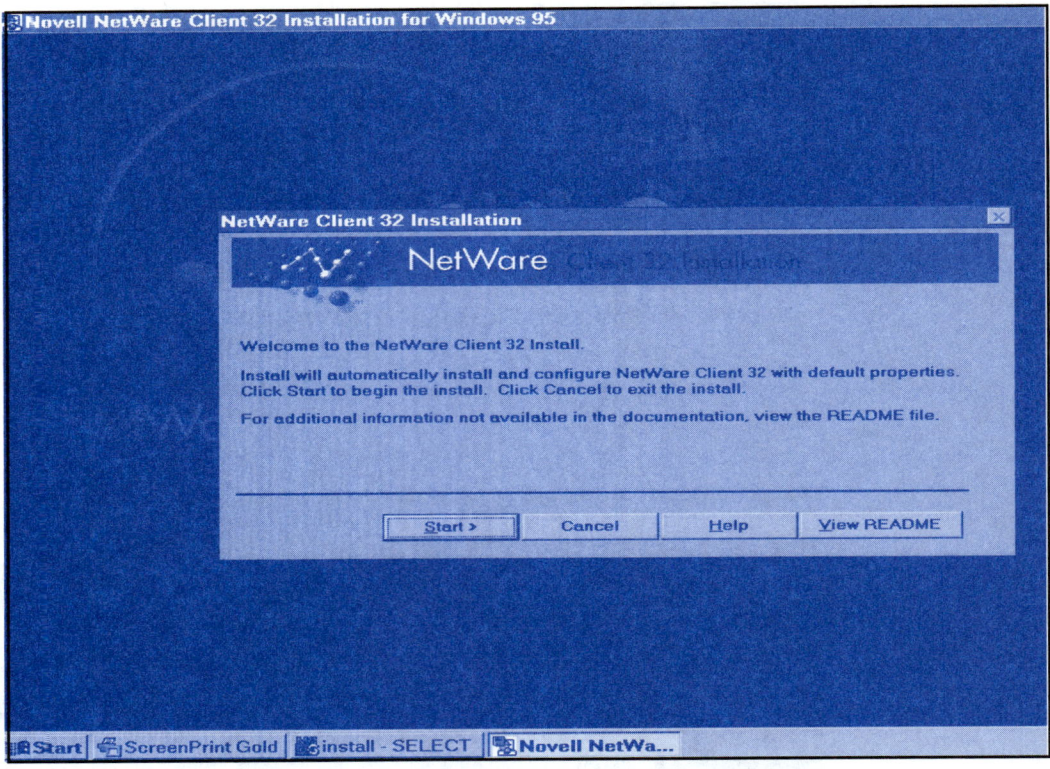

Figure 2-8. Actual start of Windows 95 Client32 installation

9. Click **Login** and make sure that the following selections are chosen:

   Display Connection Page

   Display Script Page

   Run login scripts

   Close on exit

   Save settings when exiting Login

10. Click the **OK** button and then click the **OK** button again.

11. Click the **YES** button to reboot your computer.

Testing the New Boot Process with Client 32 for Windows 95

1. Boot your Windows 95 station by either turning it on if it is off or by clicking on Shut Down and then Restart Computer if Windows 95 is already active.

2. When prompted, enter **.ADMIN.TREEXXX** for the user ID on the login tab and the password in the password box. Click on the Connections tab to make sure that the desired server is entered in the connections box.

3. Click the OK button to complete the login process. NetWare drives should now be accessible through the Explorer and through My Computer on Windows 95.

Summary

The installation process for the NetWare 4 server gets easier with each new edition of NetWare. In this chapter you learned that NetWare 4 can be installed by either the simple or the custom installation method, and you learned the strict requirements for performing a simple installation. You learned the background information needed for a successful installation, and you performed the installation.

NetWare 4.11 supports a variety of clients. Using the installation CD-ROM disk, diskette sets can be created for the VLM client, as well as the Client 32 clients for DOS/Windows and Windows 95. You also learned how to install and test each of these clients.

Questions

1. What is an enterprise-wide network and how does it differ from a single-server network?

2. What are the minimum hardware requirements for installing NetWare 4.11?

3. What are the minimum software requirements for installing NetWare 4.11?

4. What is SERVER.EXE? How can is be customized for a particular server?

5. What is the Internal IPX Network Number?

6. What is the network number (External IPX number)? How must this number be unique?

7. What are the requirements for a simple NetWare 4.11 install?

8. Why is it necessary to install a bootable DOS partition on the NetWare 4.11 server?

9. What is held in the NWSERVER directory after NetWare 4.11 is installed?

10. What is the difference between IPX.COM/NET#.COM and the VLM client?

11. What is the difference between the VLM client and Client 32 for DOS/Windows 3.1?

12. Is it necessary to have a CD-ROM on every workstation in a NetWare 4.11 network? Why or why not?

13. What is the purpose of the Open Data Link Interface model?

14. How can you determine that a NetWare 4.11 server has been properly installed?

15. How are the interrupt number, memory address, and port address used for interfacing a network interface card with a NetWare 4.11 server?

Project

Objective

There are usually multiple servers in a NetWare 4.11 network. The purpose of this project is to install a second server on top of half of the NDS directory trees created in the Hands-On section of this chapter. This exercise requires more thought than many of the projects in this book.

Outline:

1. For every second server in the classroom, go to the server console and enter

    DOWN and press <Enter>

Wait for the server to go down and then enter

EXIT and press <enter>

NetWare 4 Installation

2. On the "downed" server, boot the machine with the DOS bootable diskette, and use FDISK to remove all the partitions on the hard drive.

3. Repeat the simple installation process, including the creation of the DOS bootable partition, and when prompted for the tree name into which to install, select the tree name of your partner's NDS tree. After this project, each tree will contain two servers.

3
Novell Directory Services

Objectives

After completing this chapter you will

1. Understand the architecture of Novell Directory Services.
2. Be able to describe the major feature and benefits of Novell Directory Services in an enterprise networking environment.
3. Understand the major components of NDS.
4. Understand NDS naming conventions.
5. Be able to create a Windows 3.1x or Windows 95 icon for NetWare Administrator utility.

Key Terms

Objects

Properties

Single Login

Enterprise Network

Values

Container

Country Object

Organization Object

Organizational Unit Object

Leaf Object

Common Name

Distinguished Name

Relative Distinguished Name

NetWare Administrator

NETADMIN

CX

Introduction

Although Novell NetWare version 4 can be used to serve the needs of the small company using a single file server, NetWare 4 was actually created to serve the needs of a large company or even a global company utilizing multiple file servers connected by both local area and wide area networking media. As such, NetWare 4 is described as an enterprise system. With NetWare 3 and earlier versions of NetWare, companies could utilize multiple file servers, but each user had to be set up with a unique user account for each file server. Thus, network administration in this multiple file server environment was difficult, to say the least.

With NetWare 4 came the advent of the enterprise-wide single log in for each user through the use of Novell Directory Services and the Novell Directory Services tree concept. The purpose of this chapter is to explain the architecture of NDS and how it is used to support an enterprise-wide network. The chapter also explains the naming conventions for objects in the NDS tree and will examine several utilities used with NDS. Finally, it will present hands-on exercises on how to create an icon for NetWare Administrator on both Windows 3.1 and Windows 95.

Overview of NDS

Novell Directory Services (NDS) is a directory naming service provided by Novell as a part of all Novell NetWare 4 network operating systems. NDS keeps a directory of all network components ranging from users to file servers to printers. Each of the network components is called an **object** in NDS, and each object has **properties** or characteristics specific to the type of object. The entire database of network components and their values is organized into a hierarchical configuration, which is referred to as the NDS tree.

All users on all NetWare 4 servers in a single NDS database or tree have access to all the network resources in the tree, depending on NDS object trustee assignments, which are assigned to the user. This means that a user can have a **single login** ID and be granted rights to any NDS object in the tree and to the file system on any of the file servers that are a part of the tree.

NDS is a single global database that supports centralized management of network resources for an **enterprise network**. Additionally, it provides

Novell Directory Services

for a logical organization of network resources, which is independent of the physical location of network resources. NetWare 4 provides a series of utilities to view the components of the NDS tree for ease of maintenance. Most importantly, though, NDS allows a single user log in to provide access to all the network resources that the user needs.

NDS consists of several types of architectural components that are generically called objects. Each of these objects has characteristics called properties, and each property can then have one or more **values**. In general, objects are such things as users, printers, file servers, etc., which have characteristics or properties that are particular to the type of object. For example, a user would have a name, a password, etc., while a printer would have a name, a print queue assignment, etc. The value of a property is the actual current worth of a specific characteristic. For example, a user might be named John, and thus, the value of the name property for that user would be John. Refer to Figure 3-1 for an example of the properties and values assigned to the user John as compared to the properties and values assigned to the file server SERVER1.

USER OBJECT - John

Property	Value
Name	John
Title	Manager Accountant
Password	novell

Server Object - SERVER1

Property	Object
Name	SERVER1
Location	First Floor Computer Room
Net Address	332C4603: 000000000001: 0451

Figure 3-1. Properties and values of a user object and a server object.

NDS Architecture Overview

An NDS tree consists of various types of objects originating from an object called (ROOT). Additionally, an NDS tree can consist of various container and leaf objects as shown in Figure 3-2.

Chapter 3

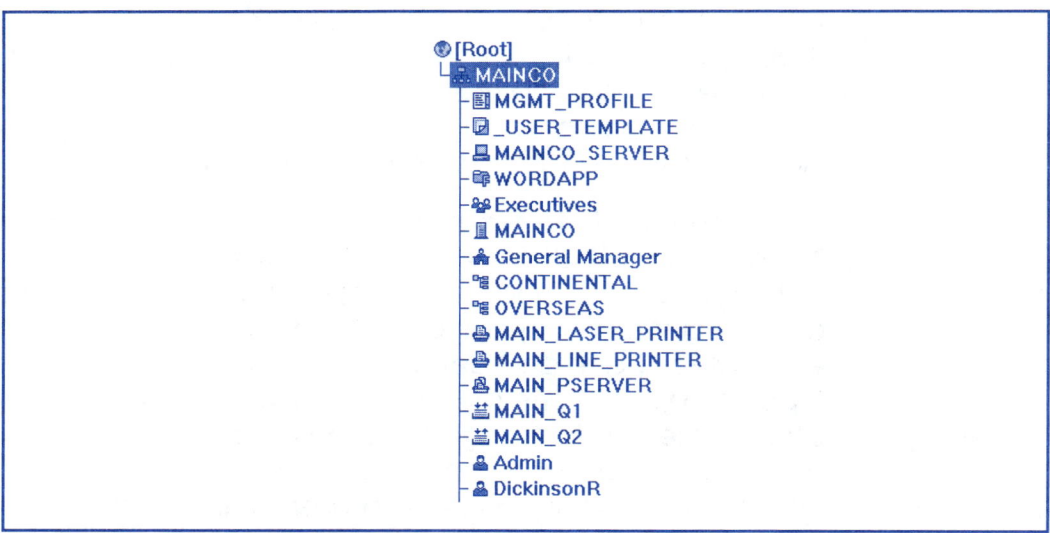

Figure 3-2. A sample NDS tree.

(ROOT)

The (ROOT) object is the highest level in the NDS tree and ultimately provides access to all other objects in the tree. There is only one (ROOT) in any NDS tree, and it cannot be moved, deleted, or renamed. It can contain only Country, Organization, and Alias objects pointing to Country or Organization objects. These objects are explained below.

Container Objects

A **container** object is a grouping object that exists for the purpose of organizing other objects in the NDS directory tree. There are three types of container objects besides the (ROOT), which is the ultimate container object, containing everything in the NDS tree.

The three types of containers are:

Country Object

Organization Object

Organizational Unit Object

Each of these objects is explained below.

Country Object

The Country object is used to indicate the country where the network resides. The object is used to organize other NDS directory objects within the country. When used, this object must be a valid two-character country code. However, since use of the object is optional and since over time it has become apparent that many companies do not organize along country boundaries, the use of the Country code is not widespread. In fact, this object is rarely used in NetWare 4 designs.

Organization

Every NDS directory tree must have at least one **organization object**. This object represents the highest level in the NDS directory tree beneath (ROOT) and can represent the entire company. Alternately, a company may have multiple divisions or organizations at the top and therefore would have multiple organization objects at the top of the tree. This object can contain leaf objects or Organizational Units. It can also contain alias objects, which point to other Organizational Units or leaf objects.

Organizational Unit

An **organizational unit** represents a subdivision of the company, perhaps a division, a department, or a workgroup. It can be contained in an Organization or in another Organizational Unit. It can also contain leaf objects and alias objects pointing to other leaf objects or Organizational Units. The purpose of the Organizational Unit is to subdivide the company from an organizational viewpoint.

Leaf Objects

The actual resources in a network are called **leaf objects**. These include such things as users, printers, computers, servers, volumes on servers, print queues, etc.

A list of the available container and leaf objects and their definition is shown in Figure 3-3.

Putting the Objects Together

Using the object definitions and rules given earlier in this chapter a particular NDS directory tree might look like the tree in Figure 3-4. In this tree, the company has

>One Organization Object called MAINCO.

>Main divisions called CONTINENTAL and OVERSEAS represented by Organizational Units.

>The CONTINENTAL Organization Unit is further subdivided into NY, SANFRAN, and DALLAS Organizational Units. OVERSEAS is further subdivided into LONDON and FRANKFURT organizational units. Each Organizational Unit contains leaf objects appropriate to the workings of the company.

Chapter 3

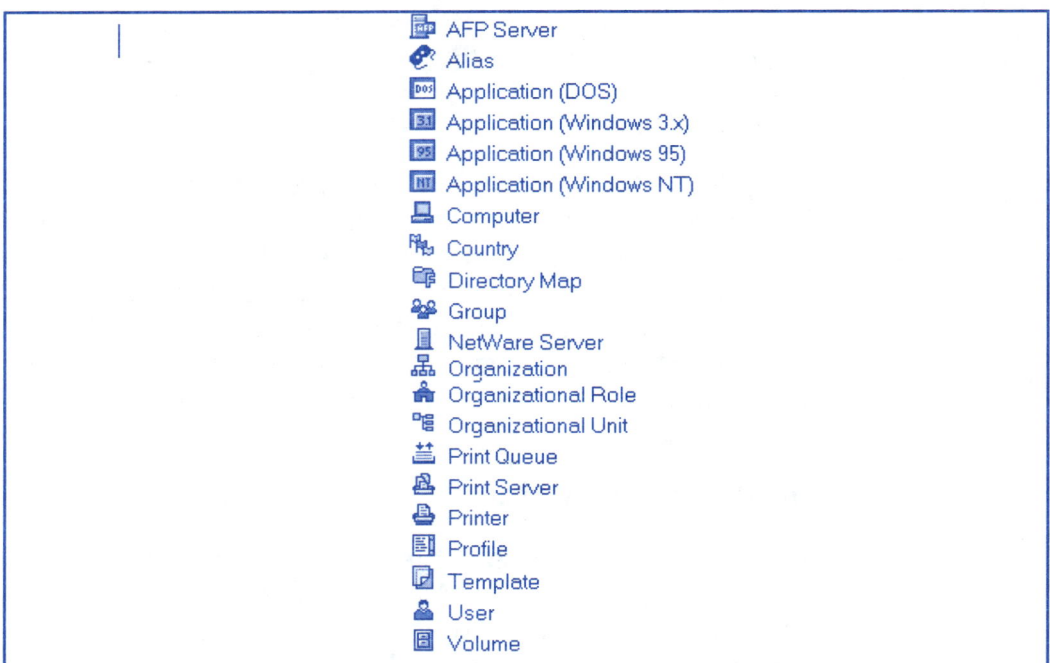

Figure 3-3. Container and Leaf Objects

Naming Conventions

Just as one must understand the directory naming conventions of DOS in order to handle DOS operations, the network administrator must understand the NDS directory object naming conventions in order to successfully work with objects in an NDS tree. In order to understand the naming conventions themselves, we must first discuss the concepts of context, current context, common name, distinguished name, and relative distinguished name.

Context

The context of an object is the NDS name of the container containing the object. It lists the containers from the container in question back to the (ROOT). The context of an object does not change regardless of who is viewing the NDS directory tree or what container is currently being viewed.

The context of the user MannS is the Accounting container, and the Accounting container's distinguished name is

Accounting.DALLAS.CONTINENTAL.MAINCO

Novell Directory Services

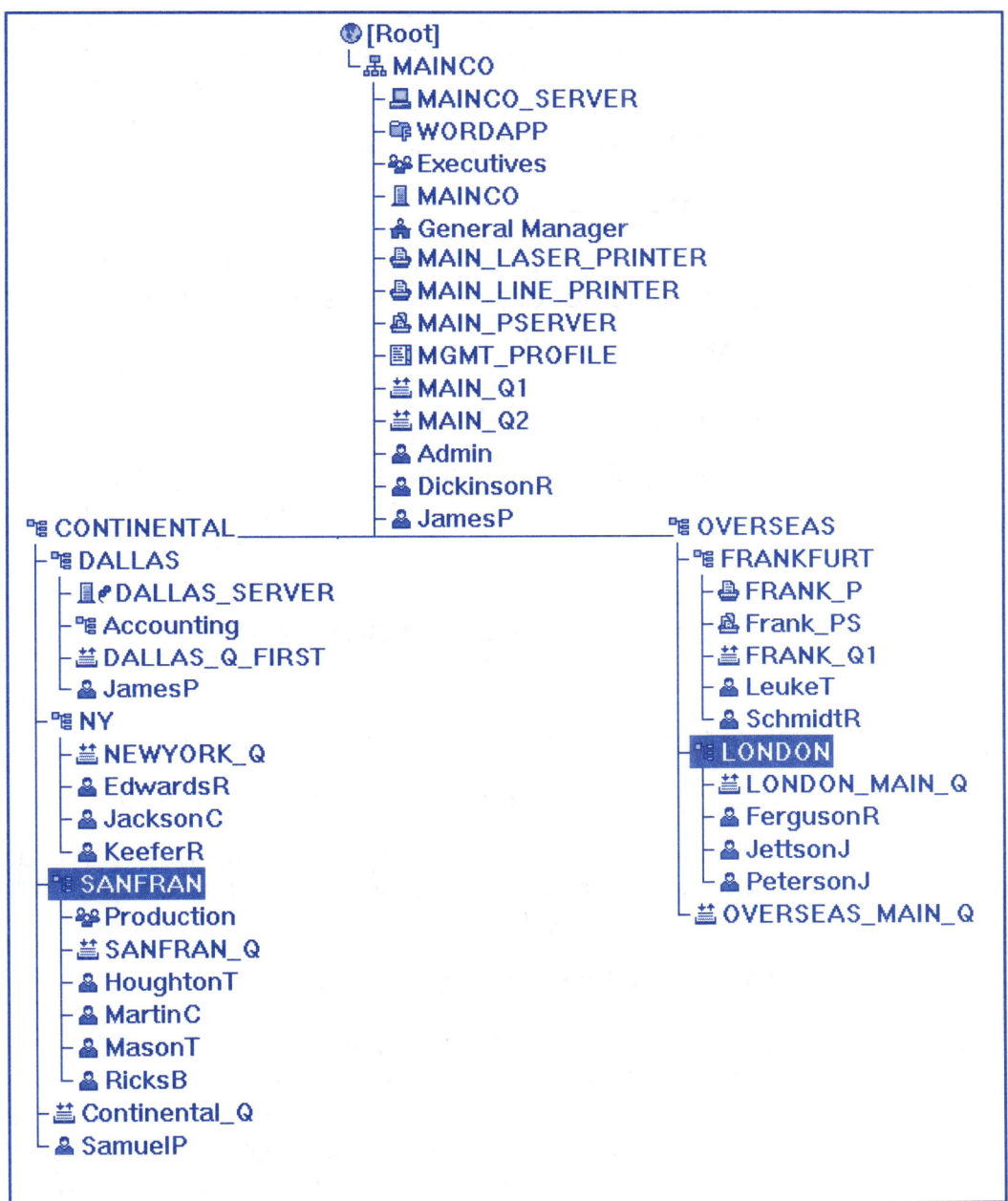

Figure 3-4. A representative NDS tree for MAINCO

Current Context

Current context is the name of the container that the person logged in and viewing the NDS directory tree is currently viewing. The current context varies by what portion of the NDS directory tree is being viewed. It lists the containers from the current container being viewed back to the (ROOT). To determine the current context, one can enter CX from the command line through either DOS or Windows 95.

For example, if the user's current context were the DALLAS container, the following would be displayed when the CX command is entered at the command prompt:

.DALLAS.CONTINENTAL.MAINCO

Common Name

A leaf object's **common name** is simply the name of the object. The common name for MannS in the Accounting container is just

MannS

Distinguished Name

The **distinguished name** for an object begins with a period and contains the common name of the object and the name of the object's context. For example, the distinguished name of JamesP in Figure 3-4 is

.JamesP.DALLAS.CONTINENTAL.MAINCO

The distinguished name of the Accounting container in Figure 3-4 is

.Accounting.DALLAS.CONTINENTAL.MAINCO

Note that each distinguished name must begin with a period. The distinguished name for an object fully and uniquely identifies the NDS object in the NDS tree.

Relative Distinguished Name

An object's **relative distinguished name** varies with the current context. It lists the name of the object and the containers from the object's context, which when combined with the fully distinguished name of the current context yields the fully distinguished name of the object. For example, if the current context were O=CONTINENTAL, the relative distinguished name for SamuelP, a user object in the CONTINENTAL Organization, is merely SamuelP. The relative distinguished name for Mason, a user in the SANFRAN Organizational Unit, is MASON.SANFRAN, given the current context is O=CONTINENTAL.

The rules for forming a relative distinguished name are:

> A relative distinguished name never begins with a period.
>
> A relative distinguished name, when appended with the distinguished name of the current context and when preceded by a period, forms the distinguished name of the original object.

Each trailing period on the right of a relative distinguished name removes one container from the left of the current context.

For example, the relative distinguished name for MannS considering the current context is the DALLAS container is determined as follows:

First determine the distinguished name for MannS:

.MannS.Accounting.DALLAS.CONTINENTAL.MAINCO

Then, determine the distinguished name for the current context:

.DALLAS.CONTINENTAL.MAINCO

The relative distinguished name is determined by calculating the part of the distinguished name for MannS not contained in the current context:

MannS.Accounting

The relative distinguished name for PetersonJ in the LONDON container, assuming the current context is the LONDON container, is determined the same way:

First, the distinguished name for PetersonJ is

.PetersonJ.LONDON.OVERSEAS.MAINCO

Then, the distinguished name for the LONDON container is determined:

.LONDON.OVERSEAS.MAINCO

The relative distinguished name for PetersonJ is therefore just

PetersonJ

Now consider determining a somewhat more difficult relative distinguished name. Consider PetersonJ's relative distinguished name considering the current context is the DALLAS container.

First, the distinguished name for Peterson J is

.PetersonJ.LONDON.OVERSEAS.MAINCO

The distinguished name for DALLAS is

.DALLAS.CONTINENTAL.MAINCO

Therefore, the relative distinguished name for PetersonJ is

PetersonJ.LONDON.OVERSEAS..

Note that the two periods at the right of the relative distinguished name remove two containers from the left of the distinguished name of the current context.

Utilities For Managing and Manipulating NDS

Novell provides three main utilities for managing and manipulating NDS. They are

NetWare Administrator

NETADMIN

CX

NetWare Administrator is a graphical user interface that runs under Windows 3.1s and Windows 95. There is also a version of NetWare Administrator for Windows NT. This textbook will focus on Windows 3.1 and Windows 95 because of their wide popularity as clients in NetWare 4 networks. Figure 3-5 shows NetWare Administrator's view of the NDS tree for the MAINCO company.

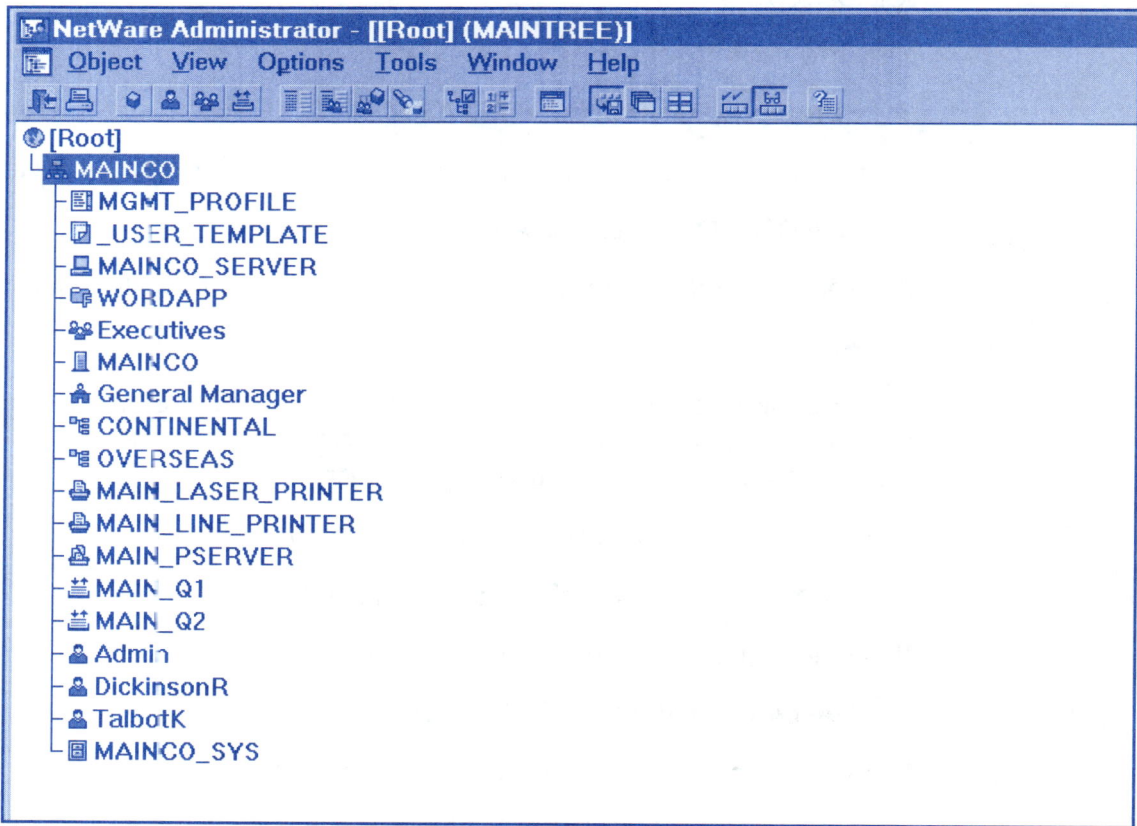

Figure 3-5. NetWare Administrator view of MAINCO NDS tree.

NETADMIN is a DOS text-base menu type utility that provides many of the same functions as NetWare Administrator. It was popular during the earlier days of NetWare 4 because of the general lack of widespread

Novell Directory Services

use of Windows. Figure 3-6 shows NETADMIN's view of the NDS tree for the MAINCO company. NETADMIN is no longer popular and will not be covered further in this textbook.

CX is a command line utility that can be used to display the user's current context and to navigate NDS. CX will be used throughout the text from time to time for convenience. If the user's current context were .DALLAS.MAINCO, the following would be displayed when the user enters the command CX at the command prompt:

.DALLAS.MAINCO

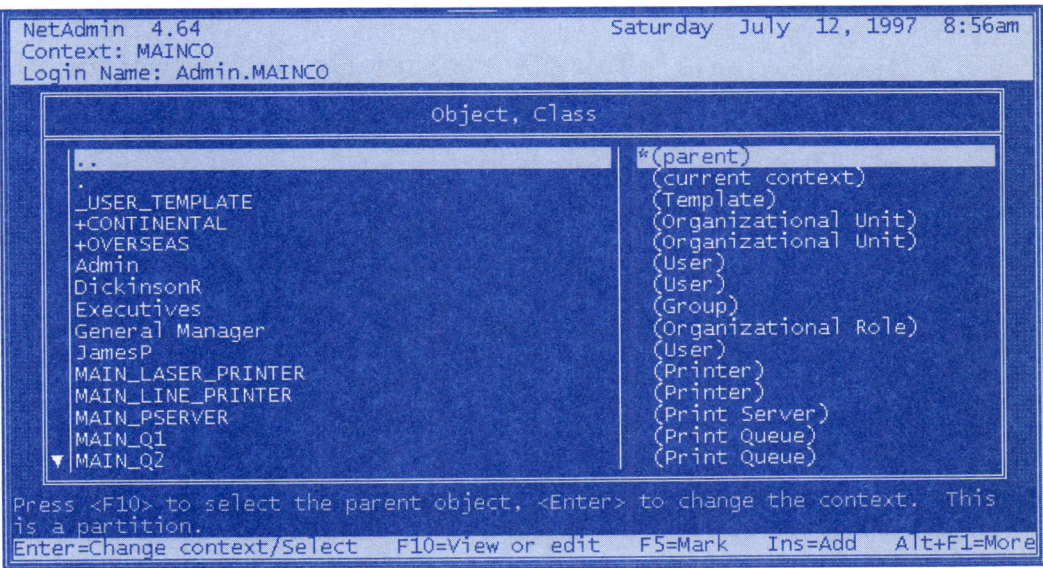

Figure 3-6. NetADMIN view of MAINCO NDS tree.

NetWare Administrator

As previously mentioned, versions of NetWare Administrator are available for both Windows 3.1 and Windows 95. The following hands-on exercises will illustrate how to create an icon for NetWare Administrator.

Hands-On Creating an Icon for NetWare Administrator in Windows 3.1

1. Boot the computer. (Consult your instructor for specifics about booting your computer. In general, this is accomplished by simultaneously pressing the Ctrl, Alt, and Del keys.)

2. Log into your NetWare 4 server with your user ID and password, which were assigned by your instructor.

3. Activate Windows. (Again consult your instructor for specific instructions. Generally, Windows 3.1 can be activated by entering WIN and pressing the <Enter> key.)

4. Click on the **Windows** selection on the main Windows menu bar and then highlight the **NetWare Window** to bring this window into focus.

5. Click on the **Name box** and enter **NetWare Administrator.**

6. Click on the **Command box** and then click on the **Browse button** and locate **NWADM3X.EXE** in the PUBLIC directory on the SYS volume of the server. (This is likely to be on drive letter Z: but it may be in another location. Consult your instructor.)

7. Click on the **OK button** to complete the function,

The NetWare Administrator Icon should now appear on the screen.

Hands-On Creating an Icon for NetWare Administrator on the Desktop in Windows 95

1. Bring up the computer in Windows 95. (Consult your instructor for specifics for brining up Windows 95. In general, it is merely necessary to turn on the computer, but different lab setups may require different use interaction.)

2. Log into your NetWare 4 server with your user ID and password, which were assigned by your instructor.

3. Activate Windows Explorer by clicking on the **Start button**, then the **Program icon**, and then **Windows Explorer**.

4. Locate **the drive that is mapped to the SYS volume of your file server**. Click it open.

5. Locate **the PUBLIC** directory and click it open.

6. Locate **the NWADMN95.EXE** program and **drag and drop it onto the desktop**.

A shortcut to NetWare Adminstrator is now shown on the desktop.

Summary

NetWare 4 is described as an enterprise system, providing a single log on fcr each user, which can be configured to grant the user access to resources on multiple servers and to NDS itself. The NDS tree structure is the crchitectural component that makes the single log on possible.

Novell Directory Services

NDS is a series of containers and leaf objects that represent the functional network. The naming convention for NDS relies on two types of names: the distinguished name and the relative distinguished name. Each of these names requires a knowledge of context and current context in order to form or interpret NDS names.

This chapter explained the architecture of NDS and how it is used to support an enterprise-wide network. The chapter also explained the NDS naming conventions for objects in the NDS tree. It also presented an exercise in which you created an icon on the desktop for NetWare Administrator, the NetWare 4.11 account and resource administration tool.

Questions

1. Identify the components of an NDS directory.
2. How does the NDS directory support a single user log in?
3. What is an object? What are examples of objects?
4. What are properties of objects? What are values of properties? Give an example of properties and values of properties for a user named Peter Jensen and a print queue named MAINCO_Q.
5. What is a country object and why is it not often used?
6. What is an organization object and what kinds of objects can it contain?
7. What is an organizational unit object and what kinds of objects can it contain?
8. What is a leaf object? List and explain at least five types of leaf objects.
9. What is an NDS tree?
10. What is the (ROOT) of an NDS tree?
11. What is the distinguished name for MartinC in Figure 3-4?
12. What is the distinguished name for JamesP in Figure 3-4?
13. What is the relative distinguished name for JamesP in Figure 3-4, assuming current context is the CONTINENTAL container?
14. What is the relative distinguished name for MartinC in Figure 3-4 assuming current context is the Accounting container?

15. What is the relative distinguished name for the DALLAS container in Figure 3-4 assuming current context is the OVERSEAS container?

Project

Objective

The purpose of this project is to give the student more practice in determining distinguished and relative distinguished names. The exercise utilizes the Directory tree in Figure 3-4:

Part I:

Give the distinguished name for each of the following:

1. FergusonR in the FRANKFURT container.
2. JettsonJ in the LONDON container.
3. RicksB in the SANFRAN container.
4. NEWYORK_Q in the NY container.
5. MAIN_PSERVER in the MAINCO container.
6. FRANK_PS in the FRANKFURT container.
7. MartinC in the SANFRAN container.
8. EDWARDSR in the NY container.
9. The Accounting container in the Dallas container.
10. MAIN_Q in the MAINCO container.

Part II:

Give the relative distinguished name for each of the following assuming the current context indicated.

Object	Current Context
FergusonR	OVERSEAS
KeeferR	LONDON
EdwardsR	CONTINENTAL
MAIN_PSERVER	LONDON
Continental_Q	LONDON
FRANK_Q1	OVERSEAS
FRANK_Q1	SANFRAN
DALLAS	LONDON
LeukeT	LONDON
MasonT	FRANKFURT

4
Creating the User Account, Mappings, and Login Scripts

Objectives

After completing this chapter you will

1. Understand how to use NetWare Administrator to create user accounts.
2. Understand the functions of each of the main option buttons for a user object.
3. Be able to define and understand the purpose of each of the four types of login scripts.
4. Understand login script commands.
5. Understand how to use login script variables.
6. Understand how to map network and search drives.
7. Be able to log in and log out of a file server.

Key Terms

File Server

Login Restrictions

Password Restrictions

Login Time Restrictions

Network Address Restrictions

Intruder Lockout

Group

Security Equal To

Postal Address

Chapter 4

>Login Script
>
>Container Login Script
>
>Profile Login Script
>
>User Login Script

Introduction

In the last chapter, Novell NetWare was installed on the **file server** and the workstation was booted with the network workstation software. That arrangement allowed the user Admin, the administrator for the network, to log in to the file server and view the files listed there. Now the file server must be set up to allow other users to log in and easily manage their files and directories.

NetWare 4.11's major system configuration utility is NetWare Acministrator. Using this utility, the Admin can begin to create user accounts, groups of user accounts, and other types of objects introduced in the last chapter. Each account or group can have different access rights, legal login times, and other attributes. Many of the controls used to set up the user's environment are executed when the user logs in through the use of a login script. It can set the user's drive mappings, check various conditions at the time the user logs in, and write messages to the screen.

NetWare Administrator

Introduction

NetWare Administrator, NWAdmin, allows the network administrators to create, change, and delete users and groups of users in addition to enabling many other functions. It is by far the most important utility Novell provides with NetWare 4.11 since it used to set up the most fundamental aspects of the network. As with many NetWare utilities, some menu options only appear for the Admin. Users can choose other limited menu options themselves to view and change their own accounts. Figure 4-1 shows NetWare Administrator's main screen.

Creation of a User Account

To create a user one would

1. Click on the container to contain the user. You should create for yourself an Administrator equivalent account that you can use throughout the course.

Creating the User Account, Mappings and Login Scripts

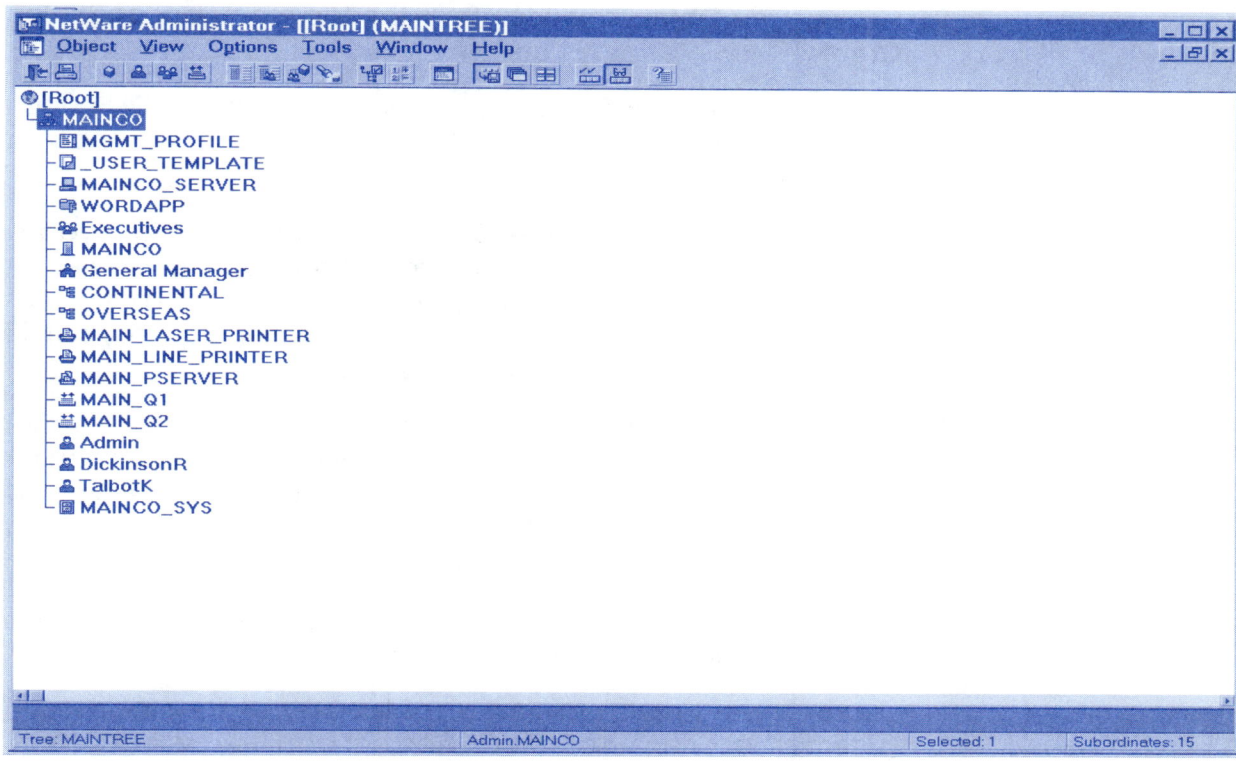

Figure 4-1. NetWare Administrator main screen.

Figure 4-2. Selecting the Create User icon.

2. Click on the **Object** selection from the top menu bar and select **Create**.

3. Select the **User type object** and then click on the **OK** button. (Alternatively, one could click the Create User icon as shown in Figure 4-2.)

4. Using either technique, the Create User screen is displayed as shown in Figure 4-3. Click on the **Login ID box** and enter the user's login ID. Click on the **Last Name** box and enter a last name. You may think that the last name is not required, but it is a critical property for a user in NetWare 4.11.

5. Click on the **Create Home Directory** box and use the second browse button to navigate and locate the Users directory on the SYS volume of the server. By default, the user's home directory will be created beneath the directory indicated, and it will be named by the user's login name.

6. Click on **Create** to create the user. (Other selections in this window are optional and will be discussed in later exercises.)

7. Locate the new user just created and double click it. (Alternatively, right click the user object and then select details.)

8. A screen such as the one shown in Figure 4-4 is displayed.

The selection buttons on the right-hand side of the screen can vary based on the Page Options chosen, but, in general, they are as follows:

Identification

Environment

Login Restrictions

Password Restrictions

Login Time Restrictions

Network Address Restriction

Print Job Configuration

Login Script

Intruder Lockout

Rights to Files and Directories

Group Membership

Security Equal To

Postal Address

Creating the User Account, Mappings and Login Scripts

Account Balance*

See Also*

Applications*

Launcher Configuration*

NetWare Registry Editor*

Note that the starred items will not be discussed as part of this introductory course. Each of the other topics will be explained before a hands-on session.

Each of the pertinent buttons listed above will be discussed as preparation for a hands-on exercise to allow the student to create his or her own user account.

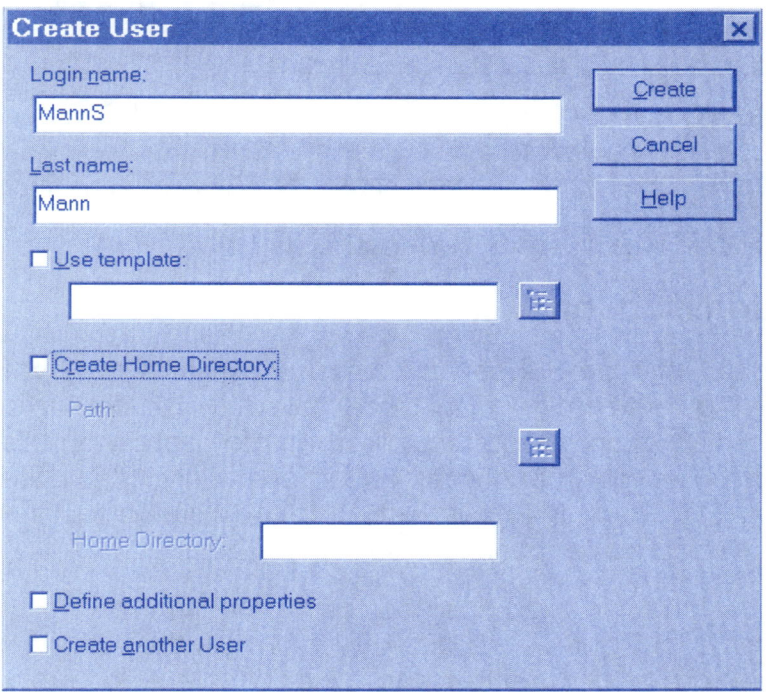

Figure 4-3. Create a new user screen.

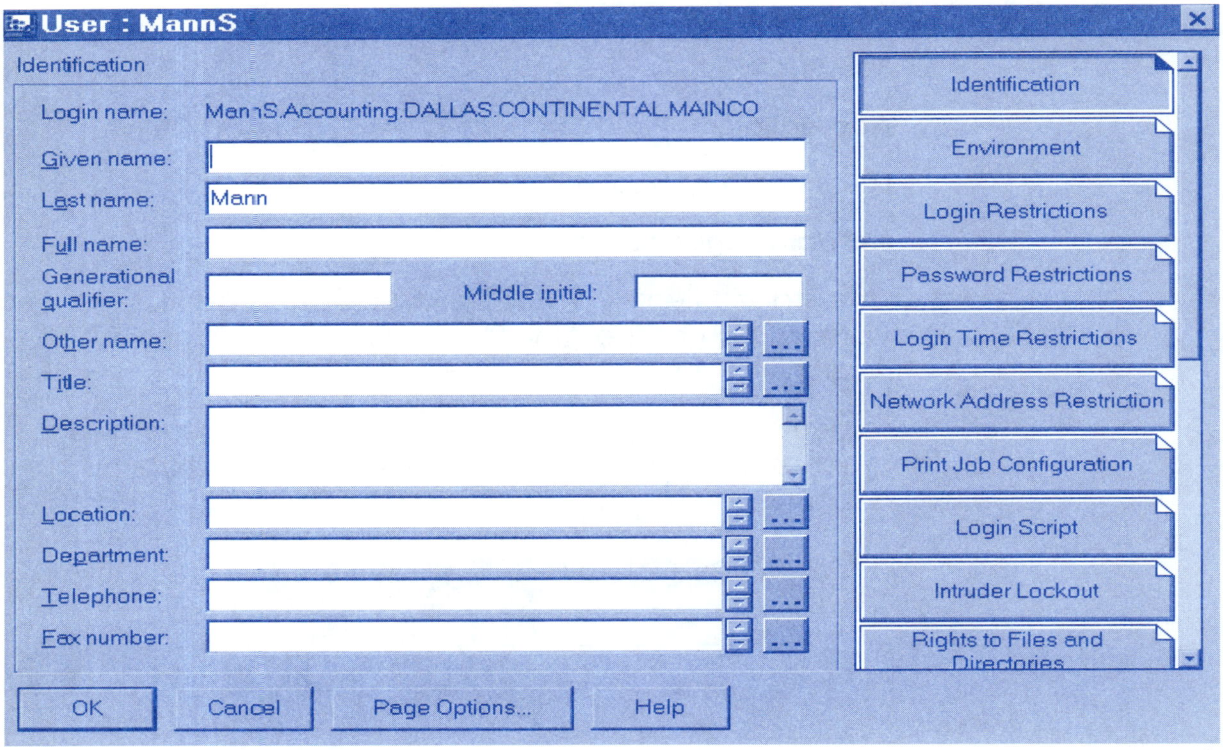

Chapter 4

Figure 4-4. Identification page for a new user.

Identification

This button produces the initial user screen where various types of identifying information can be entered. With the exception of the last name, which is required, all other information on this screen is optional and used for identification purposes only. It is noteworthy that each item that has an Ellipsis button on the right (a square with three periods in it) can have multiple values.

If we click on the Ellipsis button to the right of the Title line, the screen shown in Figure 4-5 is displayed. When the Add button is clicked, the user can enter a title for the user. If the Add button is clicked again, another title can be entered as shown in Figure 4-6. Then, when the OK button is clicked, the main identification screen is once again displayed. The two titles can alternately be displayed by clicking the up or the down arrow to the right of the title field.

Environment

The Environment page shows particulars about the user's operating environment as shown in Figure 4-7. Most notable for the beginning student is the specification for the user's home directory, a designation that can be changed from this screen if necessary.

Creating the User Account, Mappings and Login Scripts

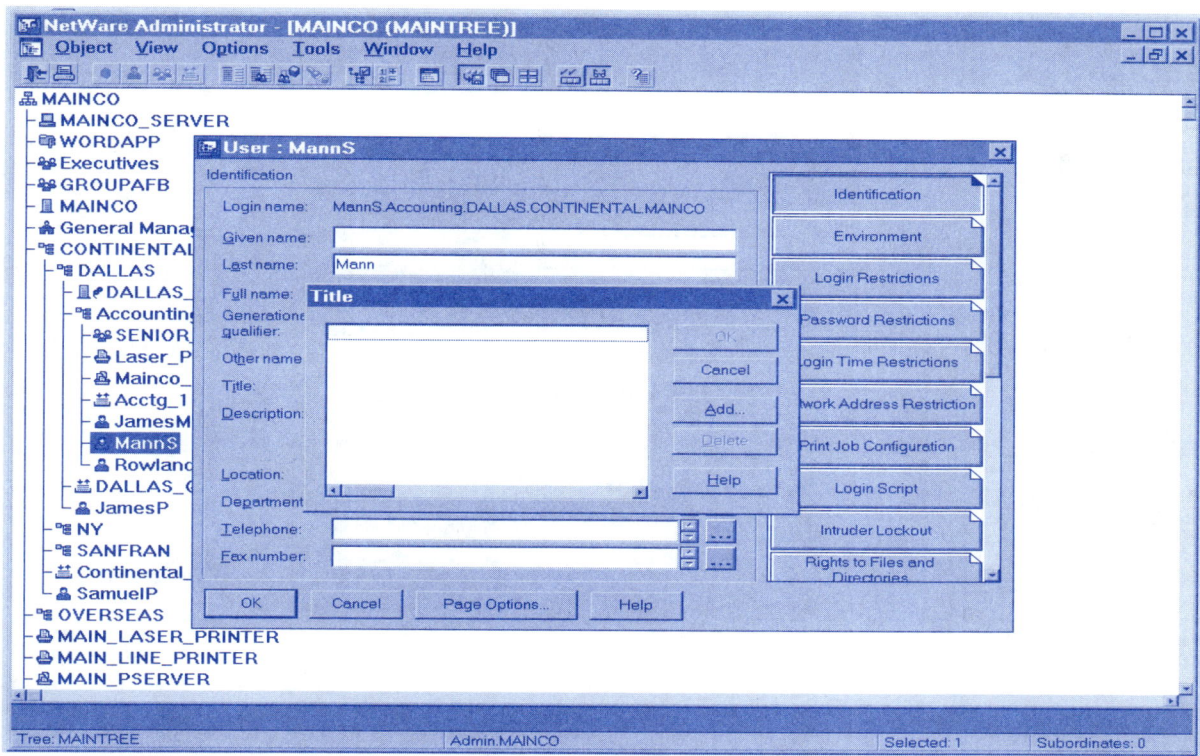

Figure 4-5. Using the Ellipsis button on the Title field.

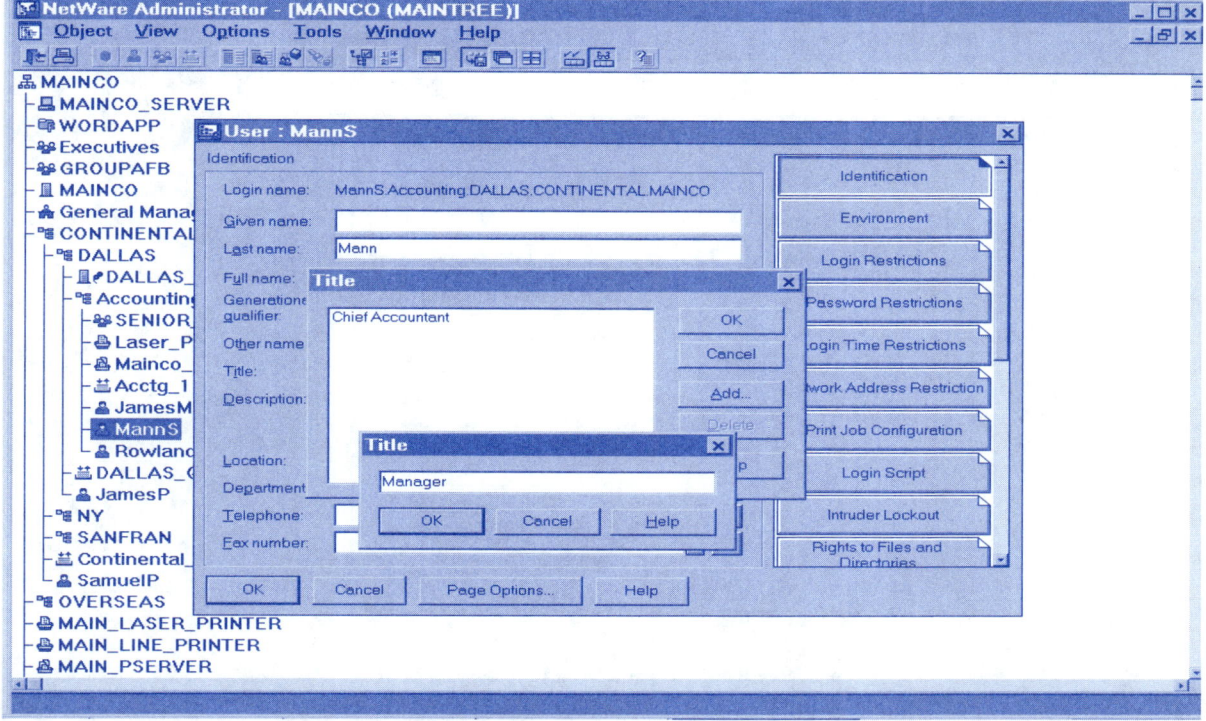

Figure 4-6. Adding a new title.

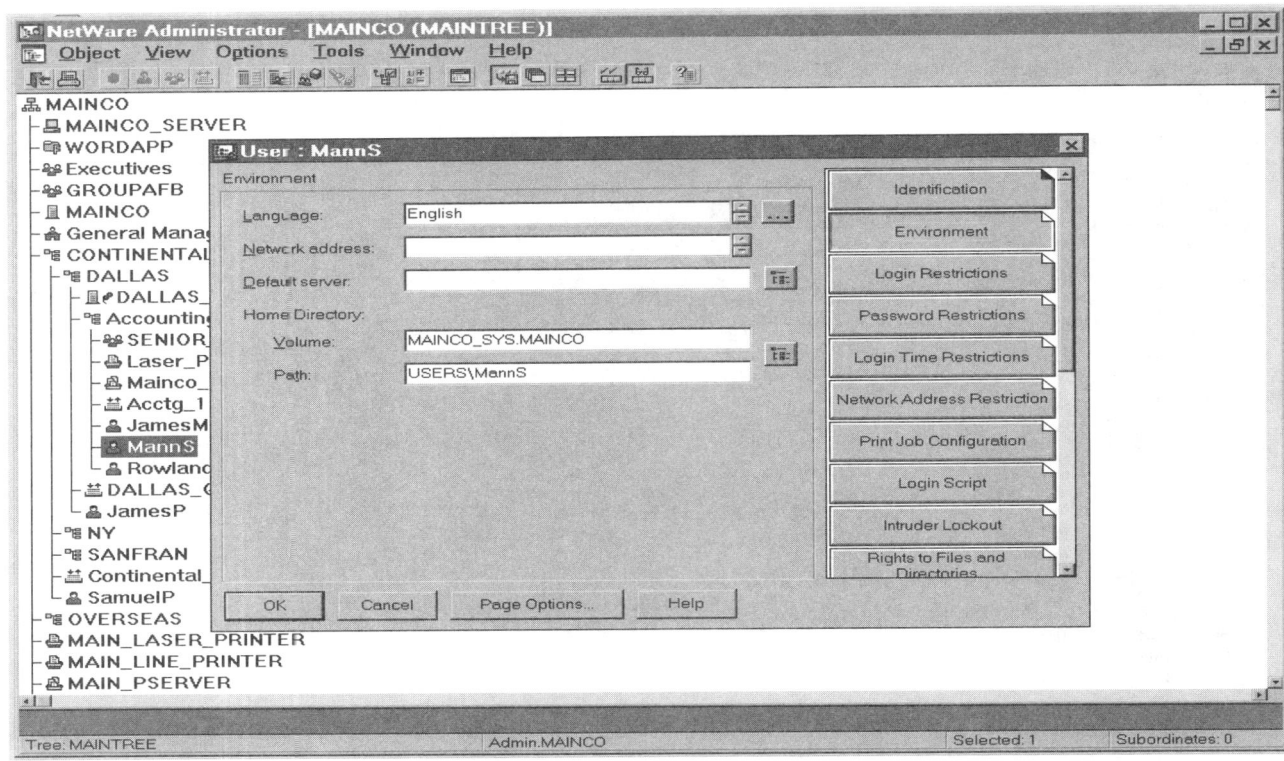

Figure 4-7. The Environment page for a user.

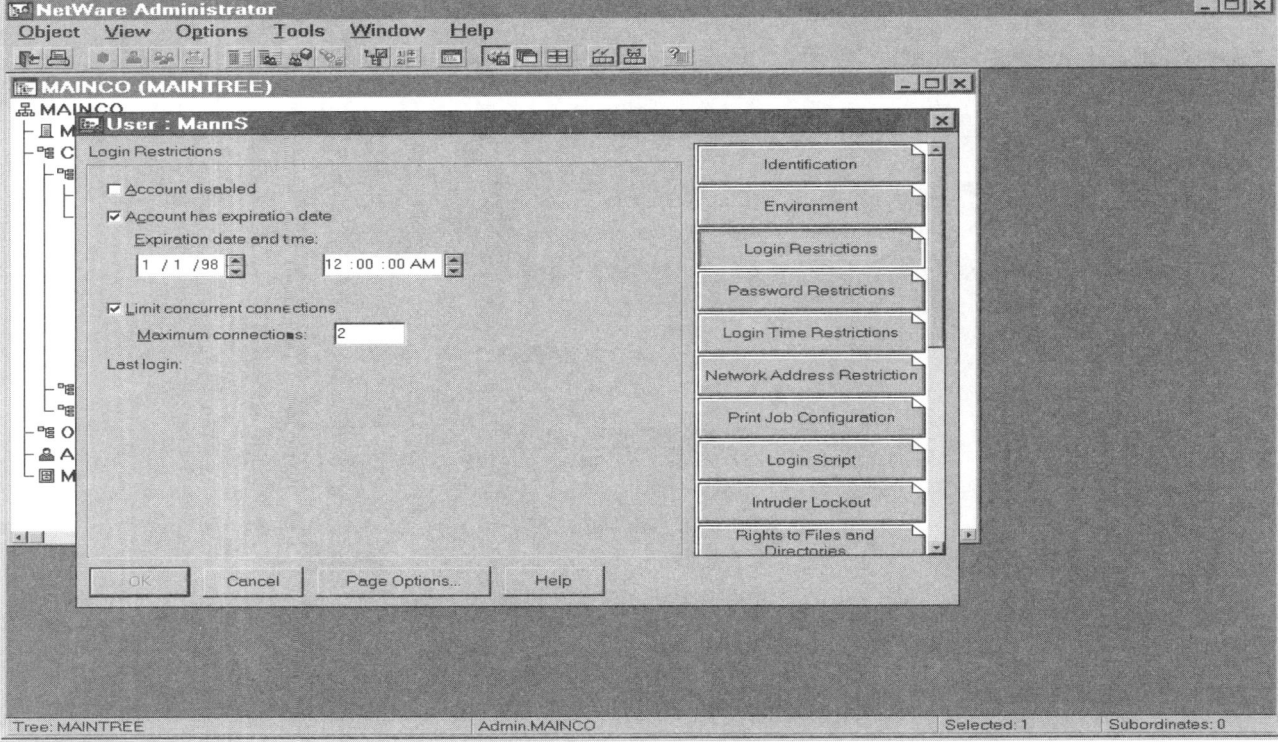

Figure 4-8. The Login Restrictions page.

Login Restrictions

The **login restrictions** page is shown in Figure 4-8. This page allows the administrator to disable the account, to set an expiration date for the account, and to limit concurrent connections.

The Account Disabled option is most often used to disable an account for a person who no longer works for the company. In most cases, it is important that the account merely be disabled rather than being deleted so that the structure and access rights that the person was using can be retained until someone else can take his or her job. Additionally, this feature can be used to allow the Administrator to create an account for a new employee but to leave it deactivated until the employee reports for work.

The Account expiration date should be set for temporary or contract employees so that the Administrator does not have to remember to deactivate these users' accounts when the user no longer works for the company. If the user's contract is extended, all the Administrator need do is to change the expiration date so that the user can once again use the account.

The Limit Concurrent Connections option is used to keep a user from using the same login ID in many places throughout the company simultaneously. There are several reasons for wanting to limit a user's simultaneous connections. Most important is that several applications utilize the user's login name to identify temporary files the application has to create in normal processing. If the user is logged in from multiple stations, there is a good chance that duplicate temporary files may be created and that they may collide. Additionally, many usage statistics are kept by user ID. Therefore, if a single user is using his or her ID at multiple stations on a regular basis, these statistics will be skewed. If the user really needs additional accounts for business reasons, the administrator can easily create additional separate accounts for the user, thus avoiding clashes.

Password Restrictions

The **Password Restrictions** page is shown in Figure 4-9. The information on this page is fully discussed in the next chapter and will therefore be omitted here.

Login Time Restrictions

The **Login Time Restrictions** page is shown in Figure 4-10. It can be used to block the user from logging in by boxing the desired block-out time with the mouse and then clicking the OK button. The Login Time

Chapter 4

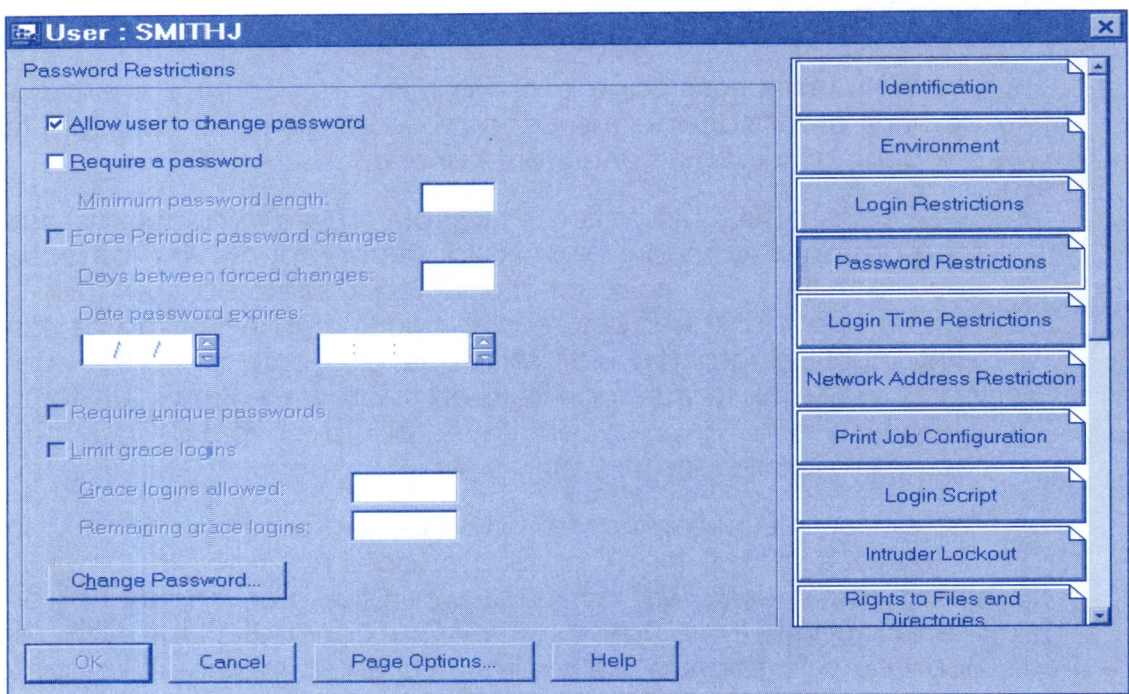

Figure 4-9. The Password Restrictions page.

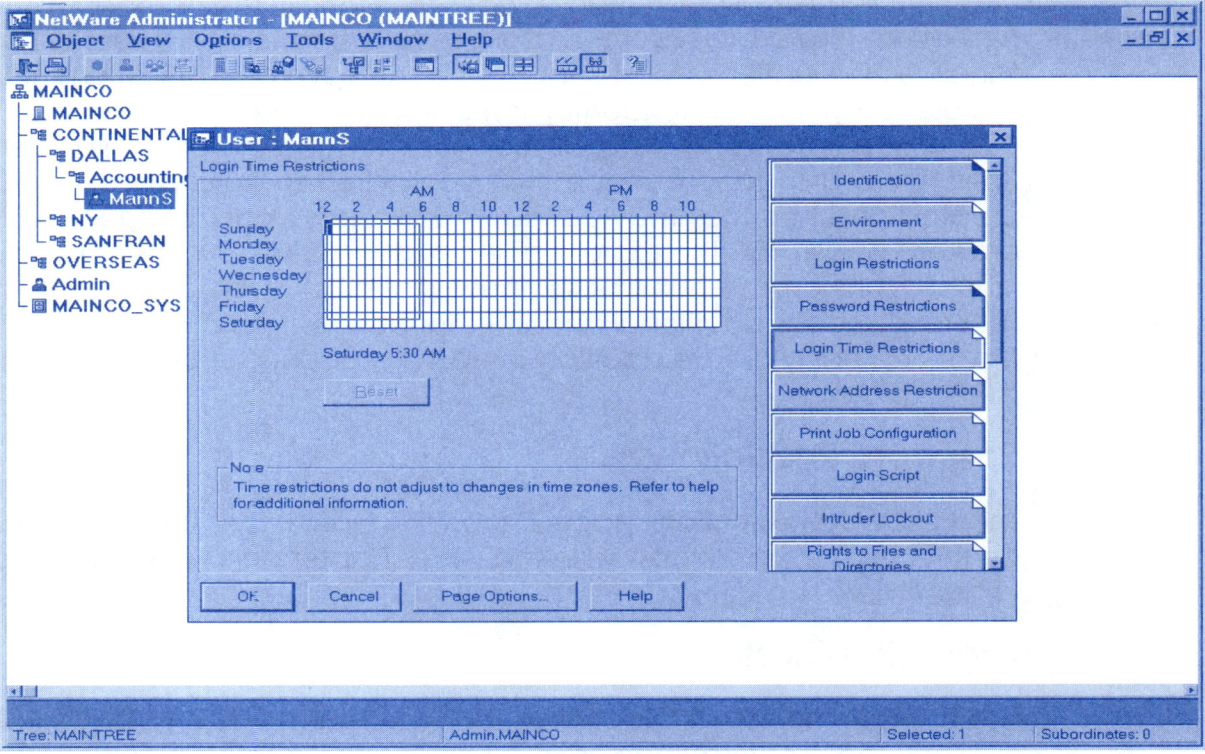

Figure 4-10. The Login Time Restrictions page.

Creating the User Account, Mappings and Login Scripts

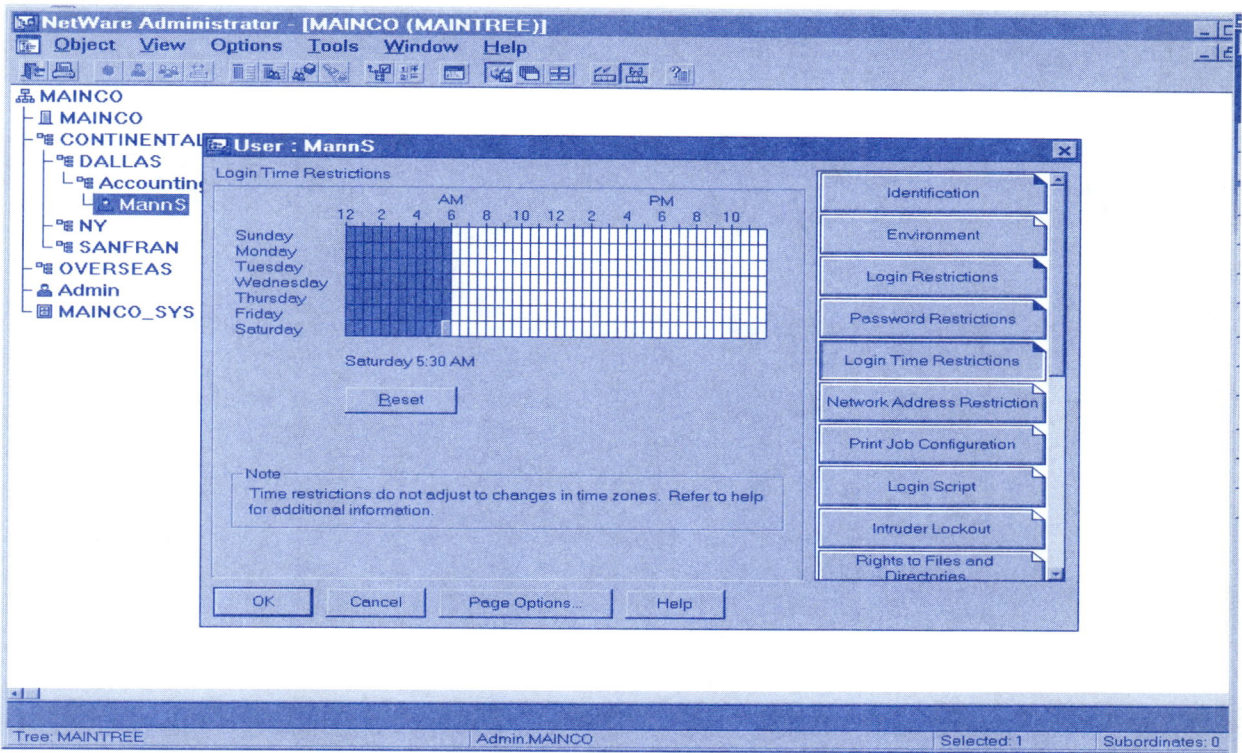

Figure 4-11. The Login Time Restrictions page with midnight to 6 a.m. excluded.

Restrictions screen is shown in 30 minute increments, 24 hours per day, 7 days per week. Figure 4-11 shows the login restrictions being set for user MannS who cannot log in from 12 midnight until 6 a.m. seven days per week.

Network Address Restriction

The **Network Address Restriction** page is shown in Figure 4-12. This page can be used to limit the physical stations that a user can use for logging in and to limit the protocols that the user can use from the station. Except in highly secure organizations, implementation of this restriction can cause more harm than good because it makes it impossible for a user to automatically use another station within the company if his or her station is inoperable.

Print Job Configuration

This page is discussed in Chapter 13 and will not be discussed here.

Login Script

This page contains information about the user's login script, and it allows the administrator to cause a profile login script to be executed

Chapter 4

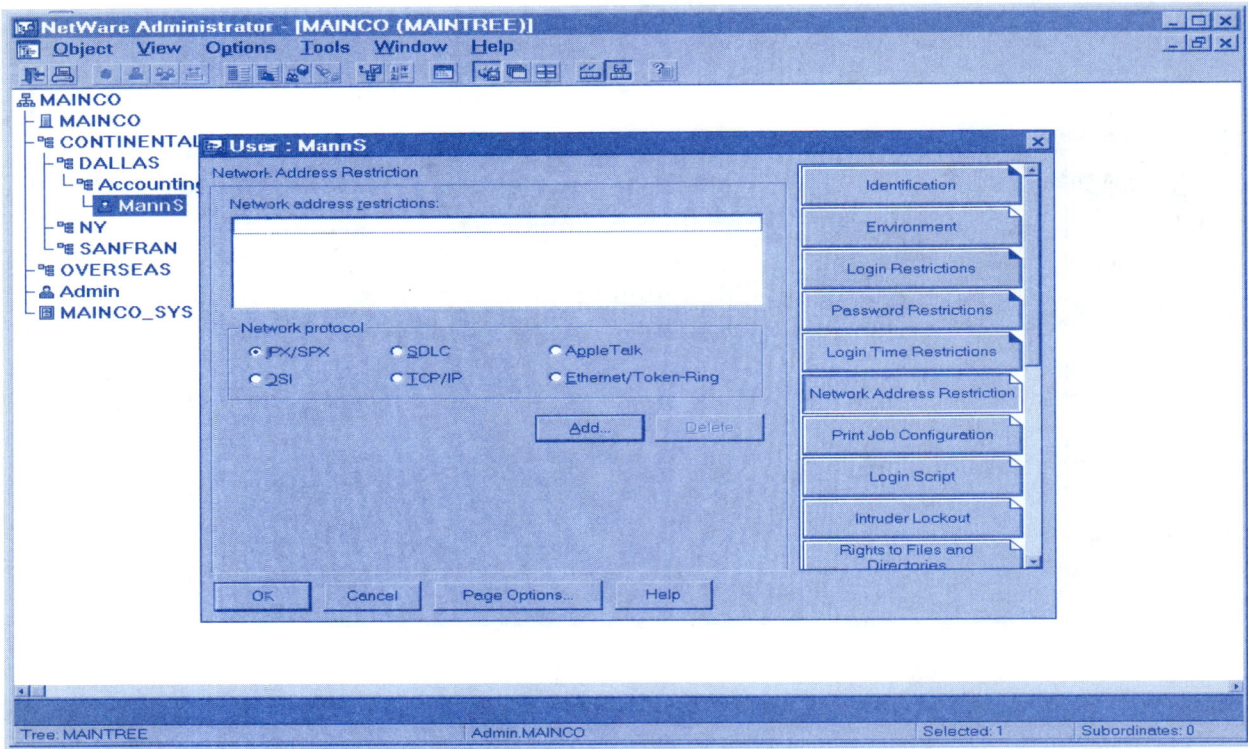

Figure 4-12. The Network Address Restrictions page.

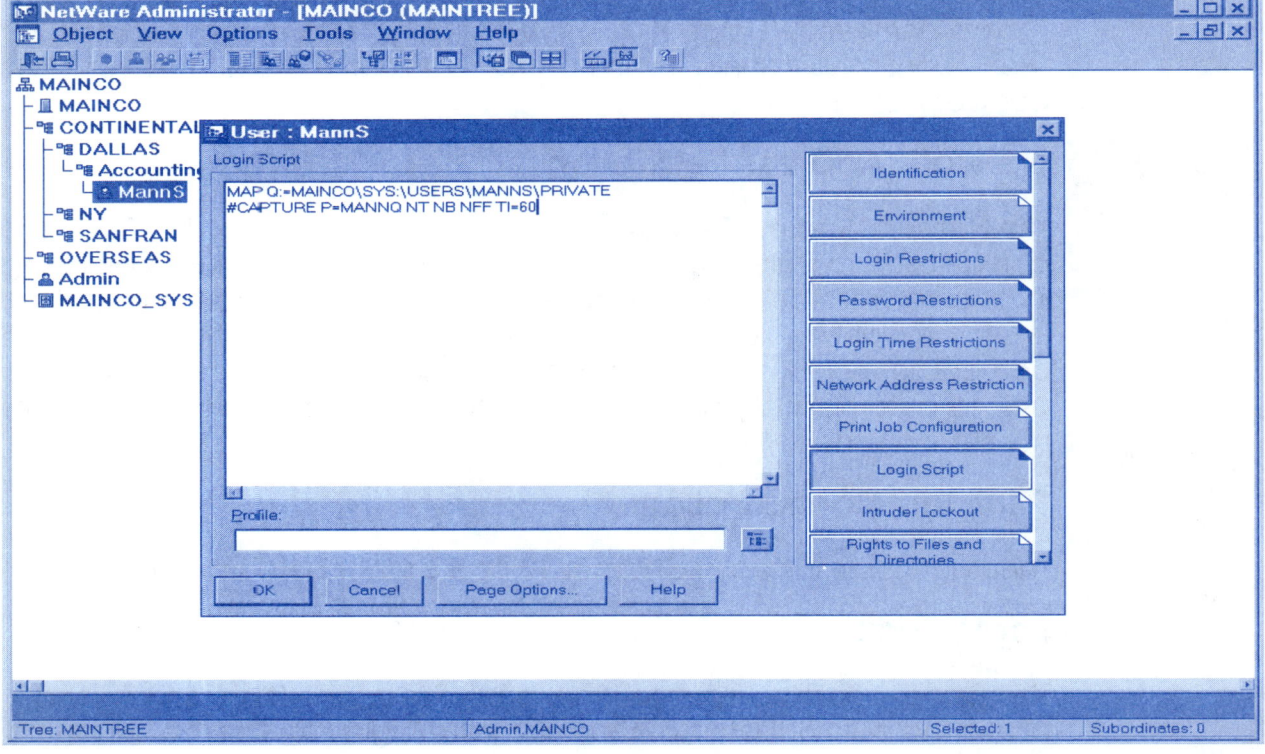

Figure 4-13. A sample login script.

for the user. A sample user login script is shown in Figure 4-13. A more complete discussion of login scripts and their usages is contained in the latter part of this chapter.

Intruder Lockout

This screen reports whether or not the user's account is locked out. The administrator can unlock the account by deselecting the Account locked box on the screen.

Intruder lockout parameters are set by container and pertain to all users in a given container. For example, a user's account can be locked if he or she uses a correct login name but an incorrect password for a particular number of times during a particular period of time. Then the account will be locked for the time indicated. All these parameters can be set for the container. In general, intruder detection is meant to keep illegal users from hacking into a system.

Rights to Files and Directories

This page, shown in Figure 4-14, is used to grant and see trustee rights assigned to a user. This page is fully discussed in Chapter 12 and is therefore omitted here.

Group Membership

Users are generally not totally unique although they usually think they are. Their needs often can be grouped according to their job functions. Therefore, rights can be assigned to a **group** and users can be placed in the group instead of assigning individual users specific directory and file system rights to each area of the server they need to access. The group membership screen shows which groups the user is a member of and allows the administrator to assign the user to additional groups by utilizing the Add button function. Figure 4-15 shows the Group Membership page.

Security Equal To

The **security equal to** page shows which users and groups that this user is security equivalent to. This means that this user can do the same things and have the same rights and privileges as all those to which the user is security equivalent. Using security equivalence is not something that should be widely done. If the user to which this user is security equivalent is deleted, and if that user were providing the new user with necessary rights, the new user would be nonfunctional.

Chapter 4

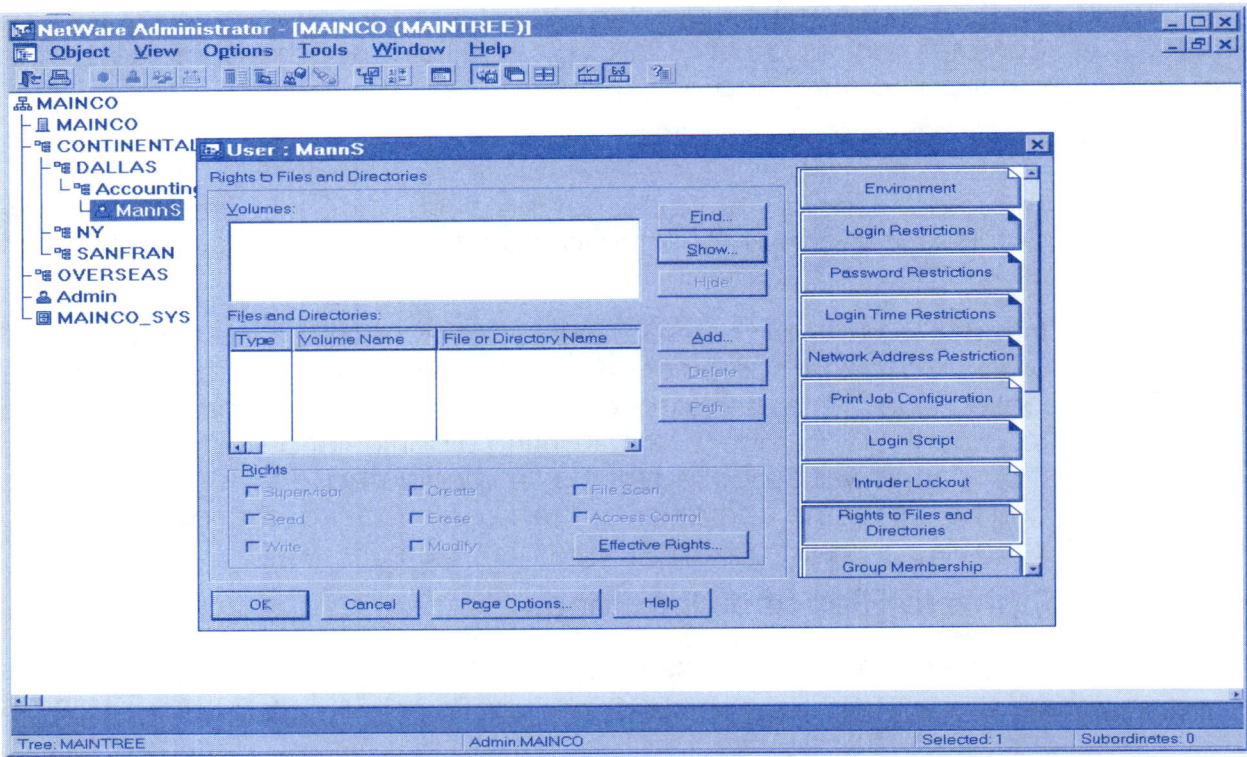

Figure 4-14. The Rights to Files and Directories page.

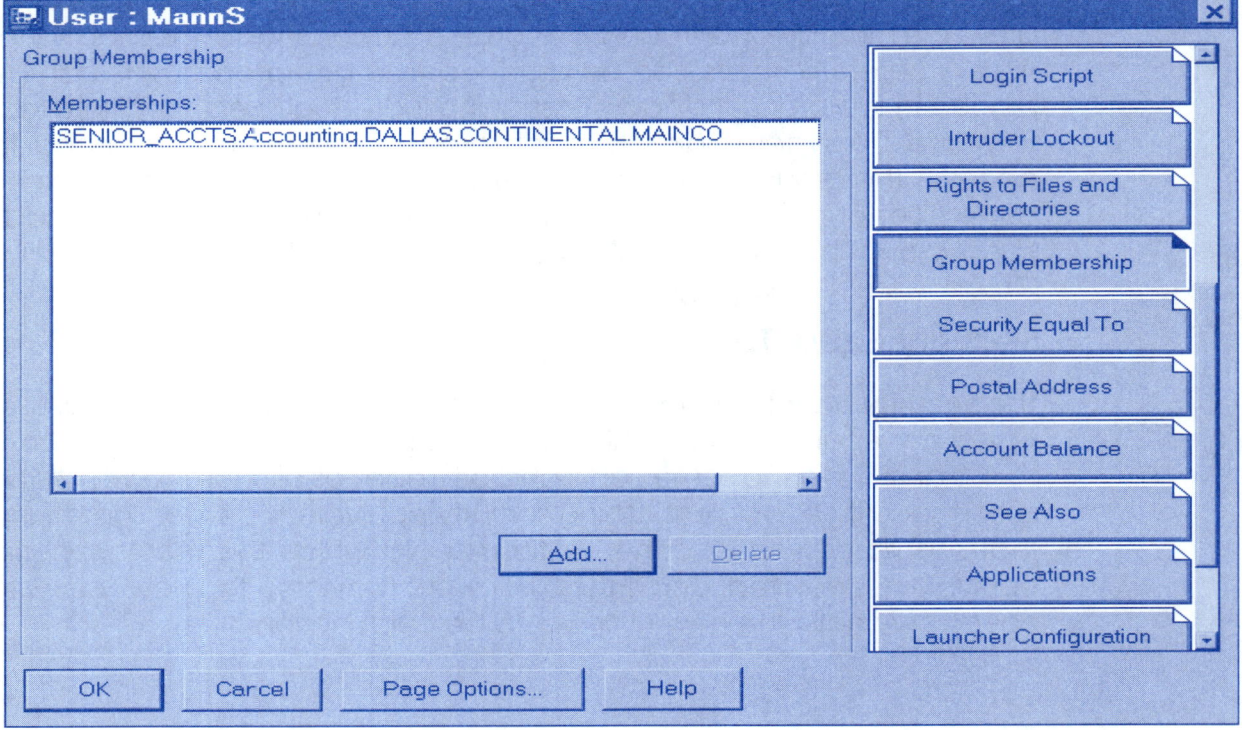

Figure 4-15. The Group Membership page.

Postal Address

The **Postal Address** page contains name and address information that can be used for mailing lists, etc.

Login Scripts

NetWare 4.11 allows each user name to have a **login script** that establishes much of the user's environment each time he or she logs in. Figure 4-16 shows the login script editor within NetWare Administrator for the user's login script. Netware Administrator provides the Admin with a simple editor similar to a text editor for creating and modifying login scripts. This login script performs several mapping operations such as mapping the \SOFTWARE\DATA directory to appear as the root directory of drive I. A message is displayed to the user, and finally the EXIT command sends a command to DOS to display a directory listing. All of these commands are executed each time the user GUEST logs in.

NetWare 4.11 does not require each user to have a login script since the Admin can set a container-wide login script in a container object, which acts as a type of system login script every time a user in the container logs in.

Login Scripts

As mentioned earlier, every time a user logs in, NetWare is capable of running one to three login scripts for the user. The function of these login scripts is to issue all the commands needed to set up the user's environment. The environment, in this case, refers primarily to the drive mappings created for the user, but there are many other commands available in login scripts for customizing the log in.

NetWare 4.11 provides 4 types of login scripts:

Container login script

Profile login script

User login script

Default login script

Container Login Script

The **container login script** is used to set up the environment for all users in a given container. The container login script runs first for all users in a container. This login script is set up by accessing the details for the container object, clicking the Login Script button, and then entering the appropriate login script commands. It is important to remember that all the commands placed in the container login script are executed for all users in the container.

Profile Login Script

Netware 4.11 provides a **profile** or group type **login script** through a profile object. The profile object has a login script property like the login script property for the user. Login script commands meant to be used by users in a particular functional category or group can be entered for the profile object. Then, the profile object's login script can be tied to execute for the user just after the container login script by entering the name of the profile object on the Login Script Properties page of the user. For example, user JamesM is set to execute the profile login script from the profile object Executives because the name of the profile object is entered into the appropriate box in Figure 4-16. The profile login script, if one exists, is executed immediately after the container login script.

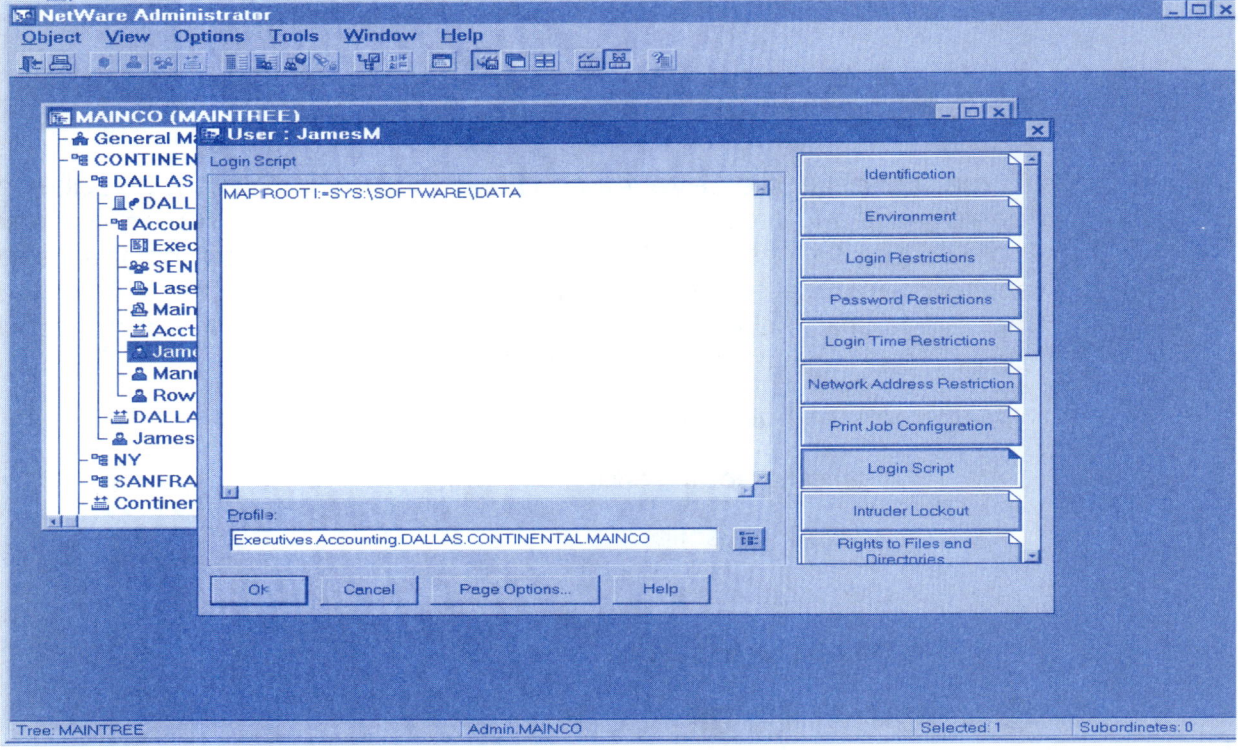

Figure 4-16. Assigning a profile login script.

User Login Script

The **user login script** is used to set up the environment for a given user. This login script is entered through NetWare Administrator by using the Login Script page for the user as shown in Figure 4-16. The user login script executes after the profile login script if there is a profile login script or after the container login script if there is no profile login script.

Default Login Script

This login script provides commands to set up a user to at least be able to do some minimal tasks within the network. If there is a user login script, the default login script does not run. Further, if the NO DEFAULT command appears in the container or profile login script, the default login script does not run. The default login script is hard-coded within the NetWare 4.11 operating system and cannot be changed.

A user might log in as user JamesM. The LOGIN program checks the user name given and executes the container login script set up by the Admin using NetWare Administrator, then executes the profile login script from the profile object Executives, and then executes the user's login script.

Many of the commands that can be used in a login script can also be used from the command line. In other words, if the appropriate PATHs have been established, a user can issue several of the commands by typing the name of the command at the F> prompt. The MAP command is a good example. The MAP command can be used in a login script or at the command prompt to map a network or search drive (explained later in this chapter).

The following is a partial list of login script commands and their uses.

1. BREAK ON | OFF

2. COMSPEC = drive:(\)file name

    COMSPEC = *n:(\)file name

    COMSPEC = Sn:(\)file name

3. DISPLAY file name

    FDISPLAY file name

4. DOS BREAK ON | OFF

5. (DOS) SET name="value"

6. DOS VERIFY ON | OFF

7. DRIVE drive letter:

    DRIVE *drive number:

8. EXIT ("file name")

9. #program name with command line options

10. FIRE PHASERS number TIMES

11. IF condition (AND condition) THEN command

    IF condition (AND condition) THEN BEGIN

    commands

    END

12. INCLUDE file name

13. MAP

14. PAUSE

    WAIT

15. REMARK remark statement

    REM, *, or ; are all remark statements

16. WRITE "comment to be displayed"

Commands

BREAK

The BREAK command controls how the keyboard responds during execution of the login script. If the command BREAK ON is used, the login script can be halted by holding down the CONTROL key and pressing BREAK. The BREAK key may also be labeled SCROLL LOCK. If the command is in the form BREAK OFF, the execution of the login script cannot be stopped with CONTROL-BREAK. Note that this command affects only the execution of the Login Script.

COMSPEC

The COMSPEC command can be very important to the proper operation of the workstation. DOS always keeps a pointer (called the COMSPEC environment variable) to the file containing the command processor program. The command processor provided with every version of DOS is a program called COMMAND.COM. DOS must be told where this file is located because it must often be reloaded into memory after the execution of a program. Ordinarily when a computer is

Creating the User Account, Mappings and Login Scripts

booted the COMSPEC variable is set to point to the COMMAND.COM that was used to boot the computer. If the computer was booted from floppy disk drive A:, the COMSPEC variable would probably read

COMSPEC=A:\COMMAND.COM.

But if the boot disk was then removed, COMMAND.COM would no longer reside where the COMSPEC variable points to. If this computer were on a network, the COMSPEC variable could be set to point to a copy of COMMAND.COM on a network drive where it cannot be removed.

The COMSPEC login script command allows the variable to be set automatically when the user logs in. In its simplest form, the command COMSPEC = drive:(\)file name sets the COMSPEC variable to a value such as

COMSPEC = F:COMMAND.COM

where F: has already been mapped to a directory containing a copy of COMMAND.COM. The drive option can indicate any drive letter that exists at the time the COMSPEC command is executed.

The two other forms of the command allow the COMSPEC variable to be set to a value that is indicated at the time the login script is executed. An "*n:" indicates a drive number that might be used in the login script. The command might read

COMSPEC = *2:COMMAND.COM

The result is to set the COMSPEC variable to point to a copy of COMMAND.COM in a directory on the second network drive, already mapped to whatever the drive letter may be.

The "Sn:" in the third form of the command indicates a search drive number. Under NetWare, a special type of drive mapping called a search drive can be made to allow the computer to automatically search a directory for a program that is not in the current directory. When mapping such a search drive, the user maps a search drive number such as S1: or S2:. NetWare designates the associated drive letter by starting at the end of the alphabet, so S1: becomes drive letter Z: and S2: becomes Y: unless those letters are already in use. By using a command such as

COMSPEC = S1:COMMAND.COM

the Admin can ensure that the COMSPEC variable points to the first search drive already assigned, without knowing what drive letter it is using.

In any of the three forms of this command, the drive letter used should point to the directory containing the COMMAND.COM program, because the command accepts only twelve characters after the drive specification. With this restriction a command such as

COMSPEC = S1:\DOS\COMMAND.COM

would not be legal. The path \DOS\COMMAND.COM is too long.

DISPLAY

Using the DISPLAY command, a message can be displayed on the screen each time a user logs in. The message is contained in a file represented by the file name option in the command. The file name can include a complete directory path such as

DISPLAY F:\PUBLIC\MESSAGE.TXT

DISPLAY is used when the file contains only the ASCII characters that are to be displayed. FDISPLAY is used when the file contains control characters placed there by a word processing program that are not intended to be displayed. FDISPLAY will filter out these characters before printing the message on the screen.

(DOS)BREAK

DOS also has a BREAK command. This login script command sets the DOS environment variable to BREAK ON or BREAK OFF.

(DOS)SET

The SET command is used to set any DOS environment variable to any value. These values can be checked later by other login script commands, batch file commands, or other programs. This command is identical in function to the DOS command SET. The only differences are the optional word DOS and the use of quotation marks around the value in the login script command. Some examples are

DOS SET USER="JANE"

SET ROOM="D229"

SET PROMPT="PG"

Several login script variables can be used to place special values in an environment variable. These variables will be discussed later.

DOS VERIFY

The DOS VERIFY flag can be set so that each time a file is copied DOS will read the newly created copy and compare it with the original to ensure it is correct. The login script command DOS VERIFY can be used to turn this feature on or off.

DRIVE

The drive command is used to set the default drive. Normally the default drive is the first network drive, usually drive F. With the DRIVE drive letter: command it can be set to any valid local or network drive letter. The DRIVE *drive number: form of the command is used to set the default drive to a number indicating the order in which the drive was mapped. For instance, the command

> DRIVE *1:

would set the default drive to the first network drive letter, which might be F.

The command

> DRIVE C:

could be used to set the default drive to be the local hard disk drive C:.

EXIT

The EXIT command is used to terminate a login script and to start another program. It is often necessary to start another program, usually a menu program, at the conclusion of the login script. When the login program finishes processing the login script, it can pass control on to any executable program named in the parameter "file name" or if there is no parameter in quotes, control passes to the client operating system. For example, if a user needed a menu program called MENU.EXE executed each time she logged in, the last line in his login script might be

> EXIT "F:MENU"

The item in quotes can actually be any operating system command as long as it is fourteen characters or less in length. Therefore, in addition to any executable program, any batch file or DOS internal command can be used. For example, suppose a user simply needed a directory listing each time he logged in. The last line in the login script would be

> EXIT "DIR /W"

When the EXIT command is used in a login script, no further login scripts run. Programs that terminate and stay resident should not be used.

#Program name with command line options

The "#" symbol is known as the External Program Execution command. This command tells the LOGIN program to temporarily suspend its operations to load and run the program named. When the program is finished, control is returned to the LOGIN program and the login script resumes execution at the next line. The program called by the External Program Execution command must have either an .EXE or .COM extension, but it can be called from any directory with any command line options it needs. The login script command

#F:\APPS\LOTUS\LOTUS COLOR.SET

loads and executes a program called LOTUS from the F:\APPS\LOTUS directory and passes the command line parameter COLOR.SET to it. As with the EXIT command, terminate and stay resident programs are excluded.

The example above, however, would be a very unusual case since after the user exited the LOTUS program, control would return to the LOGIN program and the rest of the login script would be executed.

FIRE PHASERS

The FIRE PHASERS command is used to catch the user's attention by generating a science fiction-like sound. The "number" parameter tells the login script how many times to make the sound. The command

FIRE PHASERS 3 TIMES

would cause the alarm to sound three times. This command should be used judiciously, especially if it is placed in the system login script, which is executed by all users. Execution of this command must complete prior to the login script's continuing. An alternate construction is FIRE 3.

IF Statement

This command structure allows the login script to test conditions and execute different commands based on the result. The command executed as a result of the comparison can be any valid login script command. In the diagram of the IF THEN structure, the "condition" represents a true or false comparison of two items. The comparison will always be in the form

ITEM OPERATOR ITEM

where the operator tests the relationship between the two items. In the first form of the command, a single command is executed as the result of any number of comparisons, if they are all true. In the second form of the command, the key word BEGIN is used to start a list of commands to be executed. The key word END is used to indicate the end of the list of commands. Between the BEGIN and END may be any number of commands that will be executed only if all the conditions are true. It is important to note that the IF THEN statement must be allowed to wrap naturally when it extends beyond one line of the screen. Also, the IF THEN with the BEGIN and END option must be allowed to wrap naturally until the BEGIN has been entered. Then, each additional command should wrap naturally with the ENTER key being pressed at the end of each command.

The IF THEN command will accept many different operators in the testing of the two items, as shown below:

To represent equal	**To represent not equal**
IS	IS NOT
=	!=
==	<>
EQUALS	#
	DOES NOT EQUAL
	NOT EQUAL TO

Four more relationships can be tested using the following operators. Either the symbols on the right or the words on the left may be used in the IF THEN command.

IS GREATER THAN	>
IS LESS THAN	<
IS GREATER THAN OR EQUAL TO	>=
IS LESS THAN OR EQUAL TO	<=

Several pairs of items can be compared using the AND operator. Also, the AND operator may be replaced with a comma. Comparisons such as these are possible:

   IF DAY_OF_WEEK IS "Monday" AND HOUR >= "09" THEN SET NOW="*"

This command tests whether a variable DAY_OF_WEEK is equal to Monday and checks whether a variable HOUR is greater than or equal to 9. If both conditions are true a DOS environment variable NOW is given a value of "*".

Chapter 4

> IF DAY > THAN "15", DAY_OF_WEEK IS NOT "Sunday" THEN BEGIN
>> FIRE PHASERS 2 TIMES
>
> DOS SET REMIND="Pay the bills today!"
>> END

This command checks to see if the day of the month is greater than 15 and makes sure the day of the week is not Sunday. If those conditions are met, the alarm will sound two times and a DOS environment variable is set to the string "Pay the bills today!"

The variables DAY, DAY_OF_WEEK, and HOUR are login script variables that are set before execution of the login script. Many more such variables are available for use in the IF THEN command as well as other commands. The following is a complete list of the login script identifier variables available. (Note that all are character variables and, as such, must be compared to constant values in double quotes.)

Variable	Possible Values
AM_PM	(a.m. or p.m.)
DAY	(01 - 31)
DAY_OF_WEEK	(Sunday - Saturday)
ERROR_LEVEL	(0 - 255)
FULL_NAME	(The user's full name recorded in SYSCON)
GREETING_TIME	(Morning, afternoon, evening)
HOUR	(1 - 12)
HOUR24	(00 - 24)
LOGIN_NAME	(The user's login name)
MACHINE	(The name of the workstation type of computer)
MEMBER OF	(The MEMBER OF variable is a special case in that it is not used with a comparison operator. It is used to check if the user is a member of a given group.)
MINUTE	(00 - 59)
MONTH	(01 - 12)
MONTH_NAME	(January - December)

Creating the User Account, Mappings and Login Scripts

NDAY_OF_WEEK	(1 - 7 where Sunday is 1 and Saturday is 7)
NEW_MAIL	(YES or NO indicating whether new mail is waiting for the user)
OS	(The operating system running on the user's workstation)
OS_VERSION	(The version number of a DOS workstation)
P_STATION	(The physical node number of the workstation)
SECOND	(00 - 59)
SHELL_TYPE	(A code number indicating the type of network shell running on the user's workstation)
SHORT_YEAR	(The last two digits of the year)
SMACHINE	(A shortened name for the workstation type)
STATION	(The connection number assigned to the workstation)
YEAR	(The year)

INCLUDE

This login script command tells the login script to pull in a second file as a part of the currently executing login script. When the commands are finished executing in the second login script, control is returned to the calling login script. Each script file can call other script files to a maximum of ten login scripts.

Nesting login scripts in this way can be very helpful if many different users need a section of their login script to be the same, but heavy nesting is not recommended because it makes documenting a user's actual login script unnecessarily difficult.

MAP

The MAP command is used to display or set the drive mappings of the workstation. It assigns drive letters to directories on the file server or to drives on the local workstation. It can also be used to display those assignments. There are fourteen separate forms of this command, each requiring a complete description. This command is another in which the login script variables can be used. Directory names used in the MAP command can contain login script variables preceded by a "%".

Chapter 4

Suppose that F: is mapped to volume SYS:\ and that a subdirectory under a directory called \USERS has been created for each user with the user's name being the name of the directory. For user SMANN the directory would be F:\USERS\SMANN. A directory for each user is usually referred to as a user's home directory. Each user might need a drive letter assigned to his or her home directory in the login script. To do this a MAP command could be placed in each user's login script that includes the login script variable LOGIN_NAME.

MAP H:=F:\USERS\%LOGIN_NAME

When the login program executes this command it will replace the %LOGIN_NAME with the individual user's name and, in the case of user SMANN, the result would be

MAP H:=F:\USERS\SMANN

giving the user a new drive letter H: that points to the F:\USERS\SMANN directory.

In its simplest form, the MAP command alone displays all drive letter assignments, including the drive letters assigned to local disk drives. The command

MAP drive:

displays the directory or local drive that the drive letter listed points to.

MAP drive:=directory

sets the drive letter listed to point to the directory listed. The directory may contain the volume name.

MAP drive:=directory ; drive:=directory ; ...

shows that multiple drive letter assignments may be made following a single MAP command. Each assignment is separated by a semicolon.

MAP directory

changes the current drive letter to point to the directory listed. The directory may contain a volume name.

MAP drive:=

assigns the drive letter listed to point to the current directory.

MAP drive:=drive:

assigns the drive letter on the left to point to the directory pointed to by the drive letter on the right.

MAP INSERT search drive:=directory

Creating the User Account, Mappings and Login Scripts

creates a new search drive pointing to the directory listed.

MAP DEL drive:

deletes the drive letter assignment.

MAP REM drive:

removes the drive letter assignment, exactly the same as the MAP DEL command.

MAP DISPLAY OFF

instructs the login program not to display the drive mappings made when the user logs in. Ordinarily the drive mappings are displayed.

MAP DISPLAY ON

explicitly tells the login program to display the drive mappings when the user logs in.

MAP ERRORS OFF

instructs the login program not to display any error messages that may be generated as a result of an incorrect MAP command in the login script. Ordinarily all errors would be displayed.

MAP ERRORS ON

explicitly tells the login program to display all error messages concerning MAP commands in the login script.

PAUSE

The login script command PAUSE works exactly the same as the DOS batch file command of the same name. It halts execution of the login script and displays the message "Strike a key when ready..." After the user presses a key the login script is resumed at the next command. The word WAIT may be used for the same function.

REMARK

Often the Admin will wish to place remarks or comments in the text of the login script that are not intended to be executed. These might include explanations of a particularly complex IF THEN structure, the need for various drive mappings, or a message for future administrators. Either of the four forms of the REMARK command will prevent the login program from attempting to execute the remark statement following it.

WRITE

The WRITE command is roughly equivalent to the PRINT command in the BASIC programming language or the ECHO command in a batch file. It displays the text following it on the user's screen at the time it is executed. The easiest way to use the WRITE command is to simply put a message in quotes.

>   WRITE "Welcome to file server FS_ONE."

The WRITE command above would tell the user which file server he or she just logged in to. But WRITE commands can be much more flexible. The text to be displayed can use the same login script variables that the IF THEN command can use. As in the MAP command the variable is preceded by a "%" to tell the login program to convert it to the value it represents. In the command

>   WRITE "Welcome %LOGIN_NAME, to file server FS_ONE."

the %LOGIN_NAME would be converted to the user name. In the case of user JSMITH, the message displayed would read:

>   Welcome JSMITH, to file server FS_ONE.

The login script variables can also be used outside the quotes without the preceding "%". The command

>   WRITE "Welcome ";LOGIN_NAME;", to file server FS_ONE."

is exactly equivalent to the write command above. Notice that a semicolon is used to separate the components of the text when a variable is used outside the quotes and without the "%". Also note that identifier variables must be in uppercase in most instances, so it is a good idea to use uppercase all the time.

In addition to the login script variables, there are four special symbols that may be used within the quotes to control the format of the text printed on the screen. They appear in Table 4-1.

Symbol	Description
\r	Carriage return. Causes the cursor to return to column one on the same line of the screen.
\n	New line. Causes the cursor to go to the first column of the next line. The cursor will automatically go to a new line at the end of a WRITE command.
\"	Embedded quotation mark. Must be used to display a quotation.

\7		ASCII character seven. Causes a beep sound to be generated.

Table 4-1. Format symbols.

The WRITE command below shows the effects of some of these symbols.

WRITE "HAPPY\n   \"BIRTHDAY\"\n   ";LOGIN_NAME

For user JSMITH, the output on the screen would look like this:

HAPPY

"BIRTHDAY"

JSMITH

The login script commands listed above give the Administrator a very powerful language to meet the user's needs. With them a user's environment can be constructed to allow him or her to use the network freely or to take the user directly into an application. The possibilities are endless.

In the next section of this chapter, NetWare Administrator will be used to create users, assign them various characteristics or properties, and create login scripts.

Hands-on NetWare

In the previous chapter, Novell NetWare was completely installed on a file server, and Novell client software was installed on a workstation. However, the installation of the NetWare software was only a small part of creating a usable network. The structure of the directories, the creation of user accounts, the setting up of network printers, and many other tasks will require much more work and thought. A network's administrator is the one who must consider how the network will be used and determine how best to serve each user, while maintaining overall system continuity and security.

When NetWare is installed, a user account called Admin is automatically created. It has complete trustee rights over the entire server at least initially and permission to use all options in each of the NetWare utilities. Originally the account has only the password assigned during installation.

In this section you will prepare the server and workstation for operation, log in to the network as the network Admin, start the Netware Administrator utility, and create for yourself an Administrator-equivalent account. All commands shown here are written in uppercase characters for clarity. However, they can be entered as either uppercase or lowercase.

Chapter 4

Preparing the Network for Operation

1. Prepare the server for operation by simply turning it on. A message saying that the LAN is initializing and the volumes are being mounted should appear, assuming that you have inserted the command SERVER.EXE into the AUTOEXEC.BAT file on the server.

2. At a network workstation, boot the workstation and activate the client software. A login screen similar to Figure 4-17 should appear.

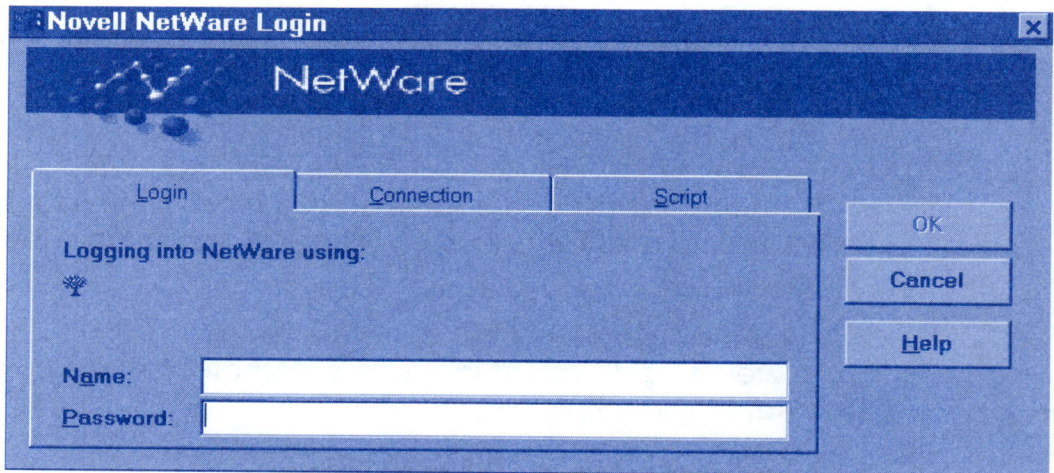

Figure 4-17. Login dialog box.

Logging In

Once the screen shown in Figure 4-17 is displayed, we know that the network drivers have been loaded, and the workstation is attached to the file server. However, no one is logged in. Logging in tells NDS who the user is and how much access that user has.

1. Click in the Name box and type in the name of the Admin. The name of the Admin account for the MAINCO company is .ADMIN.MAINCO.

2. Click in the Password box and type in the password. Notice that the password is encrypted as is should be.

3. Click the OK button to log in. The Login Results box is displayed because that is how the client was configured in the previous chapter.

Creating the User Account, Mappings and Login Scripts

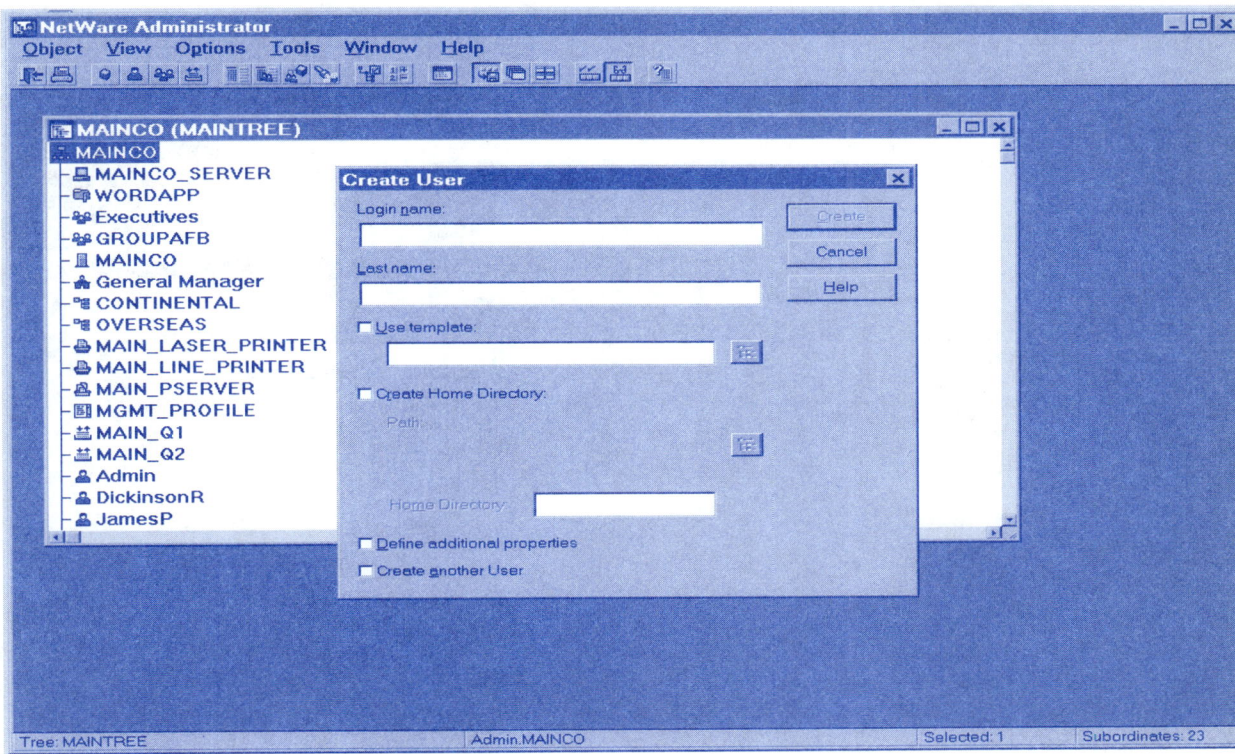

Figure 4-18. Creating a user dialog box.

Starting the NetWare Administrator Utility

If you are running Windows 3.1, locate the NetWare program group by clicking on the Windows selection in the main menu bar and selecting the NetWare program group.

1. Double-click on the NetWare Administrator icon to activate the program.

2. A screen similar to Figure 4-18 should appear.

Creating a User

1. Click on the MAINCO container.

2. Click on the Create User icon on the menu bar. (Or, alternatively, click on Object on the menu bar and then Create. Select User Object and then click the OK button.)

3. The screen depicted in Figure 4-18 appears.

4. Click in the Login Name box and enter ADMINXXX where XXX is your three initials.

Chapter 4

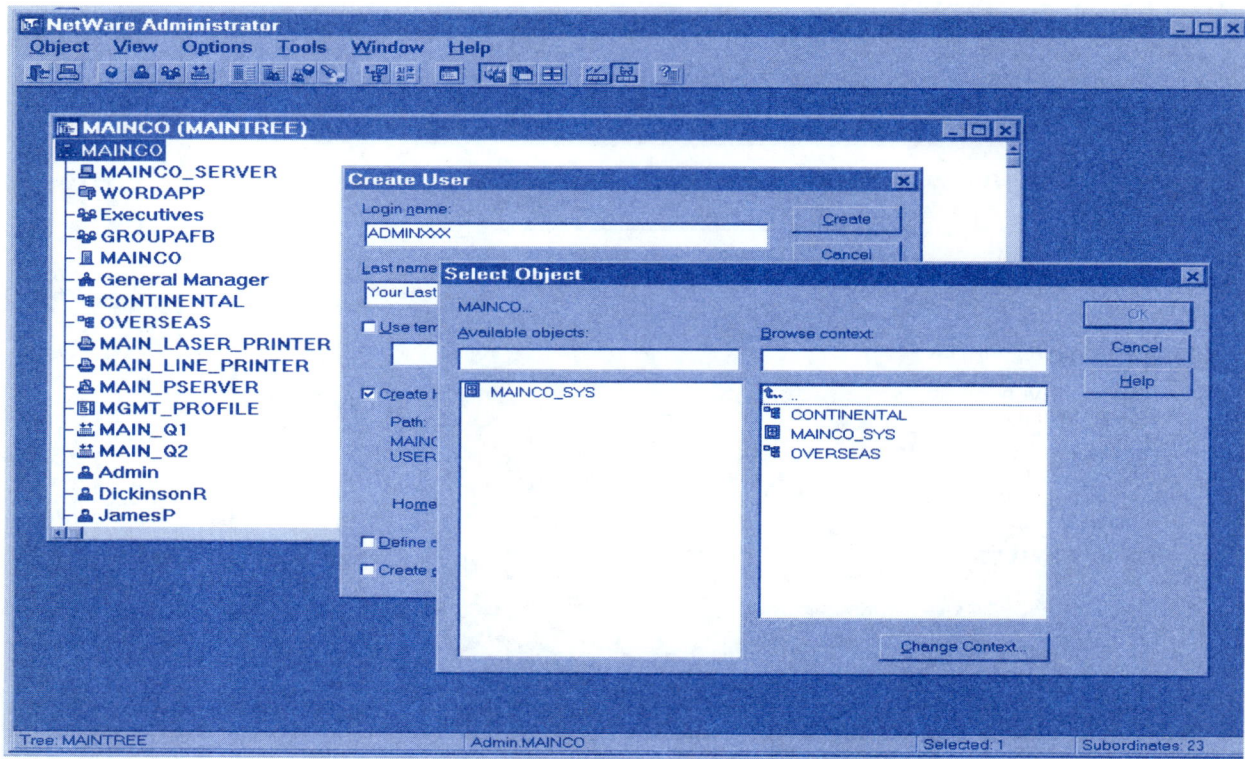

Figure 4-19. Selecting a path to the user's home directory.

5. Attempt to click the Create button at this point. This action is not possible since the Create button is dimmed. The Create button is dimmed because a critical property of the user has not been entered, the last name.

6. Click in the Last Name box and enter your last name.

7. Click the box to the left of the Create Home Directory line to indicate that you wish to create a home directory. Again, attempt to click the Create button. The Create button is now dimmed because you have indicated that you wish the user to have a home directory, but you have not specified the location of that directory.

8. Click the Browse button. (This button is the second square button in the current window.)

9. A screen similar to Figure 4-19 is displayed.

10. Double-click the MAINCO_SYS directory in the Browse context side of the screen.

11. Click the Users directory on the left side of the screen, and then click the OK button.

Creating the User Account, Mappings and Login Scripts

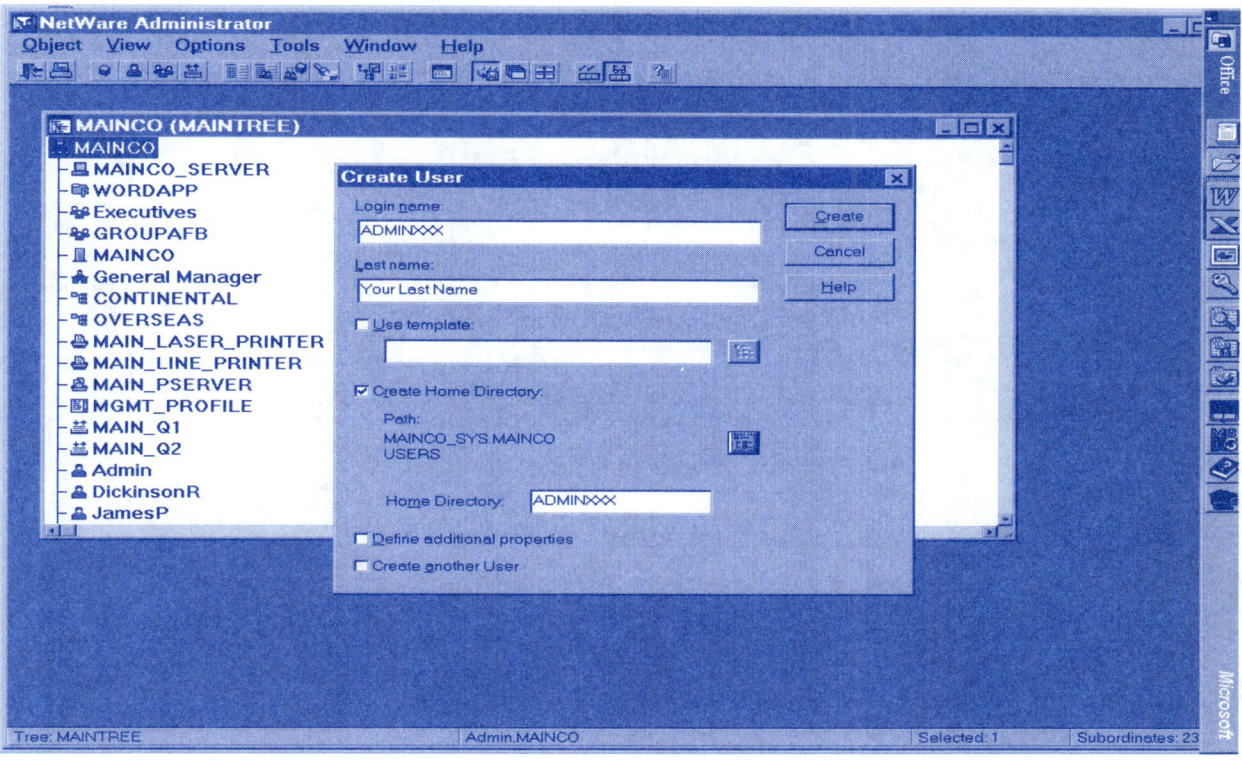

Figure 4-20. User's home directory.

12. Notice that the path to the user's home directory has been filled in, and the actual home directory name is shown in Figure 4-20.

13. Click the Create button to create the user.

Making the New User Admin Equivalent

1. Double click the ADMINXXX user you just created.

2. The screen shown in Figure 4-21 appears.

3. Arrow down until the Security Equal To button appears on the right of the screen as shown in Figure 4-22.

4. Click the Security Equal To button to display the screen in Figure 4-23.

Chapter 4

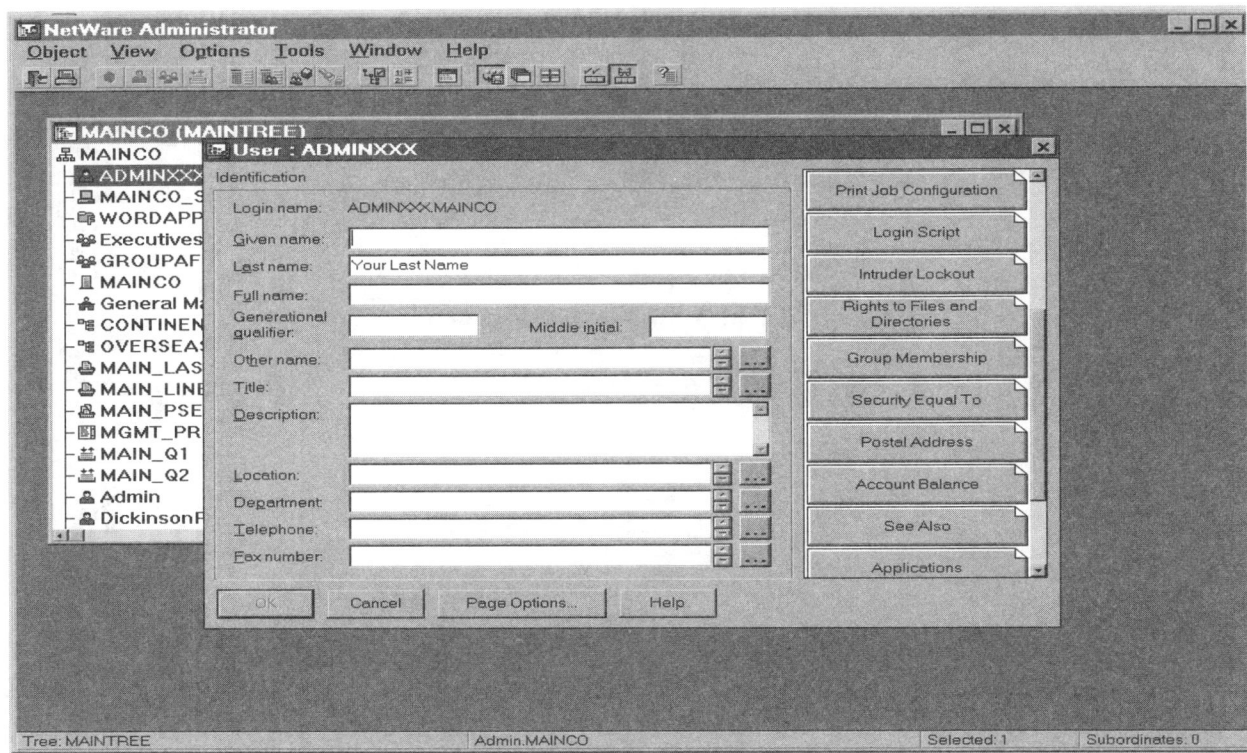

Figure 4-21. User ADMINXXX main screen.

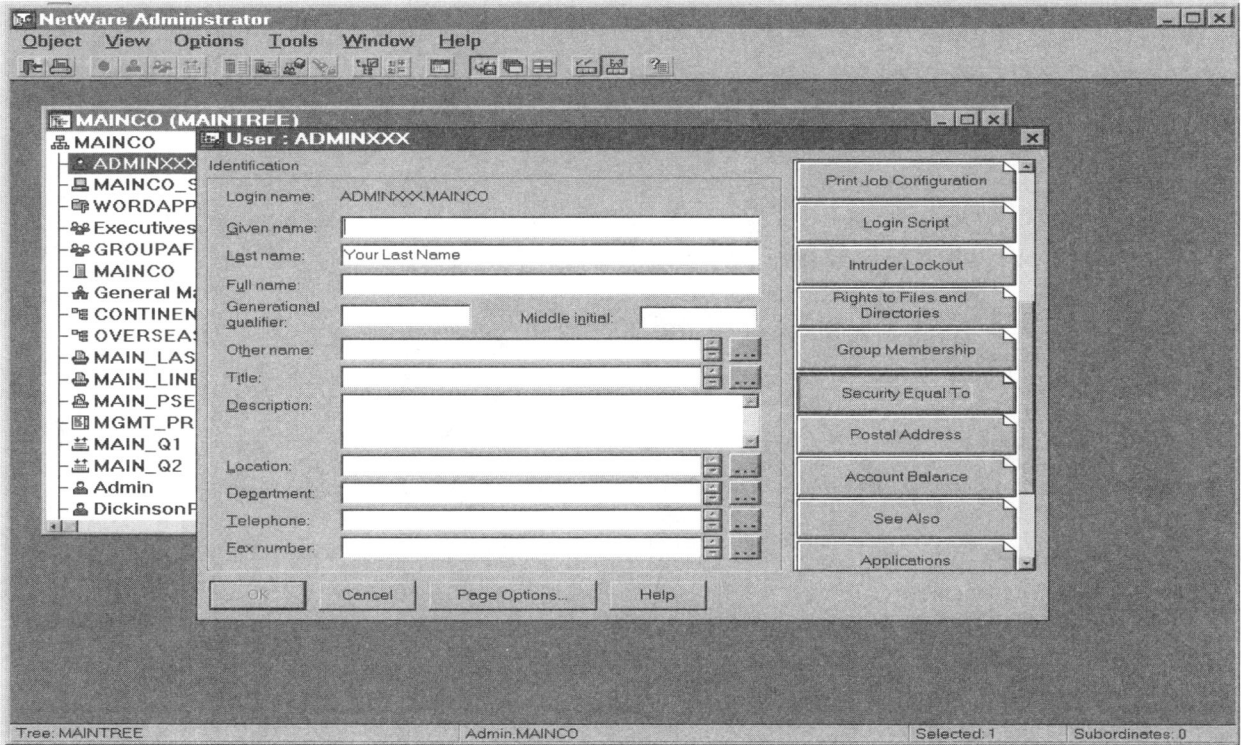

Figure 4-22. User ADMINXXX main screen showing Security Equal To button.

Creating the User Account, Mappings and Login Scripts

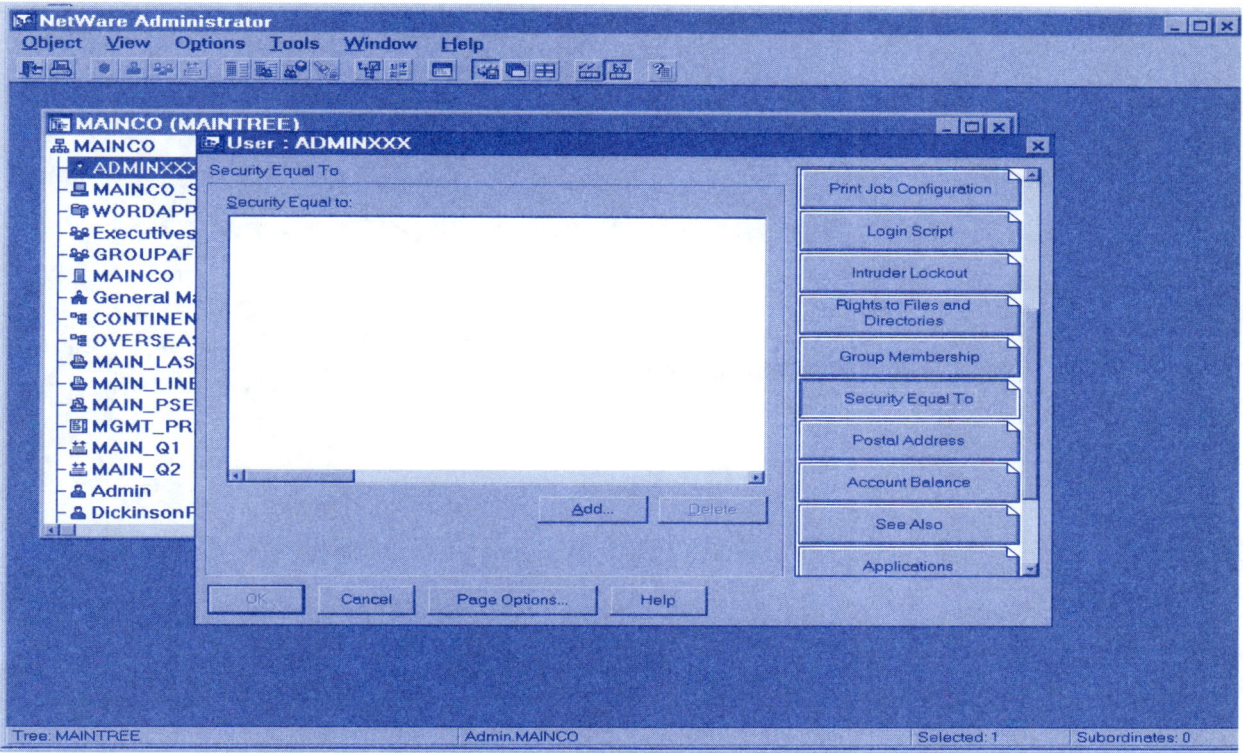

Figure 4-23. Security Equal To page.

5. Click the Add button, click the real Admin user in the left side of the screen displayed, then click the OK button in the Add screen, and then the OK button in the Security Equal To screen. Refer to Figures 4-24 and 4-25.

6. Click the Password Restrictions button on the right of the screen.

7. Click the Change Password button and enter the password FIRST in both the New and Retype password boxes as shown in Figure 4-26.

Logging in as the Admin Equivalent New User and Creating Another User

1. Log in as the new ADMINXXX user that you just created.

2. Following the above procedure, create a new user call USERXXX who has a home directory called SYS:\USERS\USERXXX where XXX is your initials. Set the password for this account to your last name.

Chapter 4

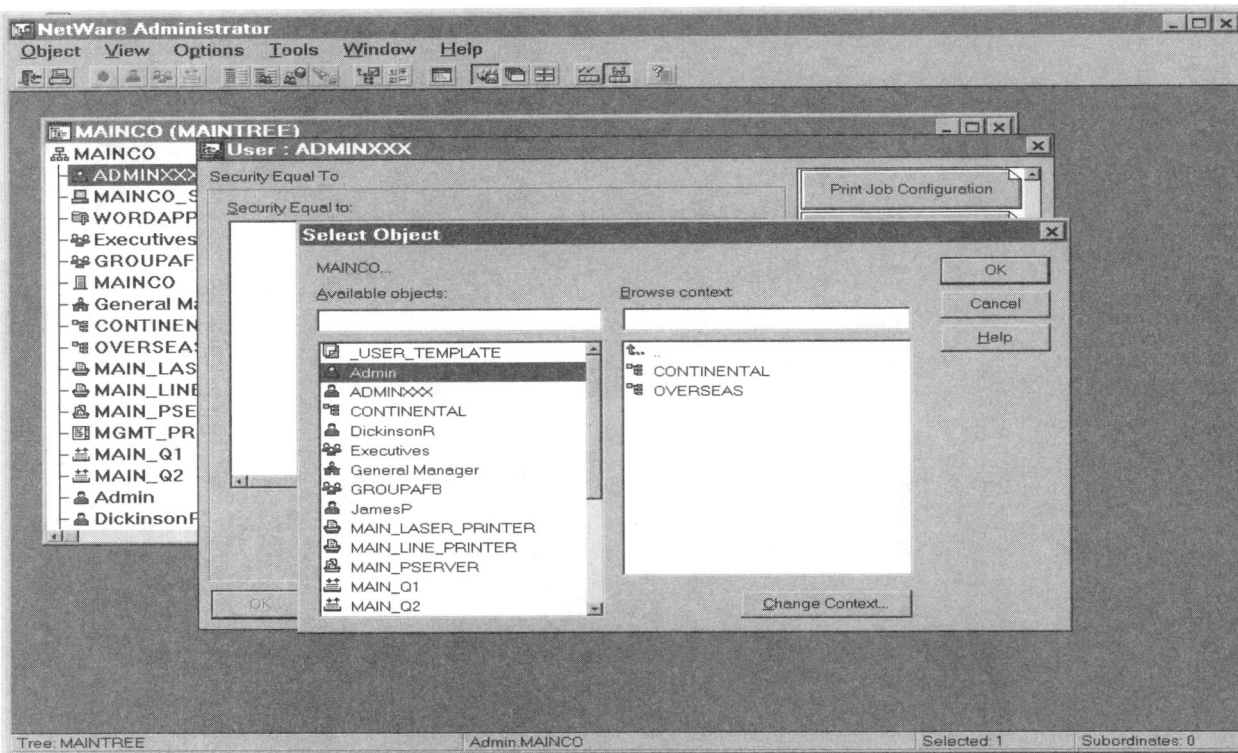

Figure 4-24. Selecting a security equivalent.

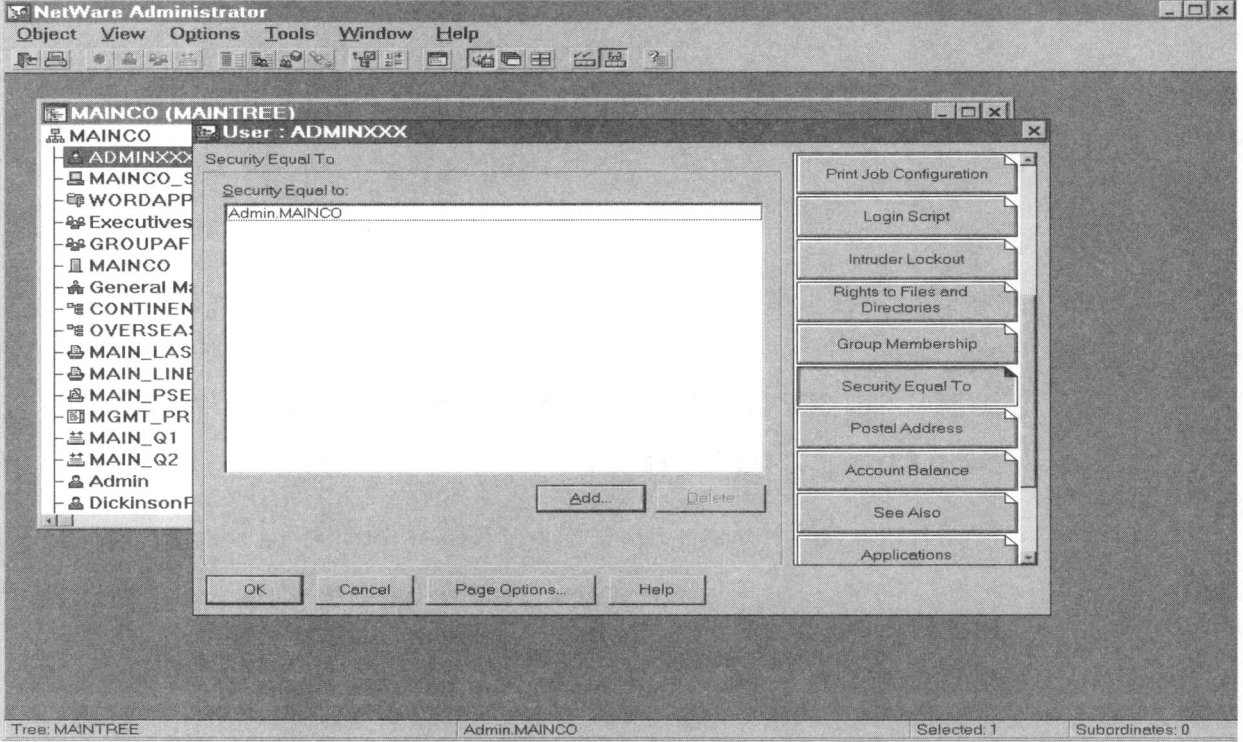

Figure 4-25. Security Equal To page showing ADMINXXX equal to ADMIN.

Creating the User Account, Mappings and Login Scripts

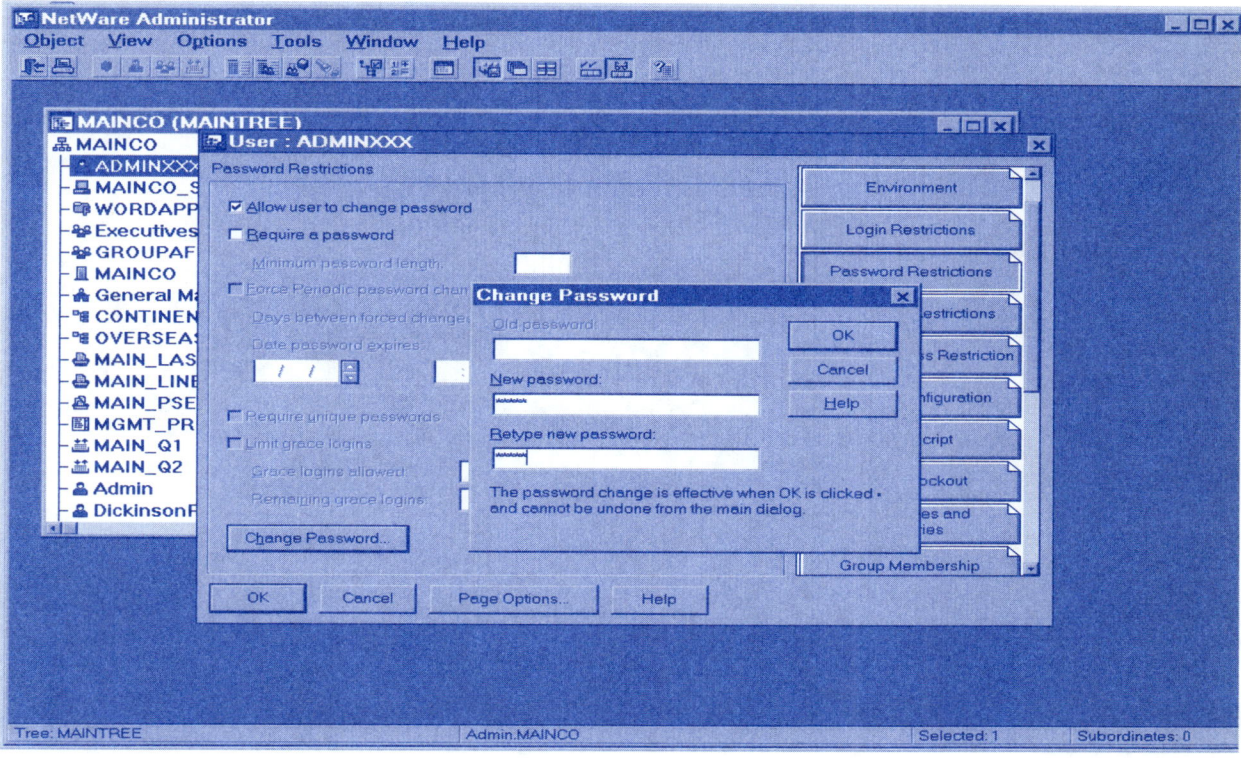

Figure 4-26. Changing the user's password.

3. Double-click the user icon.

4. Click the Login Time Restrictions button to display Figure 4-27.

5. Click in the upper left of the Time Restrictions box by Sunday and underneath the 12. While holding down the left mouse button, drag down to Saturday until you reach 1 hour AFTER the present time that you are attempting this Hands-On exercise. Release the left mouse button and click OK. Your windows should be as shown in Figure 4-28 if the current time is 3 p.m.

6. Click the OK button. The dark area of the screen indicates the times during which the user CANNOT log in.

7. Attempt to log in as USERXXX. You should receive a message as in Figure 4-29 if you have set the login time restrictions properly.

Creating a User Login Script for USERXXX

1. Log in as your ADMINXXX user.

2. Double-click the USERXXX user to expose the Details screen.

Chapter 4

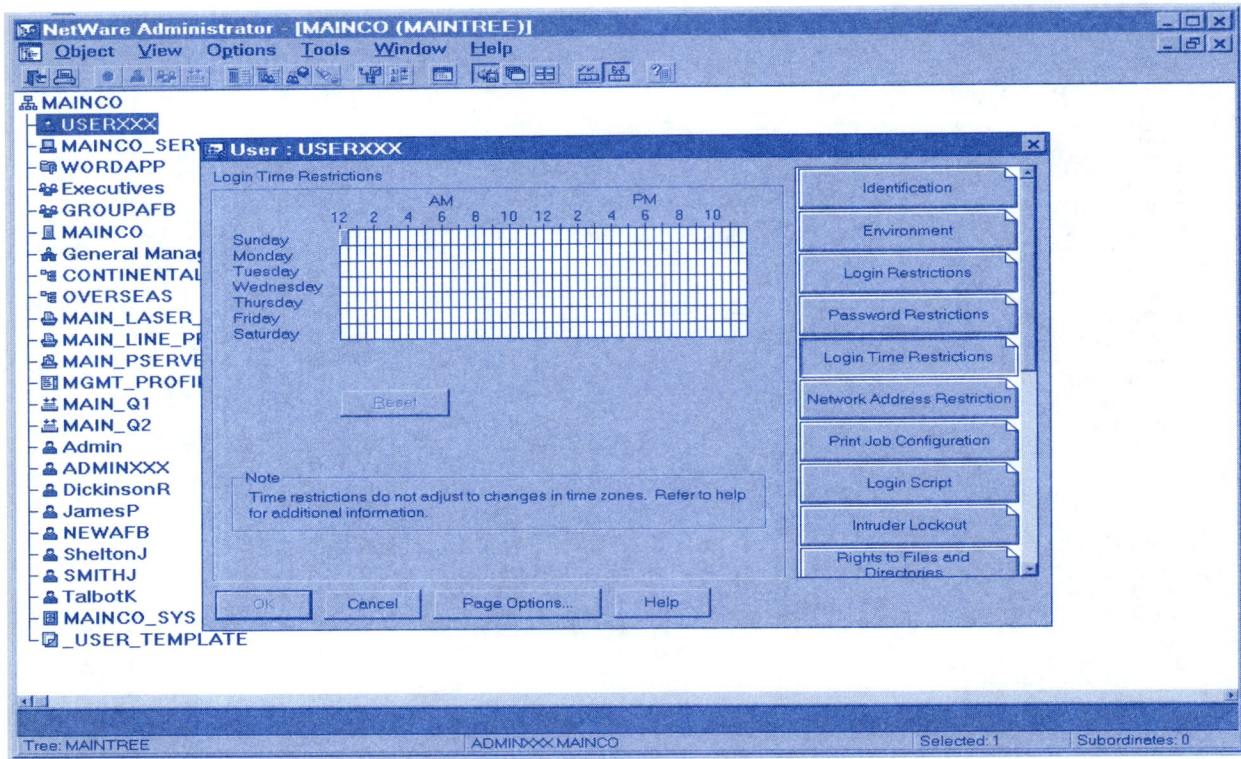

Figure 4-27. The Login Time Restriction screen for USERXXX.

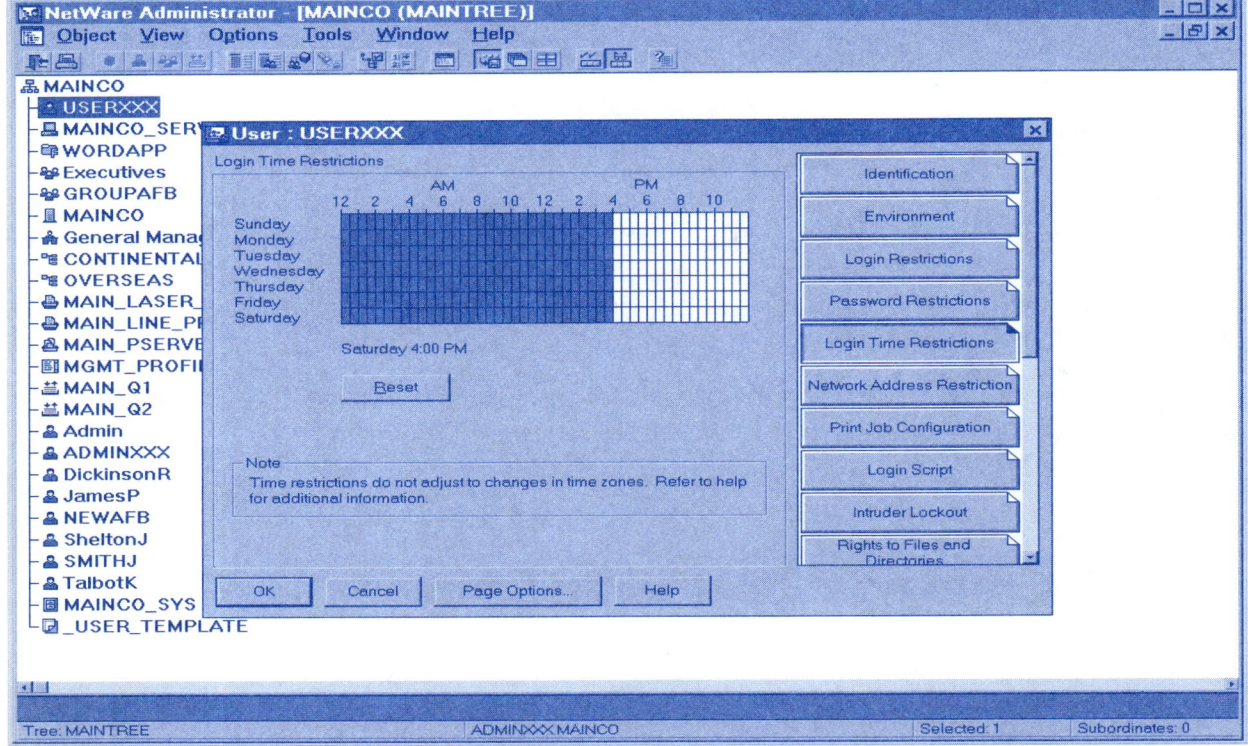

Figure 4-28. USERXXX with login time restricted midnight to 4 p.m.

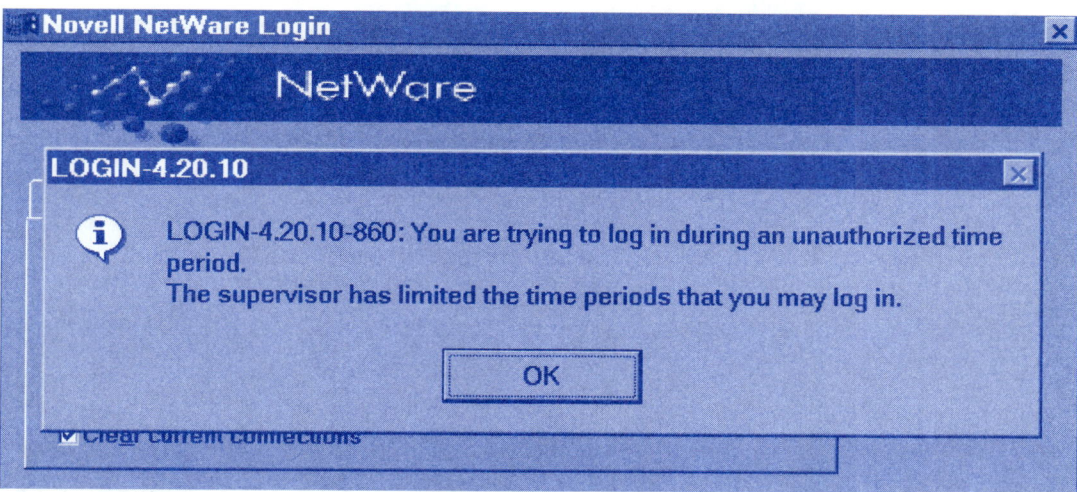

Figure 4-29. Error message USERXXX receives when trying to log in during a restricted time.

3. Reset the login time restrictions so that the user cannot log in from 12 midnight until 6 a.m. every day of the week. Be sure to click OK to save the change.

4. Click the Login Script button to display the Login Script screen as shown in Figure 4-30.

5. Click in the Login Script box and type in the following commands:

```
WRITE "Good %GREETING_TIME  %LOGIN_NAME"
PAUSE
IF HOUR24="12" then
    WRITE "TIME FOR LUNCH!"
    PAUSE
ELSE
    WRITE "TIME FOR WORK!"
    PAUSE
ENDIF
MAP ROOT H:=SYS:\USERS\%LOGIN_NAME
MAP
PAUSE
```

Your screen should look something like Figure 4-31.

Chapter 4

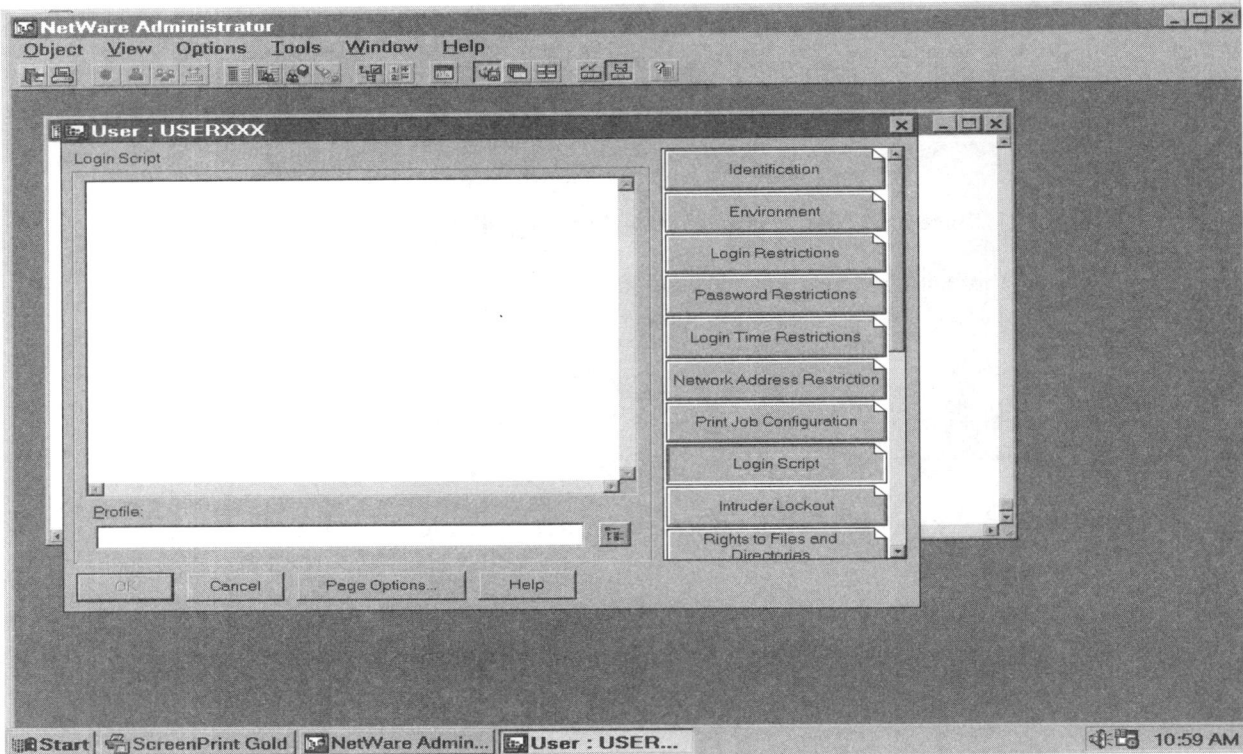

Figure 4-30. USERXXX Login Script page.

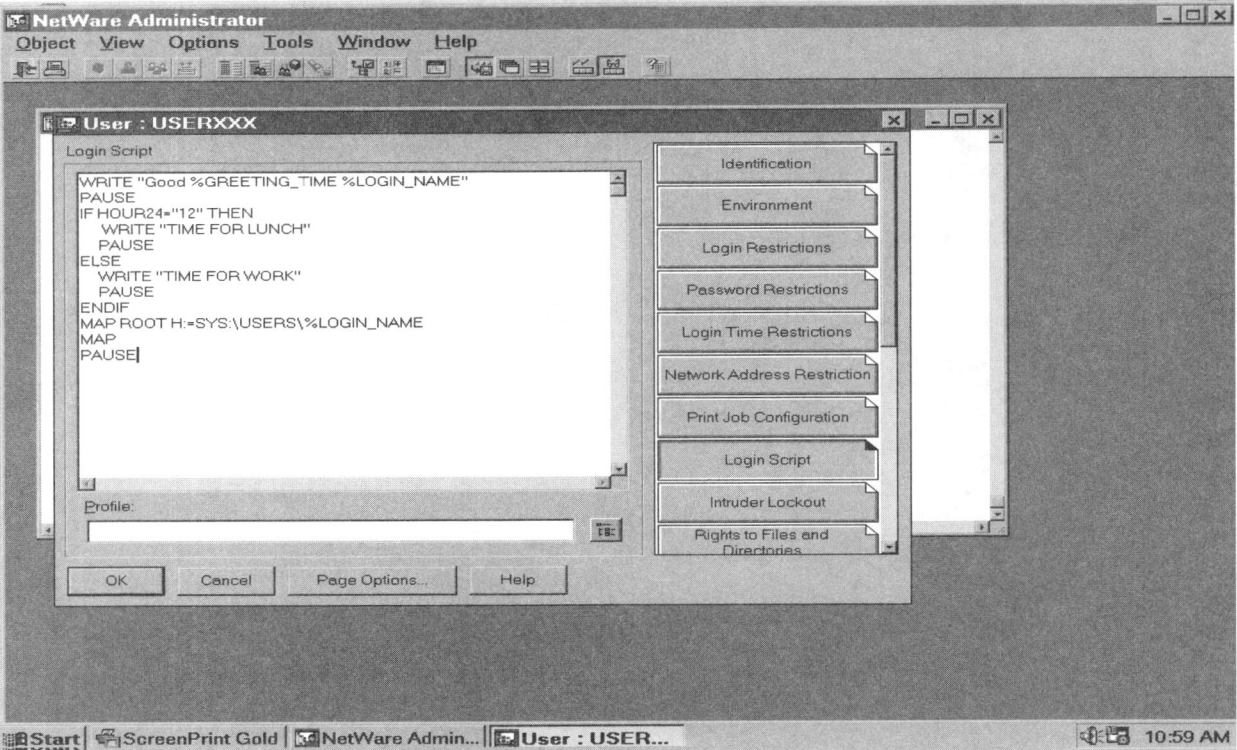

Figure 4-31. USERXXX Login Script page with login script entered.

Creating the User Account, Mappings and Login Scripts

6. Click the OK button to save the login script changes.

7. Log in as USERXXX. What messages appeared? You should see something like the screen in Figure 4-32 if the hour of the day is not 12, and something like Figure 4-33 if the hour of the day is 12.

Summary

One of the most important aspects of managing a network involves the creation of user accounts. These accounts control how and when the user will be able to use the network. With the NetWare Administrator utility, the Admin can create accounts that allow users to do the work they need to do and provide them with login scripts that set up helpful environments. The login script commands and variables available allow the Admin to create very complex programs that can take different actions based on who the user is, the time of day, and other factors.

When creating a user, the Admin can specify security equivalencies. The new user can be given security equivalence to any user or group already on the server, including the Admin. Additionally, the Admin can specify login time restrictions, login scripts, and a host of other characteristics for the user's account, All of these characteristics are aimed at making the network easier to user for the user while preserving the integrity of the network. The next chapter will examine file system security, assignments that are also made with Netware Administrator.

Questions

1. What is the purpose of a login script?

2 What are the four types of login scripts within NetWare 4,11, and how can they be used together to accomplish setting up the user's environment?

3. Which login script(s) would the Administrator use to affect the user's environment each time the user logs in?

4. What can the Admin do if a user forgets his or her password?

5. What should the Administrator do to ensure the security of the ADMIN account?

6. Explain the function of the following lines in a login script:

   IF DAY IS EQUAL TO "29" AND MONTH = "02" THEN BEGIN

   WRITE "Today is special!"

   END.

Chapter 4

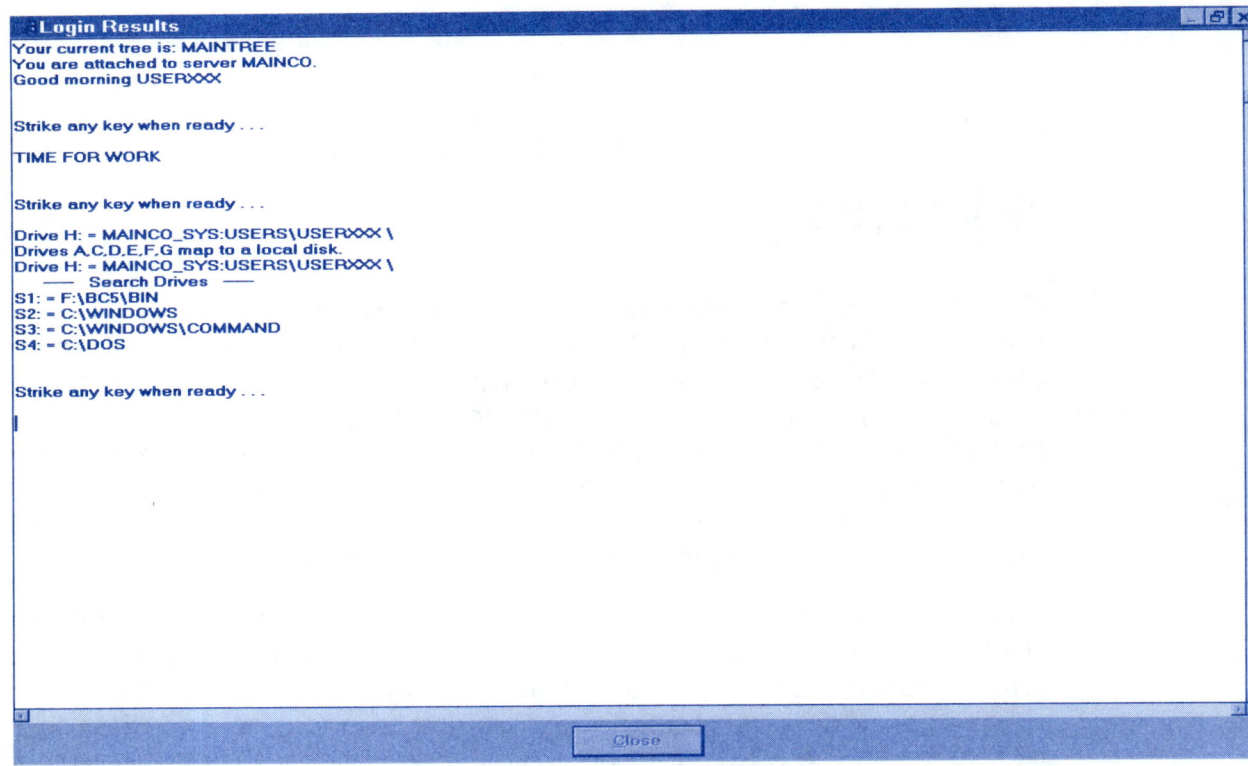

Figure 4-32. USERXXX dialog box when logging in other than with Hour=12.

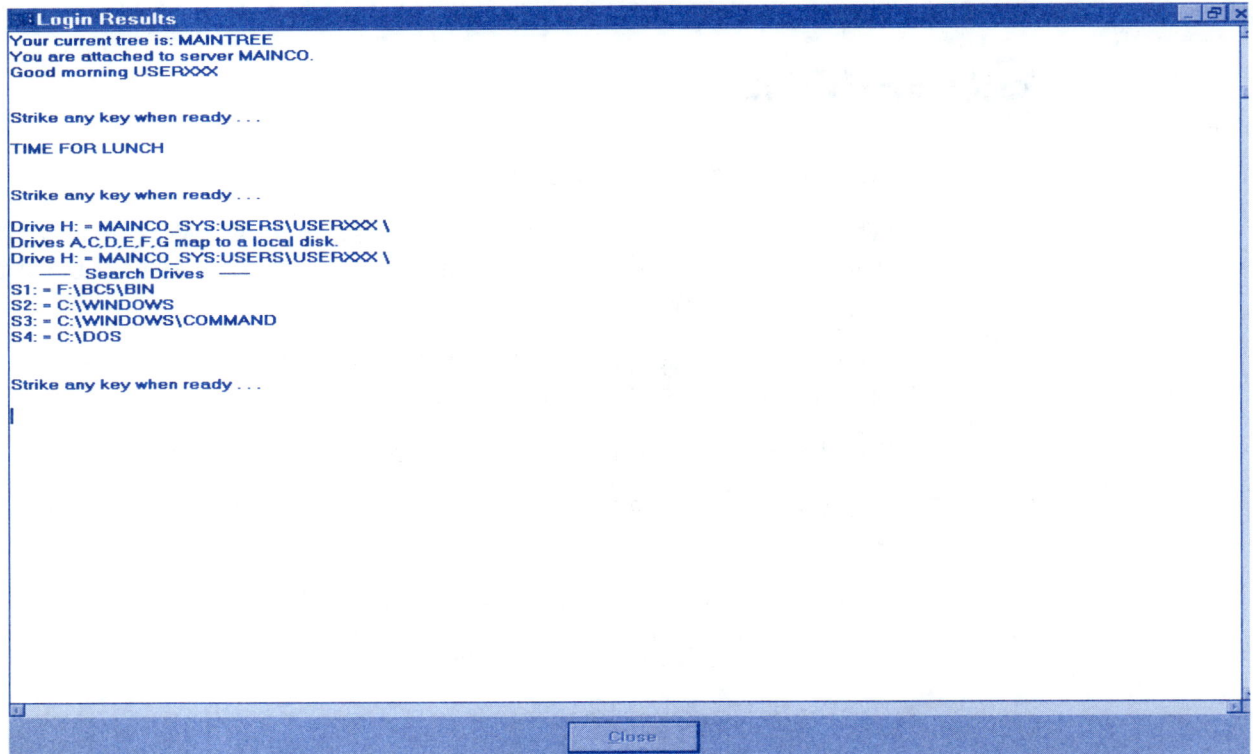

Figure 4-33. USERXXX dialog box when logging in when Hour=12.

Projects

Objective

The following projects will provide additional practice on how to create a user and login scripts. Login scripts provide a mechanism by which the system manager can customize the network and thereby make using the system easier for users.

Project 1. Using the NetWare Administrator Utility

1. Use the NetWare Administrator utility to create a new user. Use your initials as the name of the user.

2. Create a login script for the user that maps the drive letters F:, G:, and H: to the SYS:\LOGIN, SYS:\SYSTEM, and SYS:\PUBLIC, respectively.

3. Add statements to the login script that print the message "Today is the first day of the rest of your life" only if the user logs in on today's date.

4. Using SHIFT/PRINT SCREEN, print the login script just created.

5. Log in as the new user. Use the SHIFT/PRINT SCREEN keys to record the results of the login script.

6. While still logged in as the new user, start the NetWare Administrator utility and attempt to create another user. Were you successful? Why or why not?

7. Exit the NetWare Administrator utility and log in under your Admin equivalent account, ADMINXXX.

8. Start the NetWare Administrator utility and delete the new user just created.

9. Exit the NetWare Administrator utility.

Project 2. More Login Scripts

1. Using the NetWare Administrator utility, create another new user USXXX, where XXX is your initials.

2. Turn off the map display.

3. Type the basic login script commands. (MAP a search drive to the PUBLIC directory, and set up COMSPEC.)

4. Type all mappings to the basic applications installed on your file server.

Chapter 4

5. Make sure that everyone's first network drive is mapped to his or her home directory.
6. Type a greeting to be displayed when a user logs in.
7. Type the commands necessary to display the current date and time of day.
8. Type the commands necessary to remind all users of a meeting that begins at 12:00 noon every day of the week.
9. Turn the map display on and display the mappings at the end of the script.
10. Print the new user's login script.
11. Log in as the new user and test the login script.

5
File System Security and Organization

Objectives

After completing this chapter you will

1. Know the advantages of organizing users into groups.
2. Recognize the available directory and file trustee rights.
3. Understand the available directory and file attributes.
4. Be familiar with the five levels of security.
5. Know how to assign restrictions to a user's account.

Key Terms

Levels of Security

Passwords

Password Restrictions

Directory Trustee Rights

File Trustee Rights

File Attributes

Directory Attributes

Groups

Introduction

A network may have many functions. It may have electronic mail, shared printers, or shared modems. All of these functions are usually secondary to providing users with shared disk space for programs and data. In addition to the shared space, most users will need to be able to store data in a private area.

Creating a structure in which users can access the shared data they need and protect their private data is the Administrator's task. Usually programs and data must be placed in different areas with different access rights. Different users will have many different needs, and normally several groups of users will have similar needs. Under NetWare, the Administrator can grant trustee rights to these groups and still be able to customize the accounts of each user. Additionally, with NetWare 4.11, the Administrator can grant rights to the container(s) holding the user object, to organizational roles that the user occupies, to users to which the user is security equivalent, and even to a special object (PUBLIC), which supplies rights to all users connected to a file server in a NetWare 4.11 network whether or not the user is logged in.

The principle of allowing some users access to data while restricting other users is known as network file system security. NetWare 4.11 establishes system security at five levels, through passwords, trustee directory and file rights, directory attributes, file attributes, and through NDS Object and Property rights, which will be covered in Chapter 14. This multilevel approach allows the Administrator to customize the security requirements to fit any need.

Levels of Security

There are four main **levels of security**:

1. Passwords
2. Trustee Directory and File rights
3. File attributes
4. Directory attributes
5. NDS Object and Property rights

Passwords

Each NetWare account can be given a **password**. The password is a string of characters that the user types in when he or she logs in. The appropriate login program compares the login name and password to those stored by NDS. If they match, the user is allowed access to the account and the resources to which NDS provides access for that account. The login name is intended to be known by everyone while the password is kept secret by the user.

The Administrator can give the user a password or allow the user to choose one the first time he or she logs in. After it has been entered, neither the user nor the Administrator can view it. If it is forgotten, the

File System Security and Organization

only way to access the account is for the Administrator to change the password. Using NetWare Administrator, the Administrator can set defaults concerning passwords for all new accounts. See Figure 5-1 for the **password restrictions** available on a user account. You can also create a user template object with password restrictions and then use the template to create new users, transferring the password restrictions to the new user.

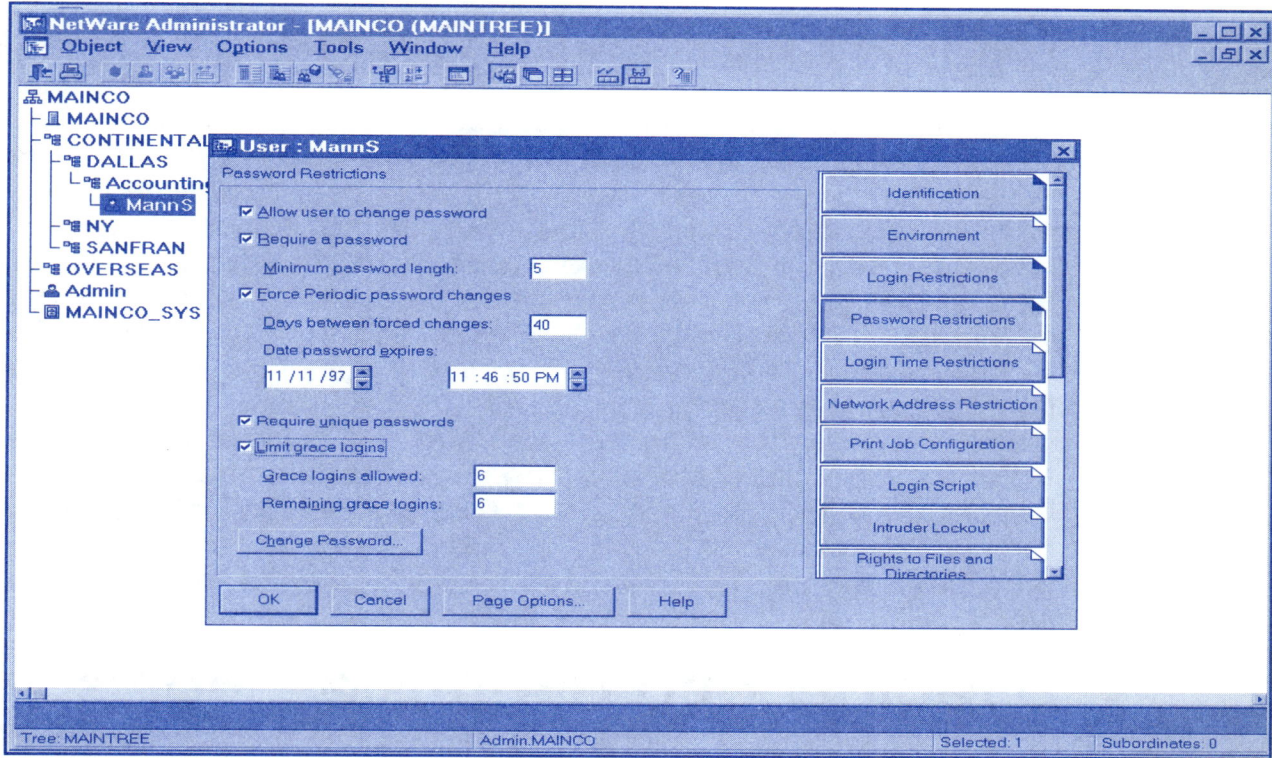

Figure 5-1. Password restrictions available under NDS.

Allowing the User to Change the Password

The user may or may not be allowed to change his or her password. In general, it is a good idea to allow the user to change his or her password; otherwise, the Administrator must take responsibility for changing users' passwords in order to help maintain security. If passwords are never changed, security is eventually diminished as users tell their peers their passwords and as passwords are written on notes taped to the users' monitors, etc. In fact, the user can be forced to change his or her password regularly as explained below.

Minimum Password Length

Each account can be required to have a password or not. If it does have a password, a minimum length can be set. The default minimum password length is 5 characters; the maximum is 128 characters. Popular and effective password lengths generally range from 5 to 10 characters.

Force Periodic Password Changes

A password is effective only if it is secret. If the same password is used for a very long time, the opportunity for an unauthorized person to discover it may be increased. This is why the account can be set to periodically force the user to change the password. If this feature is set, after the specified number of days has passed, the login program will automatically prompt the user for a new password when he or she logs in. The account can be set to allow a certain number of grace log ins that prompt the user for a new password but do not require one. If the Require Unique Passwords option is set to YES the user must enter a different password each time. NetWare remembers the last eight passwords so one could begin repeating passwords after the eighth password is used. Although using the same password for too long may allow someone to discover it, forcing the user to change it too frequently may also force the user to write it down too often or to use obvious words.

Directory and File Trustee Rights

Each user may be given trustee rights through a combination of:

1. His or her individual account
2. Each group to which the user belongs
3. Each organizational role the users occupies
4. The container(s) containing the user
5. Through being security equivalent to another user
6. Through rights given to (PUBLIC)

In NetWare 4.11, as with previous versions of NetWare, both Trustee Directory and Trustee File assignments are possible. When a user is given some access to a directory, he or she is said to be a trustee of that directory. A user's effective rights are the combination of rights at each directory obtained from any of the six sources listed above.

File System Security and Organization

Figure 5-2 shows the **directory trustee rights** for user MannS in his home directory called SYS:USERS\MannS. The only directory trustee right not given to user MannS is the S or Supervisor right to the directory. If the Administrator were to grant MannS the S right, the Admin would merely have to click the white box in front of the Supervisor right.

The rights that can be given are:

1. **Read**.

    Directory Right: The user can open and read files in the directory. The File Scan right is also needed to view the directory listing for the given directory.

    File Right: The user can see the information in a closed file to use it or to execute it even if the directory does not allow the Read permission.

2. **Write**.

    Directory Right: The user can change the contents of existing files in the directory.

    File Right: The user can change the contents of the given file even if the directory does not allow the Write permission.

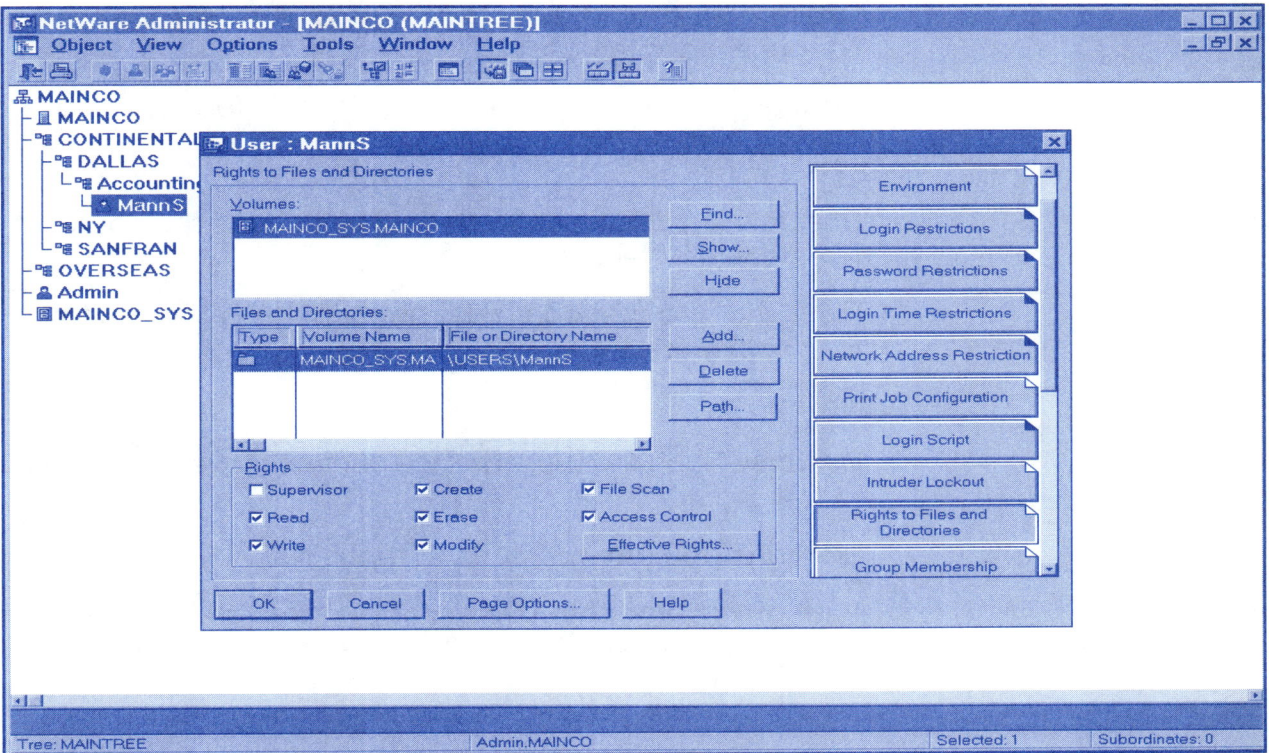

Figure 5-2. Trustee rights for user MannS.

Chapter 5

3. **Create**.

    Directory Right: The user can create files and subdirectories in the directory.

    File Right: The user can salvage a file if it has been deleted.

4. **Erase**.

    Directory Right: The user can erase files and subdirectories of the directory.

    File Right: The user can delete a file even if the directory does not allow the Delete permission.

5. **Modify**.

    Directory Right: The user can modify the Attributes and names of the files and subdirectories in the directory. The Attribute of a file indicates what access anyone has to the file.

    File Right: The user can modify the attributes and the name of the file.

6. **File Scan**.

    Directory Right: The user can see what files and subdirectories are listed in the directory.

    File Right: The user can see the file in the directory listing.

7. **Access Control.**

    Directory Right: The user can grant rights he or she has to the directory to other users.

    File Right: The user can grant any right he or she has to the file to other users.

8. **Supervisor.**

    Directory Right: The user has Supervisory, and hence, all rights to the directory.

    File Right: The user has all rights to the file.

    Trustee rights for both directories and files are given to the user and provide that user with access to certain directories.

File System Security and Organization

Directory Inherited Rights Filter

Normally, if a user has specific trustee rights to a given directory, the user inherits these rights for all subdirectories of the original directory. When a directory is created, it has the same rights as the full set of trustee rights. These directory rights, called the inherited rights filter, are attached to the directory. The inherited rights filter for a directory may be altered using NetWare Administrator and other utilities to limit any user's inherited rights to that directory, except for the Supervisor right. The Supervisor file and directory right cannot be eliminated from the Inherited Rights Filter.

Suppose a user is given Read, File Scan, Create, and Erase rights to a directory called PROGRAMS. This means that the user will also inherit the same rights for all subdirectories of the directory PROGRAMS unless the inherited rights mask for a subdirectory limits these rights. Suppose that the subdirectory called COBOL under the PROGRAMS directory has the limited inherited rights filter of Read, File Scan, and Modify. This would mean that the user's effective rights for the directory \PROGRAMS\COBOL would be only Read and File Scan because these rights are the only rights the user had to the parent directory (PROGRAMS) that are also present in the inherited rights filter of the subdirectory (\PROGRAMS\COBOL).

	Jacob's Rights
ACCTG (directory)	
IRF	--
Inherited Rights	--
Trustee Assign.	(RWCEMFA)
Effective Rights	(RWCEMFA)
SPREADSHEET (directory)	
IRF	(SRW EF A)
Inherited Rights	(RW EF A)
Trustee Assign.	--
Effective Rights	(RW EF A)
MAIN.WK1 (file)	
IRF	(SR F)
Inherited Rights	(R F)
Trustee Assign.	--
Effective Rights	(R F)

Note that the above analysis depends on Jacob's having been given the trustee assignment of all but the Supervisor right in the ACCTG directory and the Inherited Rights Filter of (RW EF A) for the SPREADSHEET directory.

Figure 5-3. Sample effective rights calculations.

Chapter 5

	Ralph as a user	Ralph as a member of the Accounting Group	Rights granted to the container containing Ralph	All Ralph's rights considered together
ACCOUNTING (directory)				
IRF	--	--	--	
Inherited Rights	--	--	--	
Trustee Assign.	(R CE F)	--	(R FA)	
Effective Rights		--		
DATABASE (directory)				
IRF	(SR F)	(SR F)	(SR F)	(R F)
Inherited Rights				
Trustee Assign.		(RWCEMFA)		
Effective Rights				
MAIN.DBF (file)				
IRF	(SRWCEMFA)	(SRWCEMFA)	(SRWCEMFA)	
Inherited Rights				
Trustee Assign.	--	--	--	
Effective Rights				

The above trustee assignments and inherited rights filters have been assigned. The effective rights at each directory and file are calculated and then added together to form the overall effective rights as shown below.

	Ralph as a user	Ralph as a member of the Accounting Group	Rights granted to the container containing Ralph	All Ralph's rights considered together
ACCOUNTING (directory)				
IRF	--	--	--	
Inherited Rights	--	--	--	
Trustee Assign.	(R CE F)	--	(R FA)	
Effective Rights	(R CE F)	--	(R FA)	(R CE FA)
DATABASE (directory)				
IRF	(SR F)	(SR F)	(SR F)	(R F)
Inherited Rights	(R F)	--	(R F)	
Trustee Assign.		(RWCEMFA)		
Effective Rights	(R F)	(RWCEMFA)	(R F)	(RWCEMFA)
MAIN.DBF (file)				
IRF	(SRWCEMFA)	(SRWCEMFA)	(SRWCEMFA)	
Inherited Rights	(R F)	(SRWCEMFA)	(R F)	
Trustee Assign.	--	--	--	
Effective Rights	(R F)	(SRWCEMFA)	(R F)	(SRWCEMFA)

Figure 5-4. Sample effective rights calculations.

Note also that when a user is given explicit trustee rights to a directory, these rights override any limitation indicated by the inherited rights filter for the directory. The inherited rights filter affects only those rights that would normally be inherited in a directory.

Trustee file rights are the same as the trustee directory rights except that they are assigned to a file, not to a directory. When specific file system rights are given, they override any directory trustee rights explicitly assigned or directory trustee rights that are inherited.

File System Security and Organization

Refer to Figures 5-3 and 5-4 for sample effective rights calculations for given scenarios. The Directory structure is \ACCTG\SPREADSHEET, and the file MAIN.WK1 is in the \ACCTG\SPREADSHEET directory.

The Directory Structure for Figure 5-4 is \ACCOUNTING\DATABASE with MAIN.DBF in the \ACCOUNTING\DATABASE driectory.

File Attributes

Information stored on the file server is stored in files. These files can have several different **file attributes** that may further control the user's access or track the use of the file. Attributes limit what a user can do with a file in much the same way that directory rights limit what can be done with the files in a directory. For instance, a file can have a Read Only attribute, which means the user cannot write to it or delete it. The file is said to be "flagged" Read Only. If the user has the Modify File Name/Flags right, he or she can remove the Read Only flag from the file using either the DOS ATTRIB command or NetWare Administrator. This allows the Administrator or the user to safeguard certain files against such actions as accidental changes or deletions, while still being able to make those changes if necessary. If the user does not have the Modify File Name/Flags right, he or she cannot remove the Read Only attribute. This would give the Administrator the ability to protect individual files in a directory. The file attributes available in NetWare are as follows:

1. **A** - Archive Needed. Identifies files modified after last backup. It is assigned automatically.

2. **Cc** -Can't Compress. The file cannot be compressed.

3. **Co** -Compressed. The file is compressed.

4. **Ci** - Copy Inhibit. The file, which must have an .EXE or .COM extension, can be executed only. The program cannot be copied. This attribute cannot be removed once set.

5. **Di** - Delete Inhibited. The file cannot be deleted.

6. **Dc** - Don't Compress. This file cannot be compressed even when compression is activated for the volume.

7. **Dm** - Don't Migrate. This attribute keeps this file from being migrated to nearline storage. (This assumes that the system has been set up to migrate files from online storage to nearline storage.)

8. **Ds** - Don't Suballocate. Do not allow this file to use the system's suballocated blocks left over when a file does not use all of the block to which it is assigned.

9. **X** - Execute Only. The file can only be executed.

10. **H** - Hidden. The file name is hidden from directory searches so it is not listed in the DOS DIR command. Unlike the DOS file attribute Hidden, a program file flagged Hidden cannot be executed.

11. **Ic** - Immediate Compress. This file will be immediately compressed when it is stored.

12. **M** -Migrated. This file has been migrated to nearline storage. (This assumes that the system has been set up to migrate files from online storage to nearline storage.)

13. **N** - Normal

14. **P** - Purge. This attribute indicates that the file will be purged from the file system after it has been deleted. It will not be possible to undelete this file later.

15. **Ro** - Read Only. This attribute indicates that the file can only be read. It cannot be deleted or updated without first resetting this attribute.

16. **Rw** - Read/Write. This file can be read, its contents can be updated, and it can be erased with this attribute set.

17. **Ri** - Rename Inhibit. The file cannot be renamed.

18. **Sh** - Shareable. The file can be read by several users simultaneously.

29. **Sy** - System. The file is one of the operating system files. It cannot be deleted or changed by the user.

20. **T** - Transactional. This attribute is a safety feature that is usually applied to a database file. NetWare ensures that changes to the file are either completed or not made at all in case of an interruption during the process.

NetWare Administrator can be used to set file attributes as shown in Figure 5-5.

Directory Attributes

Just as there are file attributes, there are **directory attributes**. Attributes assigned to the directory are inherited by the files in the directory. These attributes and their meanings are:

1. **Di** - Delete Inhibited. The directory and the files in it cannot be deleted.

File System Security and Organization

2. **Dc** - Don't Compress. The files in this directory cannot be compressed even when compression is activated for the volume.

3. **Dm** - Don't Migrate. This attribute keeps this files in this directory from being migrated to nearline storage. (This assumes that the system has been set up to migrate files from online storage to nearline storage.)

4. **H** - Hidden. The file names in this directory and the directory name itself is hidden from directory searches so it is not listed in the DOS DIR command. Unlike the DOS file attribute Hidden, a program file flagged Hidden cannot be executed.

5. **Ic** - Immediate Compress. Files in this directory are to be immediately compressed when they are stored.

6. **N** - Normal.

7. **P** - Purge. This attribute indicates that the files in this directory will be purged from the file system after they have been deleted. It will not be possible to undelete this file later.

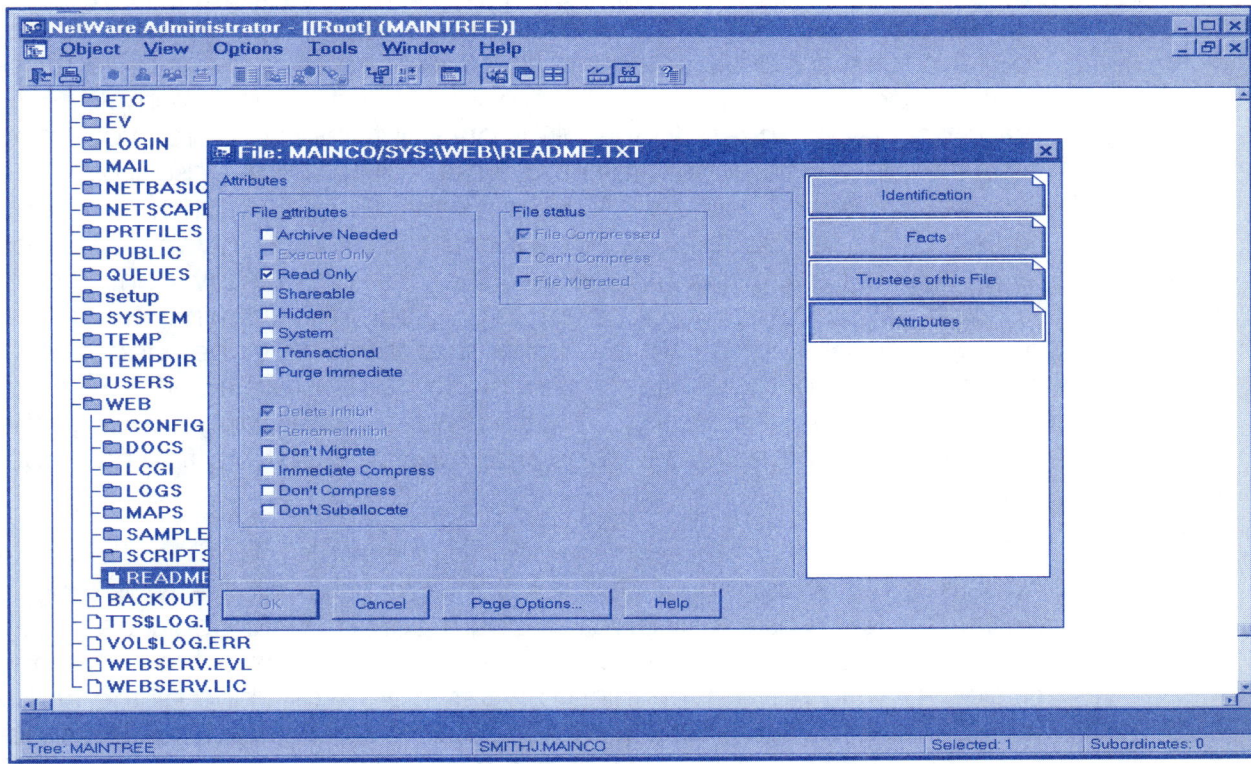

Figure 5-5. Setting file attributes through Netware Administrator.

8. **Ri** - Rename Inhibit. The files in this directory cannot be renamed.

9. **Sy** - System. The files in this directory are operating system files. They cannot be deleted or changed by the user.

NetWare Administrator can be used to set directory attributes similar to the way it is used to set file attributes.

Organization

Types of Users

When NetWare was installed, it automatically created a user account called Admin representing the Administrator. The person who assumes the role of Admin is responsible for the smooth operation of a single container up to operation of the entire network. It is the Admin's job to ensure easy and productive access to the network. As a network grows, there will likely be more than one Administrator account with each Administrator account having administration responsibility for a part of the NDS tree. For simplicity in this textbook, though, we will refer to the Admin account. A user must be given an account with access to the necessary directories and files. Most users will need drive mappings to particular directories. A typist in an office, for example, may need only read access to the directory containing a word processing program and write access to a document directory. A casual user or a user whose uses of the network are not very well defined may also need limited program groups in Windows and may not be given permission to alter his or her account. A more sophisticated user may want to control as much of his or her account as possible; the Admin may or may not want to allow the user the rights to control his or her account. In addition, this user may want to be able to configure the software he or she is using. A typist probably would not need to be able to change the configuration of the word processing program, but the office manager might.

If it is a large office there may be many people needing the same access rights and menus. One solution is to have all the typists log in under the same user name. An account called TYPIST could be set up that allows several users to be logged in at the same time. This one account could have everything a typist might want, and all the typists would share the same directory space, software, and data. This situation could work well as long as the typists could agree on how their directory space was to be handled. Having everyone log in using the same login name can be inconvenient, however. Individual typists may

File System Security and Organization

need a more customized environment to work with. Electronic mail and other messages could not be sent to individuals.

Groups

With various users needing different attributes to their accounts, individual accounts would have to be created. But since many users may need the same access rights, it is possible to create **groups** of users that can be given the same rights. A group could be created called TYPIST rather than an individual account. The group would be given the rights, and then each member of the group TYPIST in the office would be made a user in that group. Each typist in the office could have his or her own login name, login scripts, passwords, and other attributes. Each member of the group TYPIST, for example, may have programs he or she wants in addition to the word processing software provided by the company. If the Administrator sets up the accounts properly, the users could have private areas on the file server to store their programs. Some of the members of the group TYPIST may wish to share some of their private directory space with only certain other individuals, not everyone in the group TYPIST. Users can make these modifications themselves assuming the Administrator has set up their accounts correctly and they know how.

Group Hierarchy

NetWare does not explicitly provide for groups of groups, but the same thing can be accomplished logically. Suppose there were several office managers overseeing the network users. They would need access to everything the members of the group TYPIST have plus additional space for confidential employee information. A group called MANAGER could be created that has only the additional rights needed. A manager would then belong to both groups, MANAGER and TYPIST. A member of the board might need even more information available. That position might need access to pending contracts, for instance. A group called BOARD would give those members access to very critical data only, but since a member of the board might not need to see the work in progress by the members of the group TYPIST, he or she might be a member of the group BOARD and MANAGER and not TYPIST. In this way a hierarchy of users can be established so changes can be made to each group according to the functions they require.

Data Organization

The way data is organized on the file server hard disk can greatly influence the efficiency of the network. Since the Admin is responsible for providing the users with a convenient working environment, he or she must arrange the items stored on the server in a way that will make it easy for the user to access them. This implies that it must be easy for the

Admin to assign the proper rights in order to maintain security. The items on the server would need to be arranged by function, as much as possible, with data, application software, operating system software, NetWare public utilities, and NetWare system software in separate areas.

Types of Data

All of the above items may be referred to as data. However, in this context, data is the information created and stored by the user. Application software is the set of programs used to create the data. The operating system consists of DOS and its program utilities such as FORMAT.COM and CHKDSK.COM. NetWare has several public utilities that are intended to be used by any user who knows how, since they cannot harm the accounts of anyone else. Other utilities, software, and data used only by NetWare itself or the Administrator is known as system software.

Suppose a company had the same types of users as above with members of the groups TYPIST, MANAGERS, and BOARD MEMBERS. Since each user has his or her own account, the Administrator might be tempted to arrange the directories something like the way shown in Figure 5-6.

In Figure 5-6 user JACK is a member of the group TYPIST who needs access to a word processing program and a database program. JACK stores only low security letters and bills in his data directory. JILL, on the other hand, is a manager and needs to use the same type of software but must store very sensitive data such as employee evaluations and contract bids. JACK could be made a trustee with full rights in the F:\JACK\DATA directory and only read rights in the F:\JACK\APPS directory. JILL would then need similar rights in the directories under F:\JILL, but she would also need full access to JACK's data directory.

Since there are usually more members of the group TYPIST than managers supervising them, JILL would need full rights to all the members of the group TYPIST.

The network Admin would have to list each of the members of the group TYPIST data directories under JILL's trustee assignments. Also, the software that each of these users needs is being duplicated, wasting space and installation time. A more efficient approach would be to put all the software under one directory and all the data under another.

Figure 5-7 shows a better directory structure. Under this structure the group called MANAGER would have read and write access to the entire F:\DATA directory and read access to the F:\APPS directory. The group TYPIST would have read and write access to only the F:\DATA\TYPIST directory, and it would also have read access to the F:\APPS directory. With these groups created, there could be as many members of the group TYPIST and as many managers as necessary. JACK may not have any explicit trustee rights but instead belongs to the group TYPIST. JILL also might have no trustee assignments listed in her account but her membership in the MANAGER group would give her all the rights she needs.

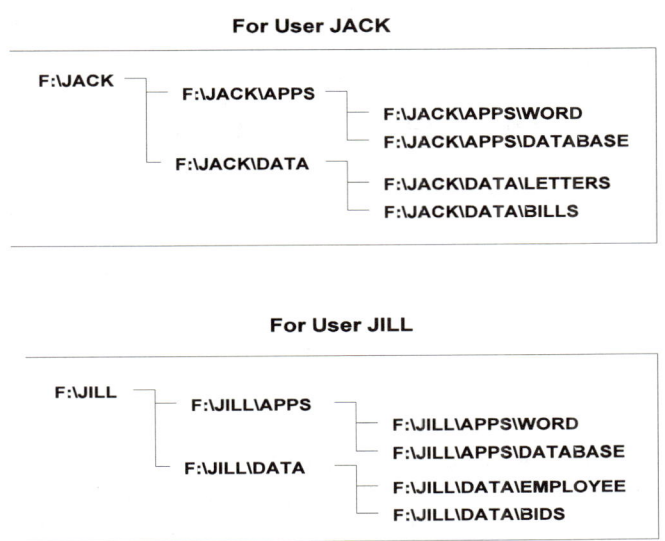

Figure 5-6. Directory arrangement.

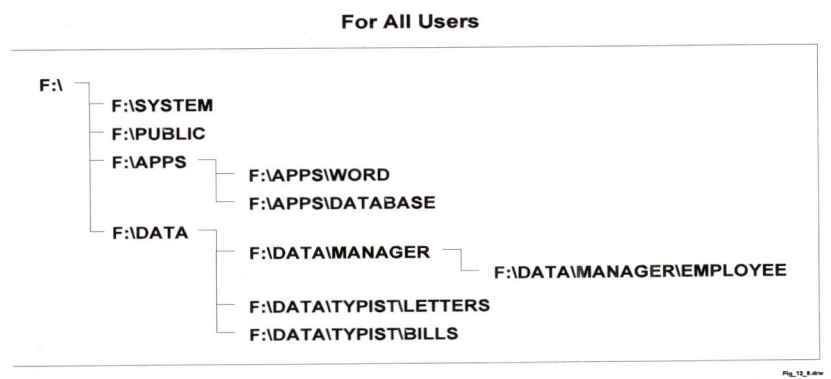

Figure 5-7. A more efficient directory arrangement.

Assigning rights to groups, in general, makes a networking system easier to maintain. For example, let's say that Jack's work doubles, and the comp-any hires an additional typist named Paula. Assuming that Jack receives all of his rights through the group TYPIST, Paula's account can be created and added to the TYPIST group rather than forcing the administrator to assign rights directly to Paula's user account.

Hands-on NetWare

In order to complete the hands-on section of this chapter, the file server and a workstation should be ready to use.

1. The file server must be on.

2. A workstation must be booted and the appropriate network drivers must be loaded.

3. Network Drive F: should be the default first network drive at the workstation.

4. The user account created in the previous chapter must still be available, and the user must be logged in.

In the example below, **TYPE THE NAME OF YOUR ACCOUNT WHERE SMITHJ IS USED**. For instance, if the instructions read "LOG IN as SMITHJ", you should LOG IN as your user account with Admin capabilities.

Each numbered set of instructions can be completed at different times, as long as they are finished in order. For instance, the exercise on Minimum Password Length must be completed before the exercise on Force Periodic Password Changes.

Levels of Security

As discussed earlier NetWare provides the Administrator with five levels of security. With these five levels, a blanket can be woven around the data providing just the right amount of access for each user. The following instructions will demonstrate the properties of the first four levels of security. The fifth level of security will be discussed in Chapter 14.

Passwords

Passwords are the "first line" of defense against intentional attempts to break network security. Two restrictions that can be placed on the password are Minimum Password Length and Force Periodic Password Changes as shown in Figure 5-8.

File System Security and Organization

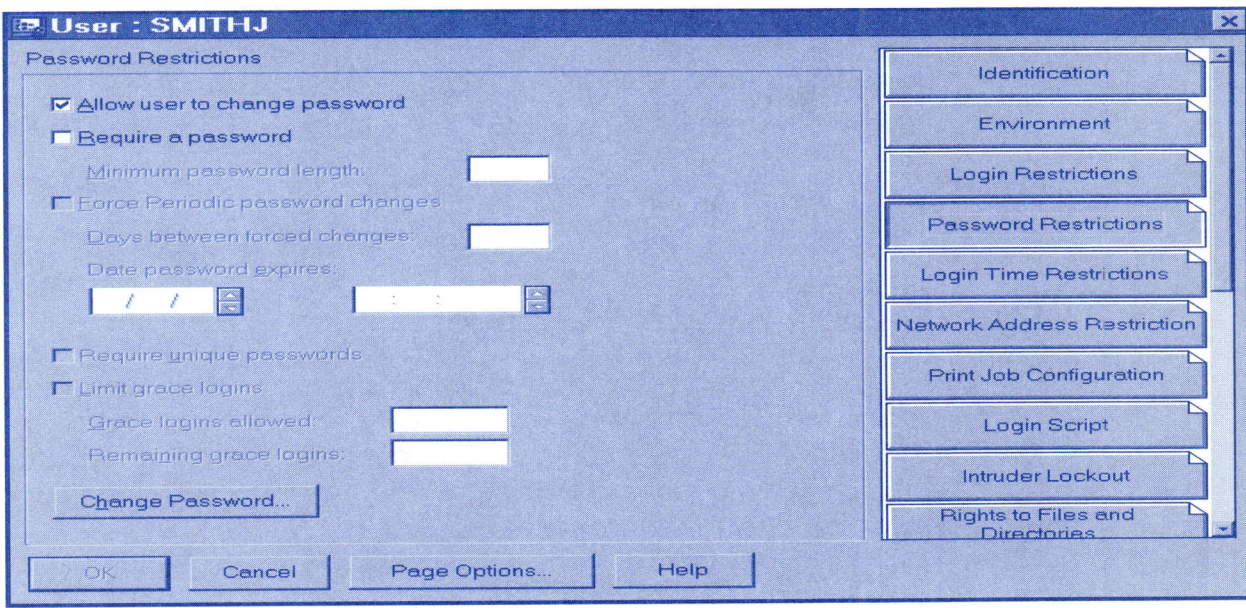

Figure 5-8. NetWare Administrator Password Restrictions screen.

Changing the Password and Minimum Password Length

If a user is allowed to change the password, he or she may be tempted to use very short words to make memorizing it easier. Unfortunately, it also becomes easier to guess. For this reason a minimum length can be set on the password. A program called SETPASS can be run at the command prompt. This program requires the user to enter the old password and then to enter the new password two times to verify its accuracy. The SETPASS program is self-explanatory and is not discussed further here.

The password can also be changed by using NetWare Administrator.

1. Log in with **your user name**.

2. Activate Windows 3.1 if necessary. If you are logging in from Windows 95, Windows 95 is already activated.

3. Double-click on the **NetWare Administrator** icon previously created.

4. Double-click on the **MAINCO container** and open other containers until your user ID is visible.

5. Right-click on **your user ID** and choose **Details.**

6. Click on the **Change Password button**. Figure 5-9 appears.

7. Enter **the old password and the new password** in both new password boxes and click OK. The password is changed.

125

Chapter 5

8. If you are not going to do further work, close NetWare Administrator by double-clicking on the box at the upper left of the NetWare Administrator screen. (In Windows 95, you can alternately click the X box in the upper right-hand corner of the screen.)

9. **Log out**.

Force Periodic Password Changes

Forcing a user to periodically change his or her password is considered an important component of password security. However, changing the password too often makes it difficult to remember. The following steps illustrate the process of setting Force Periodic Password Changes and what happens when the password expires.

1. Log in with **your user name**.

2. Activate Windows 3.1 if necessary. If you are logging in from Windows 95, Windows 95 is already activated.

3. Double-click on the **NetWare Administrator icon** previously created.

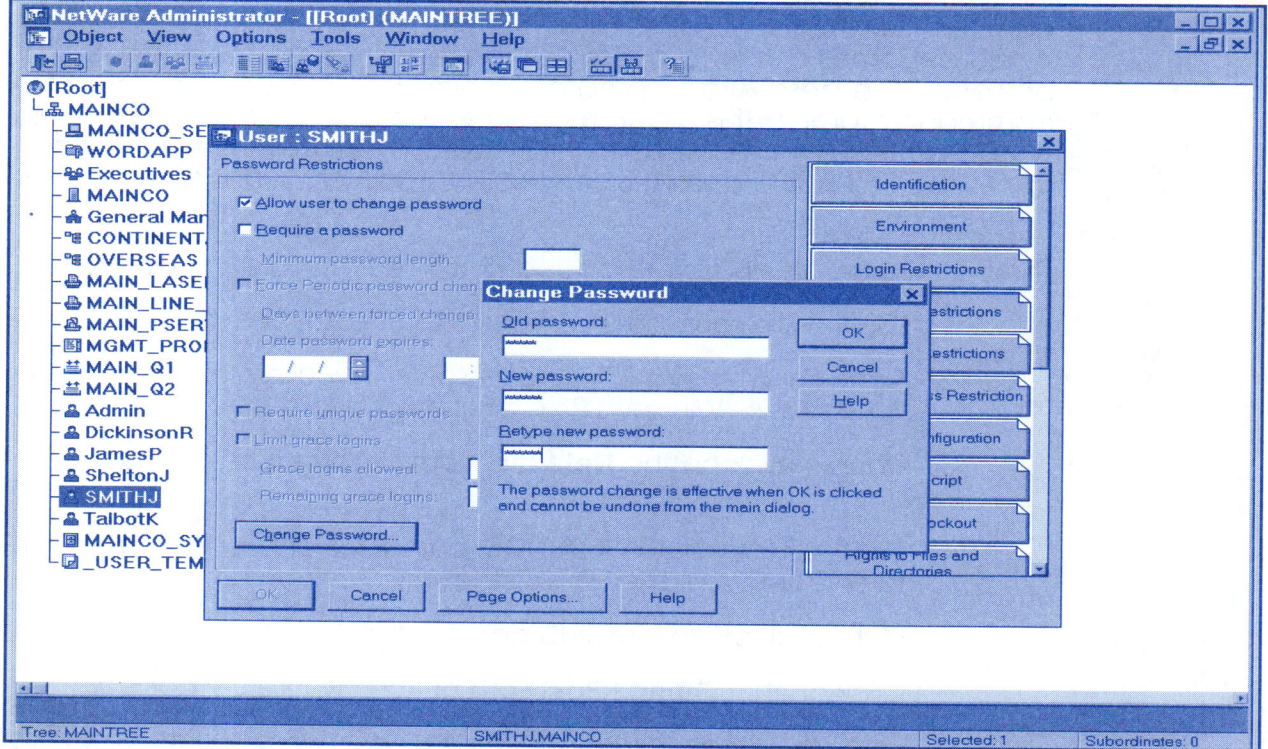

Figure 5-9. Change Password dialog in NetWare Administrator.

File System Security and Organization

4. Double-click on the **MAINCO container** and open other containers until your user ID is visible.

5. Right-click on **your user ID** and choose Details.

6. Click on the **Password Restrictions button.**

7. Refer to Figure 5-8 to require a password and to force period password changes every 30 days starting today a minute or two from now. Be sure to click **OK** to save the changes.

8. If you are not going to do further work, close NetWare Administrator by double-clicking on the box at the upper left of the NetWare Administrator screen. (In Windows 95, you can alternately click the X box in the upper right-hand corner of the screen.)

9. **Log out.**

10. Wait a few minutes (long enough for the expiration date and time to take effect) and **log in** again. What happened?

Trustee Rights

The second level of security, trustee rights, requires the most work on the part of the Administrator. NetWare Administrator is used to identify each directory the user or group has trustee rights in. In the following steps you will use your account to give yourself trustee rights in a new directory. Depending on how NetWare 4 is installed, the ADMIN is usually given the Supervisor right to the root of each volume of each server. However, since NetWare 4 is usually an enterprise network with many subadministrators, the Admin customarily will need to grant rights to subadministartors as well as users in a manner similar to what is shown below.

1. Log in with **your user name**.

2. Activate Windows 3.1 if necessary. If you are logging in from Windows 95, Windows 95 is already activated.

3. Double-click on the **NetWare Administrator icon** previously created.

4. Double-click on the **MAINCO container** and open other containers until your user ID is visible.

5. Right-click on **your user ID** and choose **Details.**

6. Click on the **Rights to Files and Directories button** on the right side of the screen.

7. Figure 5-10 is displayed. Don't be misled into thinking that the user has no rights. Click on the **Show button** and then navigate until you find the SYS volume listed on the Available Objects list as shown in Figure 5-11.

Chapter 5

8. Click on **MAINCO_SYS** and click **OK**. (Click on your SYS volume whatever its name happens to be.)

9. The existing file and directory rights on this volume are displayed as in Figure 5-12.

10. Click on **each File or Directory** to see what rights are assigned to that selection as shown in Figure 5-12.

11. Add a trustee assignment to the WEB directory that gives your user rights to read and update files in that directory. To do this, first click on **Add**. Then double-click on **the SYS volume**, MAINCO_SYS in this case, in the right side of the screen.

12. Click on **the WEB directory** in the left window of the screen as shown in Figure 5-13. Then click the **OK button**.

13. Click on **the Write right**, and then click the **OK button**. See Figure 5-14.

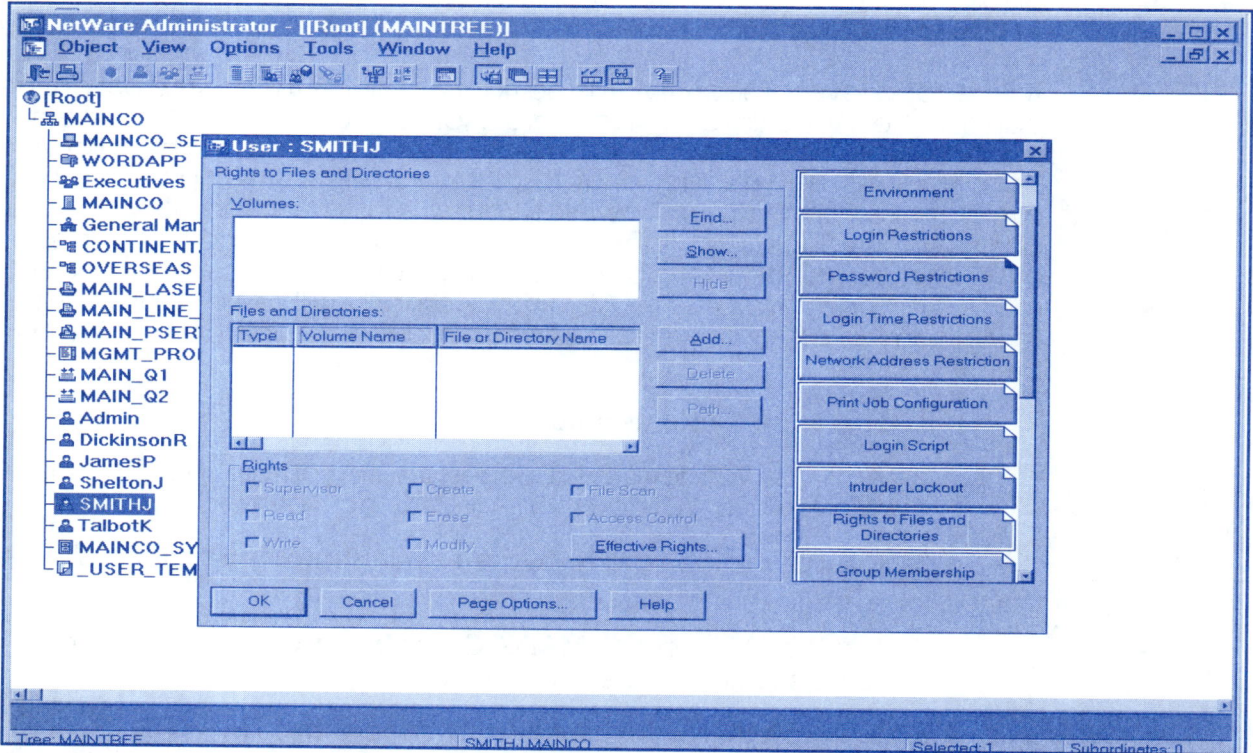

Figure 5-10. Rights to Files and Directories screen.

File System Security and Organization

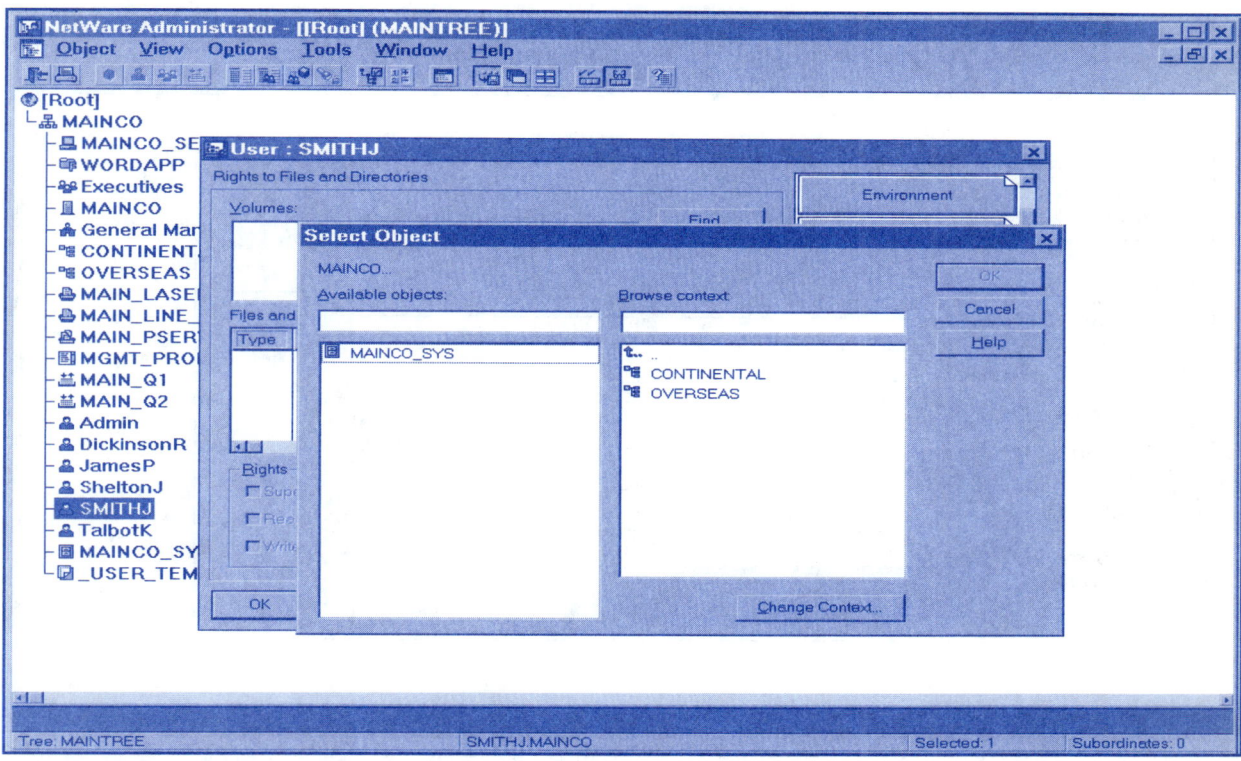

Figure 5-11. Available Objects screen.

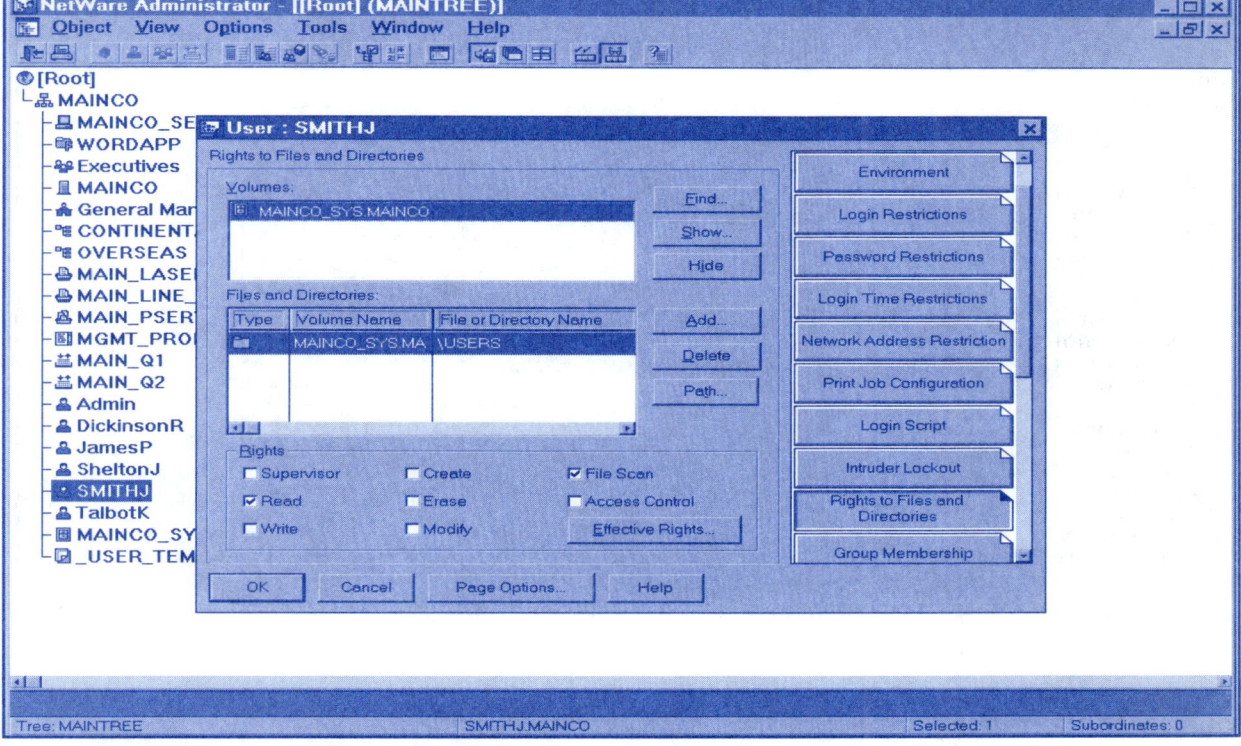

Figure 5-12. Showing rights assigned on MAINCO_SYS.

129

Chapter 5

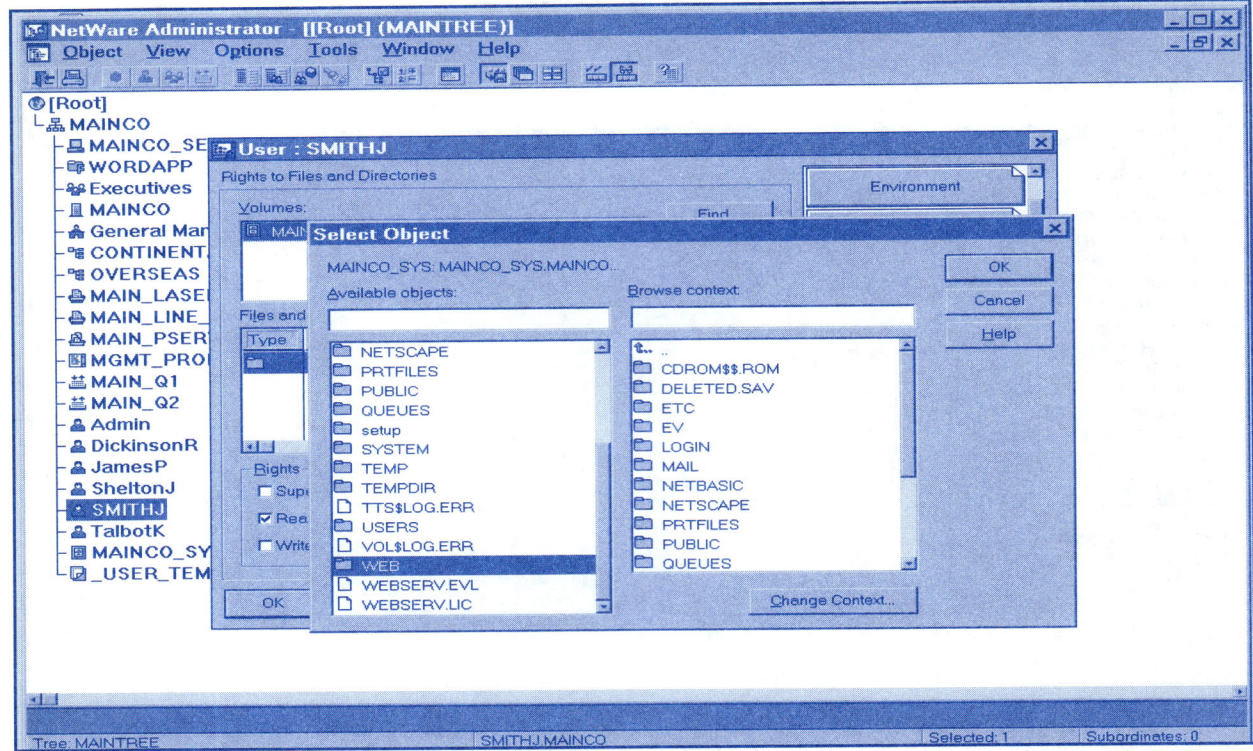

Figure 5-13. Selecting the directory for which rights are to be assigned.

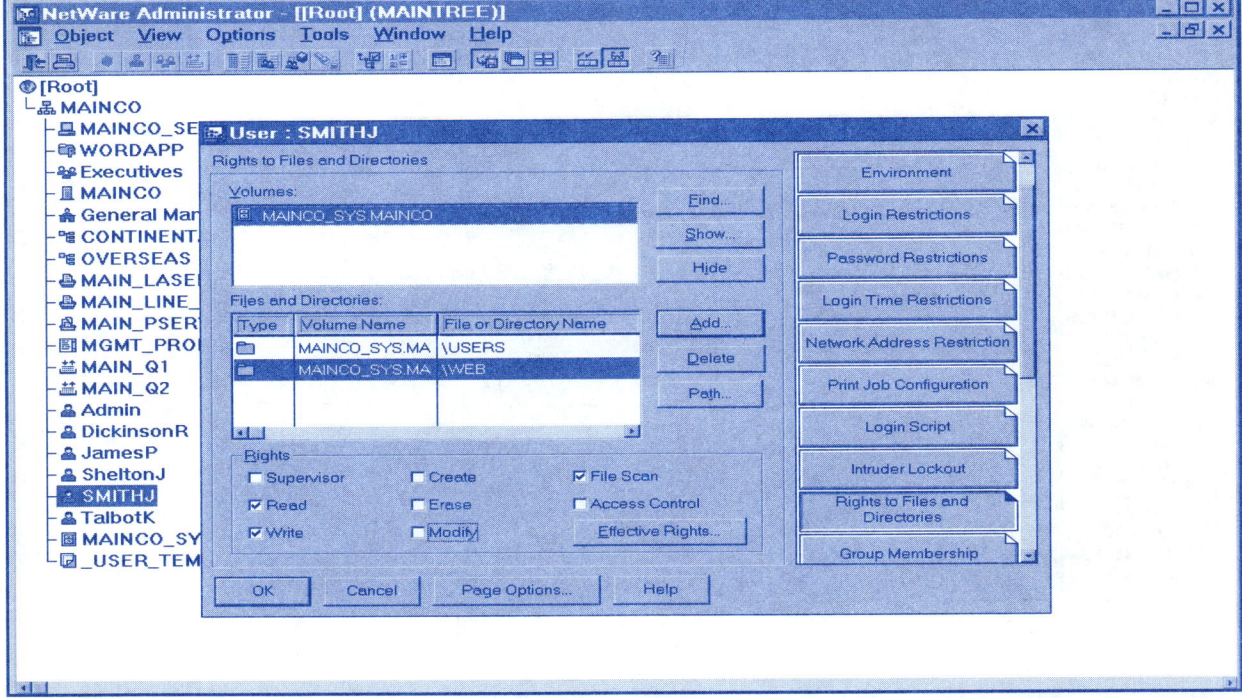

Figure 5-14. Directory rights granted for the WEB directory.

File System Security and Organization

14. If you are not going to do further work, close NetWare Administrator by double-clicking on the box at the upper left of the NetWare Administrator screen. (In Windows 95, you can alternately click the X box in the upper right-hand corner of the screen.)

15. **Log out**.

Directory Attributes

The Administrator can set each user's access rights to particular values in particular directories. The user automatically has the same rights in any subdirectory. For instance, user SMITHJ in the preceding example was given complete rights to the MAIL directory. If any directories are created below the MAIL directory, user SMITHJ will have complete rights to those as well.

Often, in a large directory structure, one or two directories may need to be restricted so that users have rights to these directories only when they are explicitly given by granting Trustee Directory Rights. Inherited Rights can be restricted by creating an inherited rights filter that restricts all users except those with Supervisor file system authority. The following directions illustrate how the NetWare Administrator program is used to make the directory rights changes.

1. Log in with **your user name**.

2. Activate Windows 3.1 if necessary. If you are logging in from Windows 95, Windows 95 is already activated.

3. Double-click on the **NetWare Administrator icon** previously created.

4. Double-click on **the MAINCO container** and open other containers until the MAINCO_SYS volume to display its contents.

5. Right-click on **the WEB directory** and choose **Details.**

6. Click on **the Attributes button** on the right of the screen.

7. Click **the directory attributes desired** and click the **OK button**.

File Attributes

File attributes could be said to be the last line of defense in security since often they are used to prevent accidental erasure or changes to files. With a file flagged as Read Only, no user, including the Administrator, can change or delete the file. If the user has the Modify File Names/Flags right in the directory, the Read Only attribute can be set to Read Write, which then allows changes. The following short exercise demonstrates this point.

1. Log in with **your user name.**

2. Activate Windows 3.1 if necessary. If you are logging in from Windows 95, Windows 95 is already activated.

3. Double-click on the **NetWare Administrator** icon previously created.

4. Double-click on **the MAINCO container** and open other containers until the MAINCO_SYS volume to display its contents.

5. Position on **the Readme.txt file under the WEB directory.** Right-click and select **details.** Figure 5-15 is displayed.

6. Click on **Attributes.** The file is already set to Read Only. Click **Cancel** to leave this screen.

7. To prove that the read-only attribute keeps the file from being erased, click on **the Readme.txt file** and the press the **Del key**. Click on the **Yes button** to confirm the delete. The message shown in Figure 5-16 shows that the file cannot be deleted.

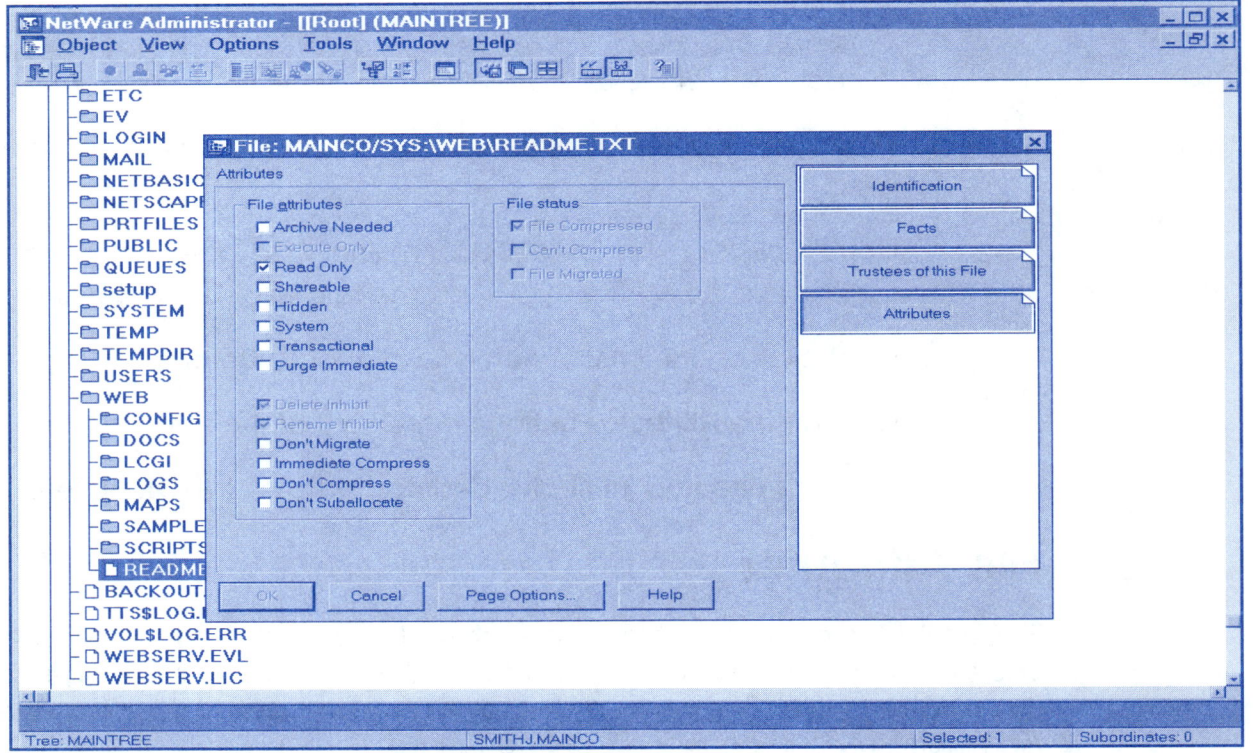

Figure 5-15. Directory attributes.

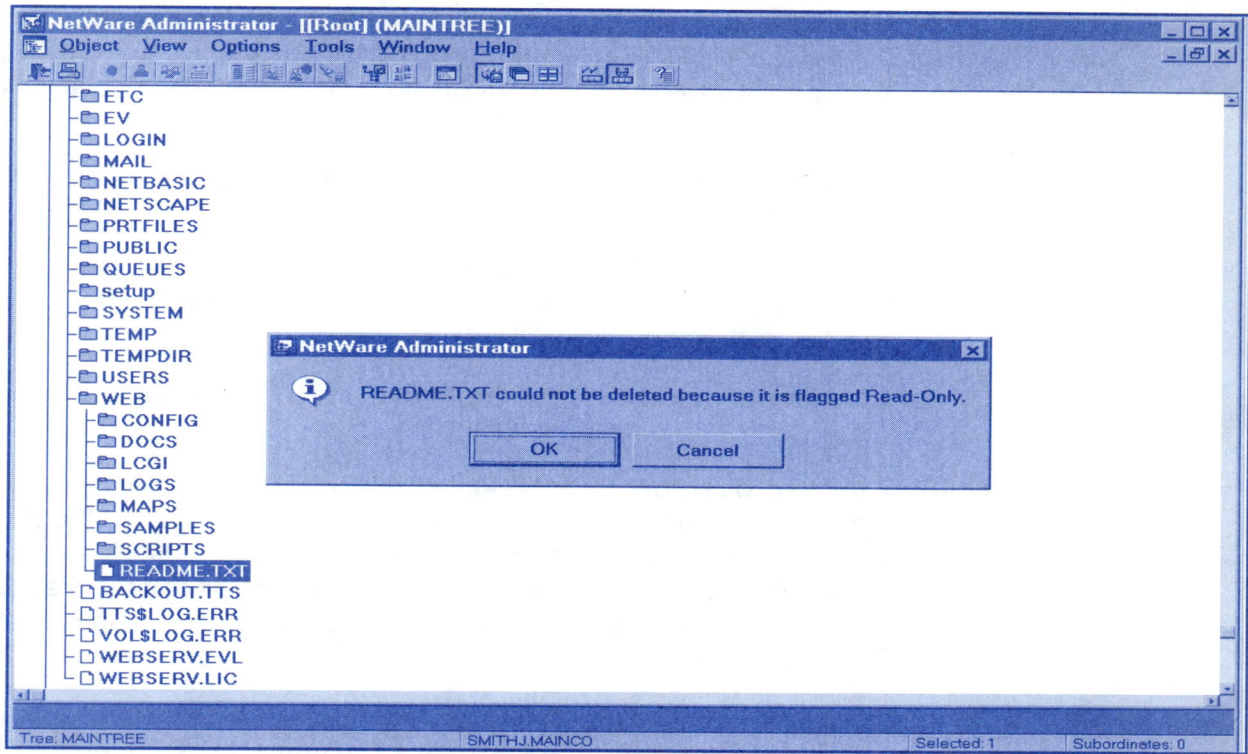

Figure 5-16. README.TXT cannot be deleted.

Effective Rights

The combination of trustee rights and directory rights is called a user's effective rights. The effective rights are those rights that are granted specifically in the user trustee assignments and/or inherited by a combination of rights inherited from the parent directory which are not limited by the inherited rights mask. To show this, a user account that is non-Administrator-equivalent is needed. The following steps create such a user.

1. Log in with your user name.

2. Activate Windows 3.1 if necessary. If you are logging in from Windows 95, Windows 95 is already activated.

3. Double-click on the NetWare Administrator icon previously created.

4. Create a new user. This user should be called NEWxxx where XXX is your initials.

5. Create a directory under SYS: called DIRxxx where xxx is your initials.

Chapter 5

6. Give directory file system rights at the DIRAFB directory that consists of all rights except Supervisor to the new user. Do this by right-clicking on **the new directory** and selecting **details**. A figure similar to Figure 5-17 is displayed.

7. Click the **Trustees of this Directory button** to obtain the screen shown in Figure 5-18.

8. Click on the **Add Trustee button** and then locate your new user in the Select Object dialog box as shown in Figure 5-19. Click the **OK button.**

9. Click on **all rights except Supervisor** as shown in Figure 5-20. Click **OK.**

10. Create **a directory under DIRxxx called SUB1.** Set the inherited rights filter for this directory to Read and File Scan only. Do this by right-clicking **the directory name**, clicking on **trustees of this directory** and then **removing the checks from all but the Read, Create, File Scan, and Access Control** boxes as shown in Figure 5-21. Note that the Supervisor right cannot be removed. Click **OK**.

11. Create **a directory under SYS:\DIRxxx\SUB1 called SUB2** and give the user NEWxxx the Read, File Scan, Modify, and Access Control trustee assignments.

12. Log in as **the new user** you just created. Position on the new directory called DIRxxx. Right-click, select **details**, and click on **trustees of this directory.** Click on **the Effective Rights button.** Browse to find **the user NEWxxx** to show the effective rights of the user in the new directory DIRxxx. Note that the rights are the same as the trustee rights that you specifically granted to the new user NEWxxx.

13. Click the **Close** button and then the **Cancel** button.

14. Double-click **the DIRxxx directory** to display the \DIRxxx\SUB1 directory. Right-click on **the SUB1 directory** and select **details.** Click on **the trustee list of this object**. What user(s) have explicit rights to \DIRxxx\SUB1?

15. Click the **Effective Rights button** to display the user's effective rights in \DIRxxx\SUB1. Observe that the effective rights are (RCFA). The rights have been limited by the inherited rights filter on the SUB1 directory.

16. Click the **Close button**, and click the **Cancel button**.

17. Double-click **the SUB1 directory** to expose the SUB2 directory. Right-click on **the SUB2 directory** and select **details.** Click on **Trustees of this Directory.** Click the **Effective Rights button** to display the new user's effective rights to the directory.

File System Security and Organization

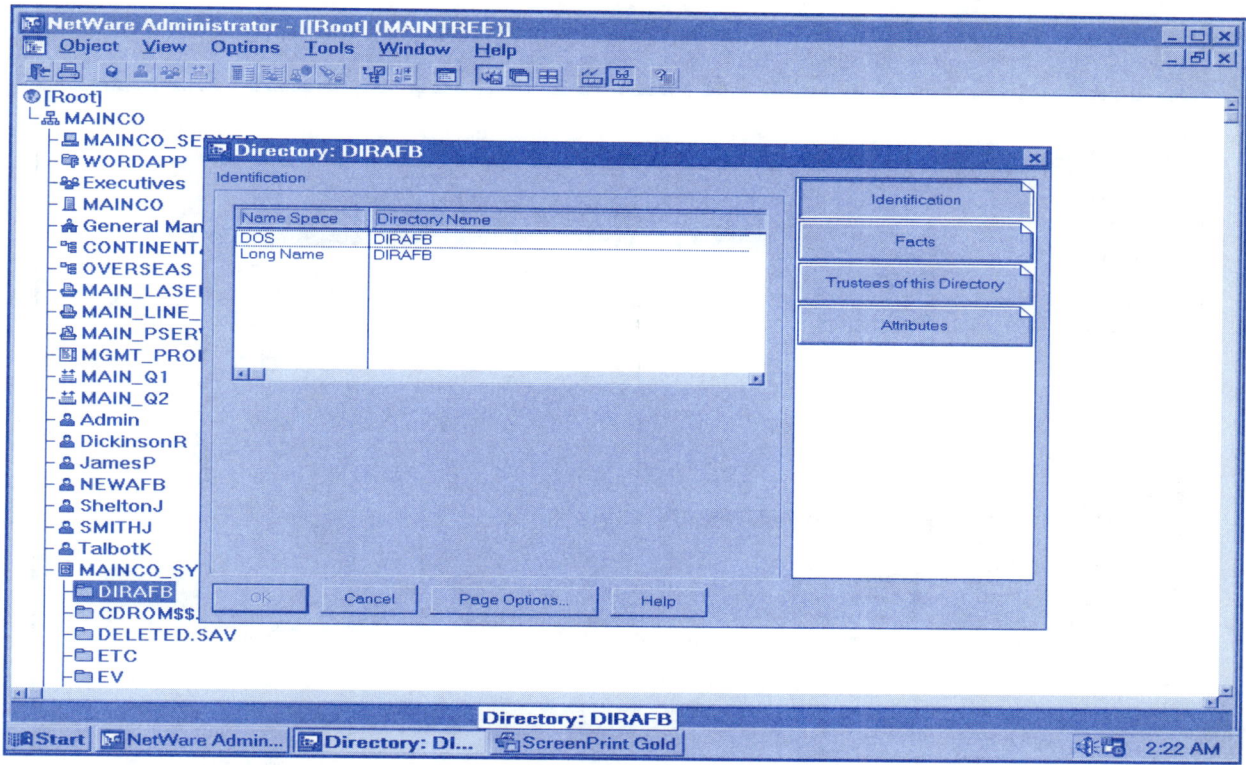

Figure 5-17. Details of DIRAFB.

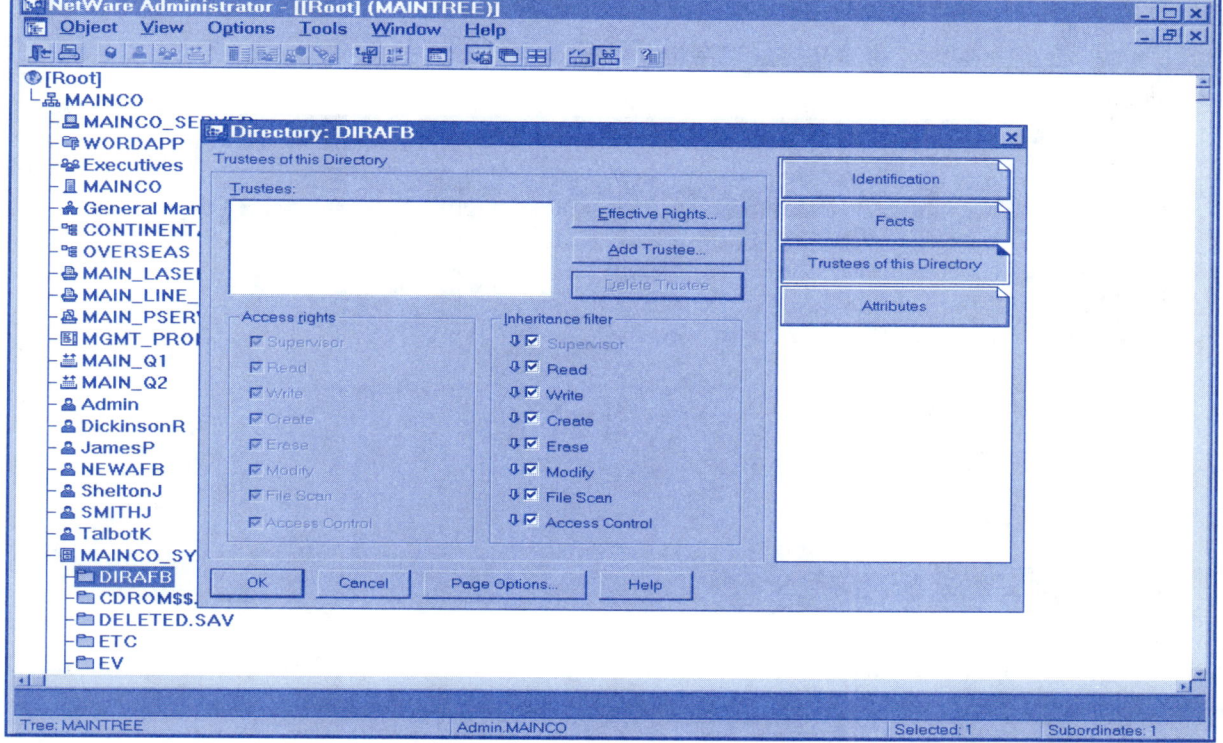

Figure 5-18. Trustees of DIRAFB.

135

Chapter 5

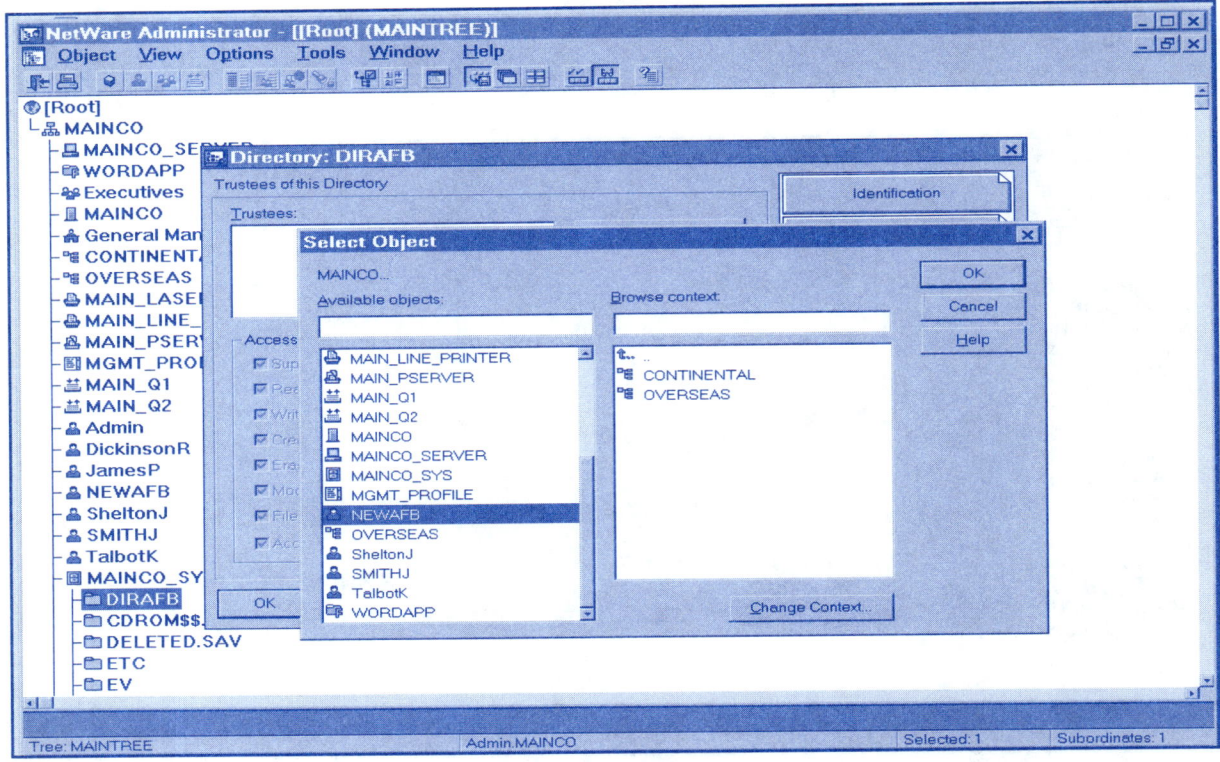

Figure 5-19. Selecting NEWAFB to be a trustee of DIRAFB.

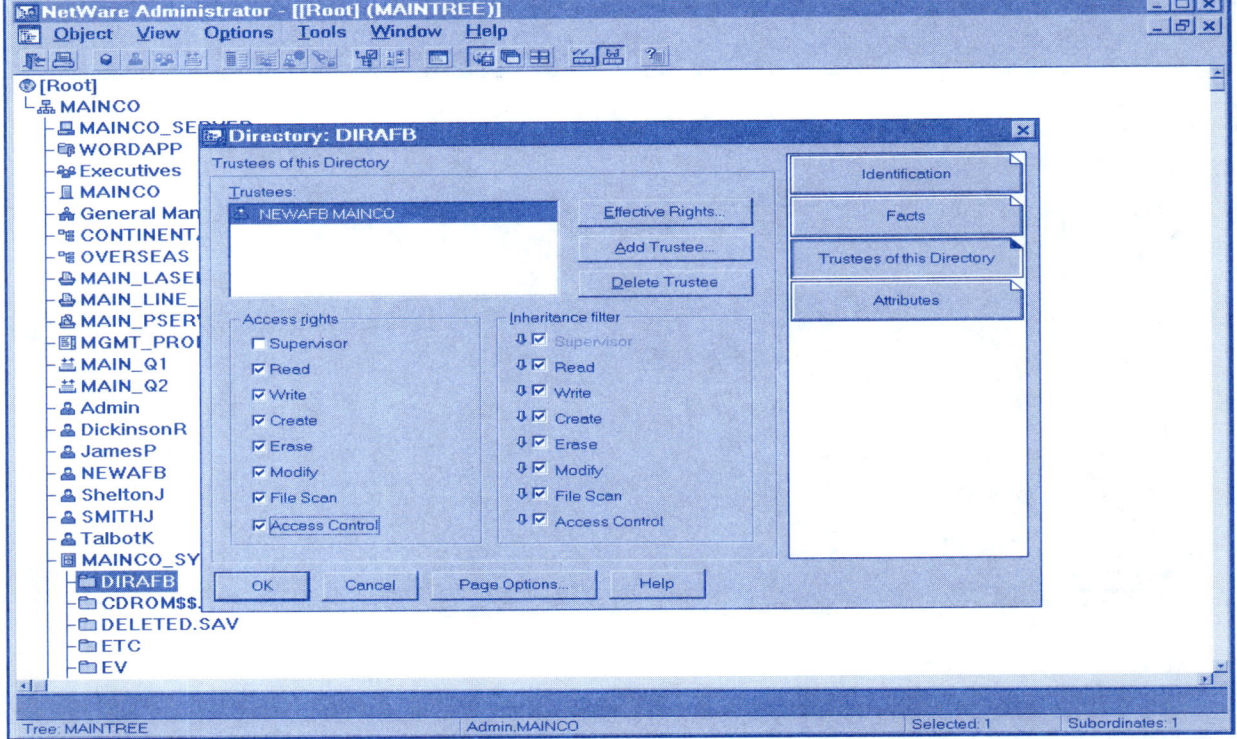

Figure 5-20. Rights to DIRAFB given to NEWAFB.

File System Security and Organization

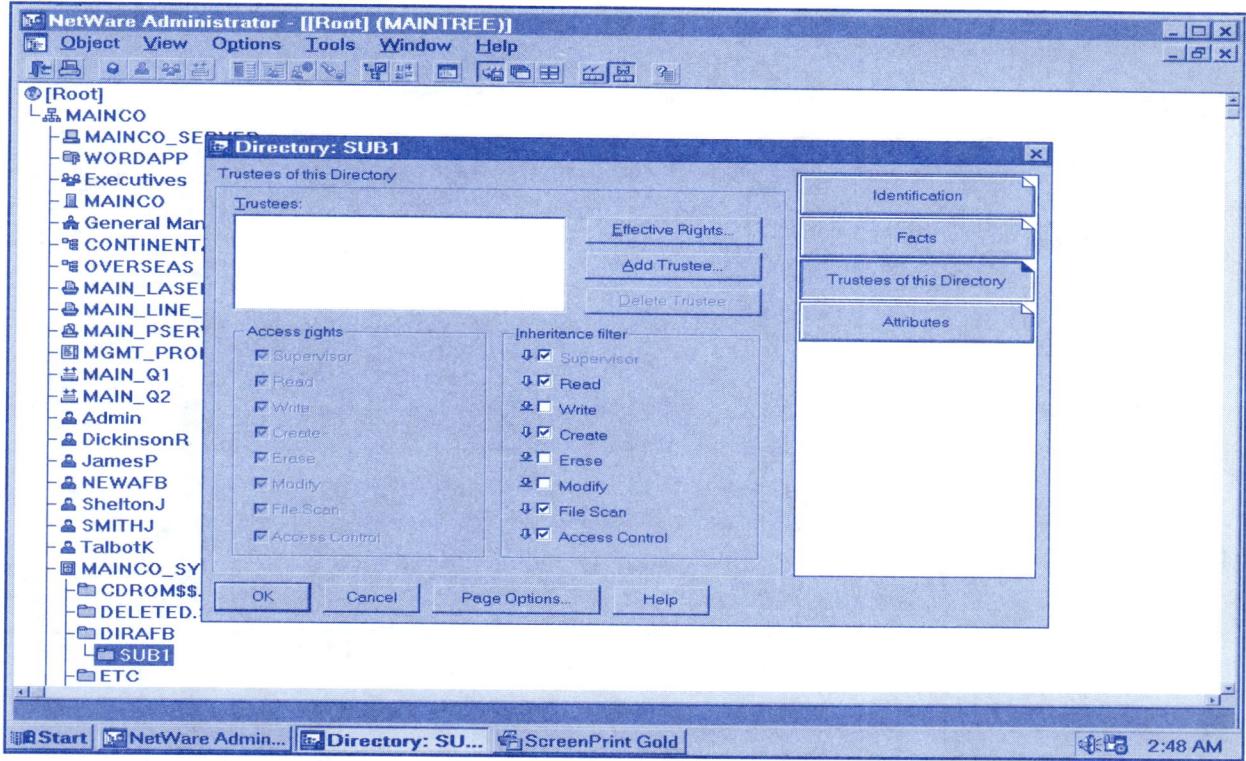

Figure 5-21. Inherited Rights Filter setting for \DIRAFB\SUB1.

Groups

The new account created in the previous section was not given Administrator equivalence. Therefore, the only rights available were those granted in the Trustee Assignments list. Since it can become tedious to maintain many users' accounts when new directories are added, NetWare provides the ability to assign users to a group, and then simply grant the group trustee rights. The following example illustrates the use of groups when assigning trustee rights.

1. Log in with **your user name**.

2. Activate Windows 3.1 if necessary. If you are logging in from Windows 95, Windows 95 is already activated.

3. Double-click on the **NetWare Administrator icon** previously created.

4. Create **a group under MAINCO called GROUPXXX** where xxx is your initials. Place your new user in the group by clicking the Members button as in Figure 5-22.

5. Click on the **Add button** and select the new user as a member. Click **OK** as in Figure 5-23.

137

Chapter 5

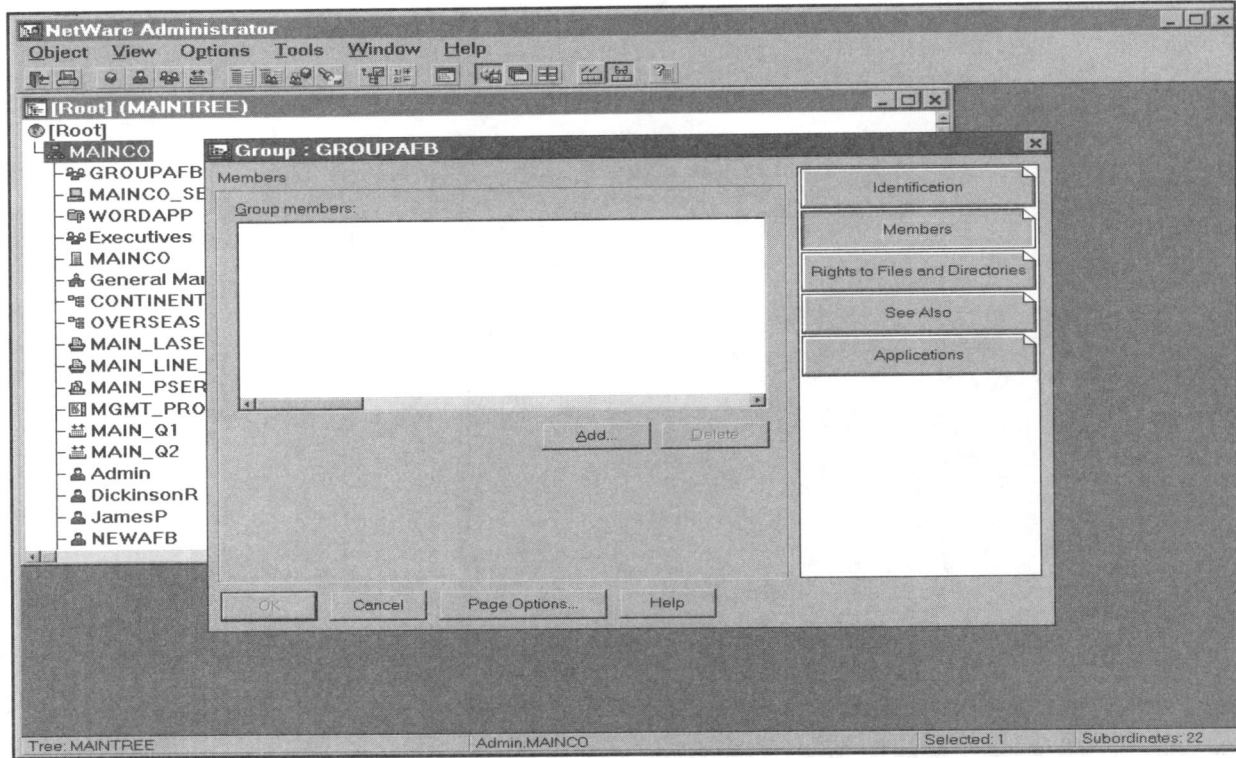

Figure 5-22. GROUPAFB initial group membership screen.

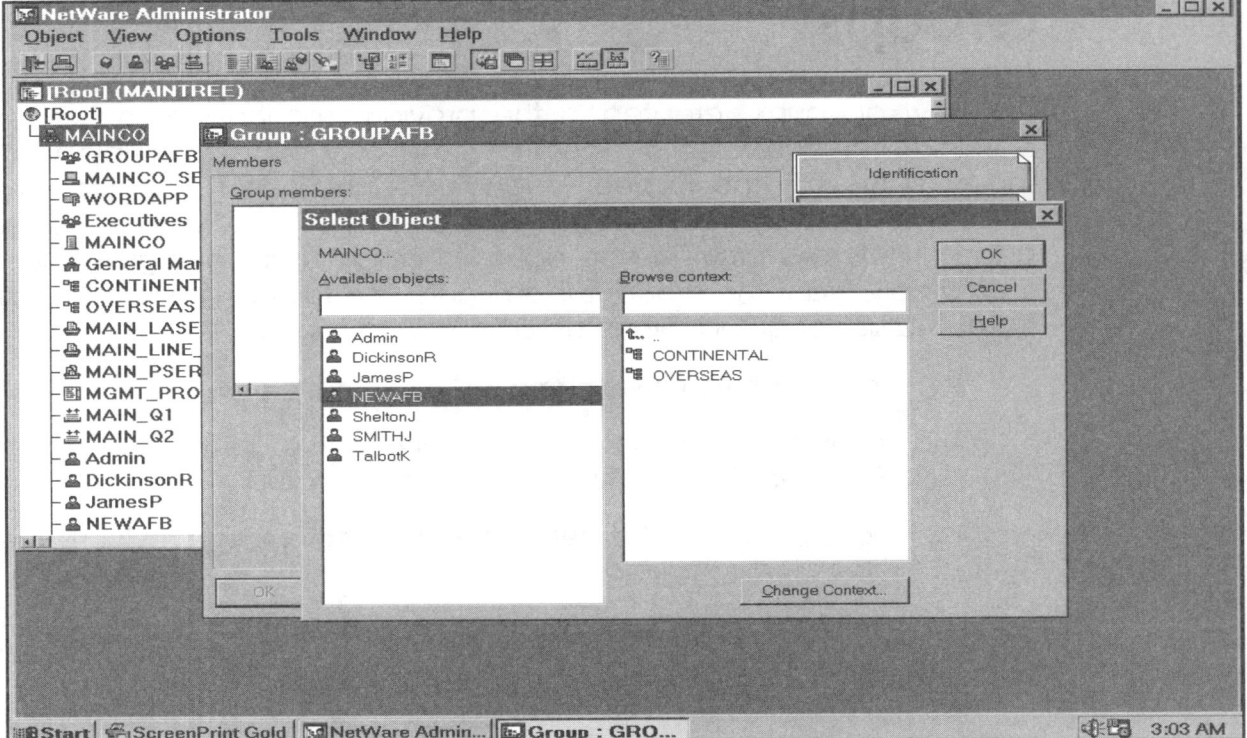

Figure 5-23. Adding NEWAFB to GROUPAFB.

File System Security and Organization

6. Click on **Rights to Files and Directories** and then click on the **Add button**. Navigate on the right of the screen until you can select the \DIRxxx\SUB directory on the left of the screen and click **OK**.

7. Click on **all rights including the Supervisor right** and click the **OK button.**

8. Repeat the above process, logging in as the new user and checking rights to directories

    DIRxxx

    \DIRxxx\SUB1

    \DIRxxx\SUB1\SUB2

    Note that the group rights from the new group were combined with the user's rights to form the effective rights.

Summary

Network security is broken down into five levels; passwords, trustee rights, directory attributes, file attributes, and NDS Object and Property rights. The first four levels were covered in this chapter, and NDS rights will be covered in Chapter 14. The Administrator can place certain restrictions on the password that are intended to force the user to maintain a secure password. The only rights a user has in a given directory are those granted by the Administrator. These rights will be listed in the user's trustee assignments.

Additionally, the user could obtain rights from groups to which he or she belongs, Organizational Roles he occupies, other users to which he is security equivalent, the container(s) that contain the user, and from the special object (PUBLIC). Rights from each of these sources are filtered by the inherited rights filter to filter out unwanted inherited rights, and then they are combined together on a directory by directory basis to form the user's effective rights. The inherited rights for all users except the Administrator are restricted by the inherited rights filter placed on a directory. File attributes are primarily used to prevent accidental damage to files because the attributes apply to the Administrator as well as the other users. With the proper rights in a directory, the file attributes can be changed. The combination of all the rights and restrictions a user has in a given directory is known as the effective rights.

Users usually fall into categories that require different rights and restrictions. NetWare provides the ability to put these users into groups that can be given the same rights as the users. The groups can then be structured to allow the Administrator to make changes easily to many user accounts by changing only the group account. Additionally, a user can receive rights from being an occupant of an organizational role, from being security equivalent to another user, from rights assigned to the container(s) that hold the user and from rights assigned to the special object (PUBLIC).

Information on the server must be organized as well. Programs and operating system software should be placed in one region and data created by the users in another. This structure has several advantages. The software and data can be more easily shared. The trustee assignments can be more easily standardized, and the Administrator can more easily isolate the data that must be backed up on a regular basis.

Questions

1. Describe the four levels of security discussed in this chapter.
2. What is the fifth level of security?
3. Can any user change his or her password?
4. What trustee rights are automatically granted to any user?
5. A user has all trustee rights in a directory but still cannot access the files in it. What could be preventing him from using the files?
6. A user checks her own Trustee Assignments list and finds that the only directory listed is her MAIL directory, yet she is able to use many different programs on the server. How can this be?
7. What are the six ways that a user can obtain directory and/or file trustee rights?
8. What are the minimal directory trustee assignments given when a user is made a trustee of a directory?
9. What directory rights are needed to change the contents of a file?
10. What is the effect of the Ic Directory Attribute?

Projects

Objective

The following projects provide additional practice in establishing security and trustee rights.

Project 1: Practicing the Login Script Commands

1. Given the following directory structure, write the MAP commands needed to map the drive letters H:, I:, J:, and K: to the numbered directories. Do not attempt to perform these operations on the computer unless appropriate directories have been established.

    ```
    F:\___|
          |-ACCOUNTS
          |   |
          |   |-RECEIVE (1)
          |   |-PAY (2)
          | - APPS
          |-PERSONEL
          |   |
          |   |-ARCHIVE
          |   |   |
          |   |   |-FULLTIME (3)
          |   |   |-PARTTIME
          |   |
          |   |-CURRENT
          |       |-FULLTIME
          |       |-PARTTIME (4)
    ```

2. Write the MAP command needed to give a search drive to the APPS directory.

3. Create a new user. Give the new user a login script that prints "Happy Birthday" on your birthday.

Chapter 5

4. Using the network, create a directory structure similar to the following:

   ```
   F:\___|
          |-(Your User Name)
                 |
                 |-SECURE
                 |
                 |-DATA
   ```

   Using the NetWare Administrator create a new user with all trustee rights to the directory (your user name) except Supervisor and Access Control. Use NetWare Administrator to make the contents of the SECURE directory inaccessible to the user. Use the SHIFT/PRINT SCREEN keys at each step and remove the directories and the user when you are finished.

5. Test your activities. How do you know that what you have done actually works?

Project 2: More Practice with Effective Rights

All questions in this project are based on the following file system directory structure:

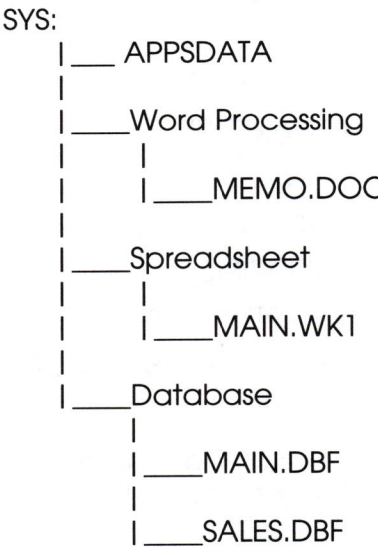

File System Security and Organization

A. Sam is given all rights except the Supervisor directory right to the APPSDATA directory. The Spreadsheet directory has an Inherited Rights Filter of (R C FM}

What are Sam's effective rights to the MAIN.WK1 directory? Can he update the file?

B. Jackie is given (R C MF) to the APPSDATA directory. She also belongs to the Accounting group, which is given (RWF) to the Database directory. The Inherited Rights Filter on the Database directory is (RF). What are Jackie's effective rights within the Database directory?

C. Determine the effective rights at each level for Jackie and for the group Accounting. Then add the effective rights together at each level to determine Jackie's overall effective rights.

6
Network Printing

Objectives

After completing this chapter you will

1. Understand the concepts of network printing.
2. Know how network printers can be attached to the network.
3. Know how to install and configure a print queue, printer, and print server.
4. Know how to activate and control a print server.
5. Be able to send data to a network printer.

Key Terms

Print Queue

PCONSOLE

Print Server

Printer

Auto Load

PSERVER

Manual Load

NPRINTER.NLM

Remote Printing

NPRINTER.EXE

CAPTURE

Introduction

Often an important function of a network is printer sharing. Printing across a network involves loading special software on the workstation that remains resident along with the other network drivers. The software intercepts output that a normal application such as a word processor sends to the workstation's printer port. That data is then sent across the network to a printer attached to another computer, which is either the file server running the print server software, another file server running remote printer software, or a workstation running remote printer software. With a network, many users can send output to the same printer. Also, for different purposes, users may wish to select among different types of printers available on the network.

NetWare has supported network printing since its earliest versions, but earlier printing support lacked many important features. Several third-party products offered capabilities that made network printing a much more valuable resource. With later versions of NetWare, however, some of these features have been introduced as separate utilities.

Printers can be attached to the network in several ways:

>**Attached to the file server that is the print server**
>
>**Attached to another file server in the enterprise**
>
>**Attached to a workstation**

In addition, several third party vendors have produced products that allow even more flexibility in printing. Only the first three methods will be discussed here.

To accommodate the many users and printers that might be on a network, NetWare 4.11 has three main printing objects with various properties attached to each one. These are:

>**Print Queue**
>
>**Printer**
>
>**Print Server**

These three objects are linked together to provide the printing function, and each of these objects has properties or characteristics that are defined to customize network printing for the entire enterprise.

Print Queue

Obviously, if everyone on the network sent data to a printer at once, problems would arise. A system had to be created to allow the data

Network Printing

from each user to be stored and printed when the printer becomes available. Print queues provide this function and more. Essentially, a **print queue** is a file on one of the volumes of a server that holds a print job until it can be serviced by a print server to be sent to an appropriate printer. The NetWare Administrator utility and the DOS text-based printing utility, **PCONSOLE**, can be used to create and configure a print queue. The following steps will create a print queue named Acctg_1 in the Accounting container.

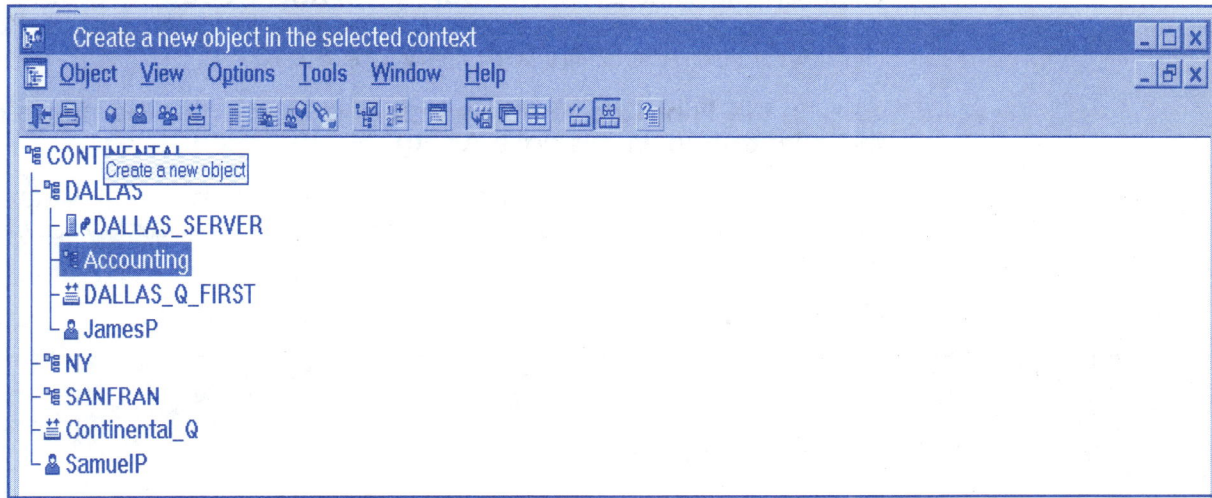

Figure 6-1. Create a new object.

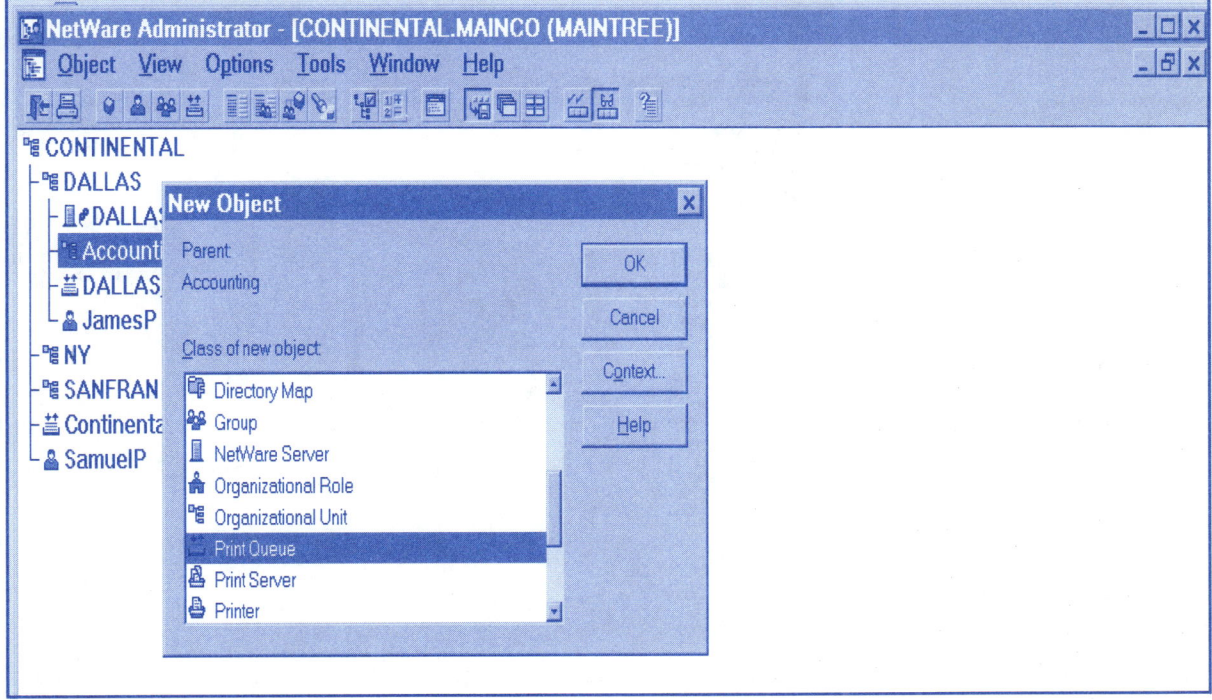

Figure 6-2. Selecting the print queue as an object to create.

Chapter 6

1. Click on **the container in which the print queue is to be created**, and then click on the **Create a New Object icon** on the menu bar at the top of the screen as shown in Figure 6-1.

2. Select the **Print Queue object** and click the **OK button** as in Figure 6-2.

3. The Create a Print Queue main dialog box appears as in Figure 6-3.

4. Click on **the box beside Directory Service Queue** to create a new Directory Service Queue. (A reference bindery queue is for backward compatibility with NetWare 3.x.)

5. Click in **the Print Queue name box** and then enter **the name of the print queue, in this case Acctg_1**.

6. Click on the **Browse button** to the right of the Print Queue Volume box and navigate to find the volume on which you wish to place the print queue.

7. Click the **Create button** to create the print queue.

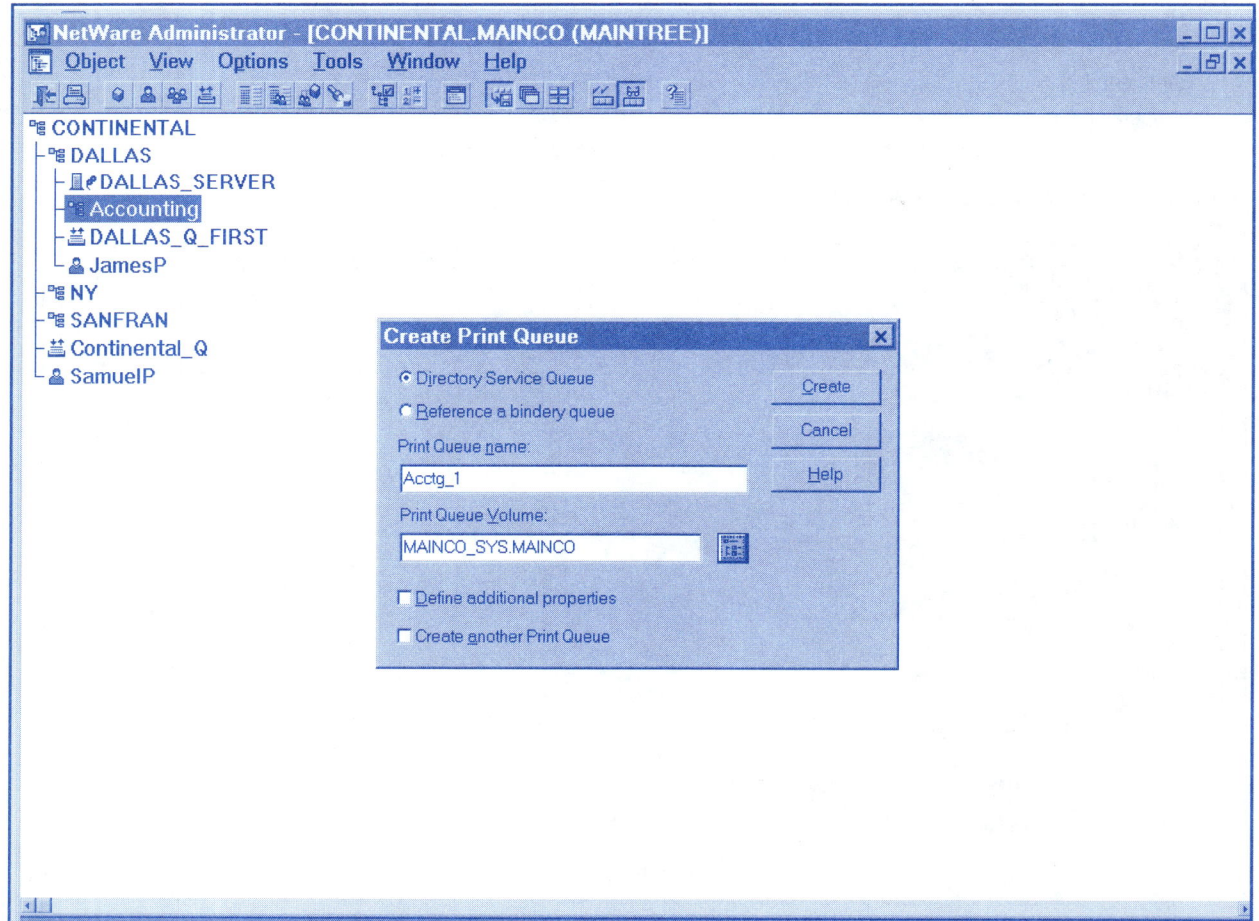

Figure 6-3. Create a Print Queue main dialog box.

Print Server

A **print server** in NetWare 4.11 is a program that runs on a file server in the form of an NLM. This program monitors the queues and printers assigned to it and directs each completed job in each print queue to the appropriate printer. The following steps will create a print server object called Acctg_PS in the Accounting Container.

1. Repeat the steps used above to create an object, except this time, create a print server object.

2. The Create Print Server dialog box appears as in Figure 6-4.

3. Click in t**he Print Server Name box** and then enter **the name of the print server, in this case Acctg_PS**.

4. Click the **Create button** to complete the creation of the Print Server Object.

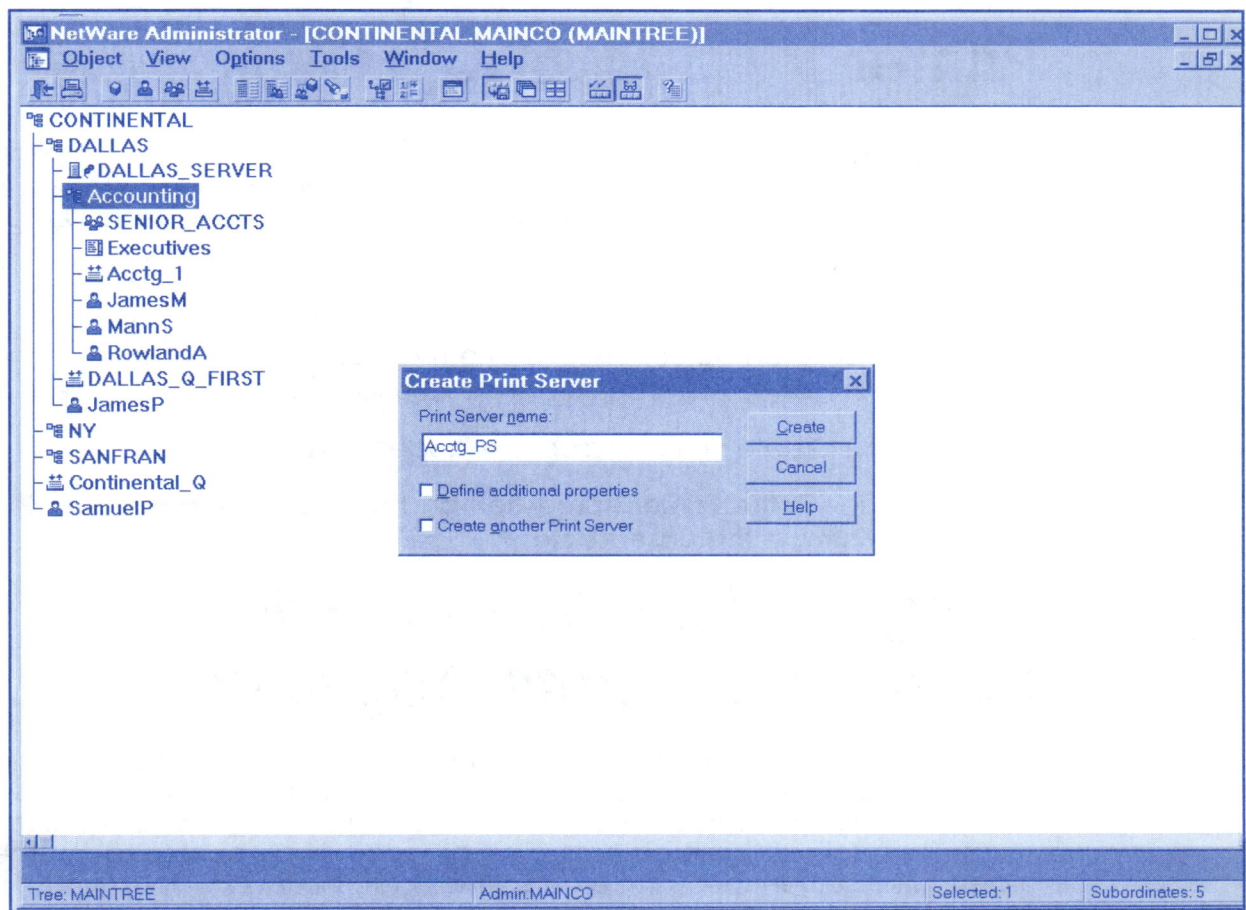

Figure 6-4. Create a Print Server.

Chapter 6

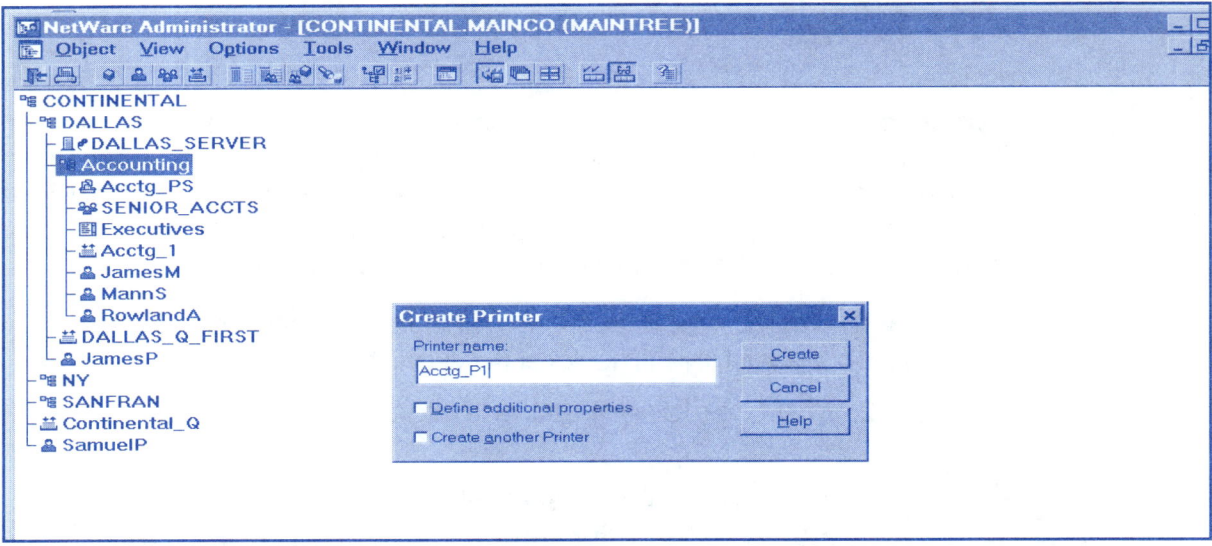

Figure 6-5. Create a Printer.

Printer

A **printer** is the ultimate recipient of a print job. For our purposes, a printer is an NDS object that represents the physical printer and contains the configuration information necessary to tie the printer to the print server. The following steps are used to create a printer named Acctg_P1 in the Accounting container.

1. Create an object in the same manner as the print queue and print server objects, except be sure to create a printer object.

2. The Create Printer dialog box appears as in Figure 6-5.

3. Click in **the Printer name box** and then enter **the name of the printer, in this case Acctg_P1**.

Tying the Print Queue, Print Server, and Printer Together

At this point, the three printing objects have been created, but they are not yet associated with each other so that printing can occur. Now, these objects will be tied together by creating the appropriate associations for each of these objects. The objects will be configured in the order: print server, then printer, and finally print queue.

Network Printing

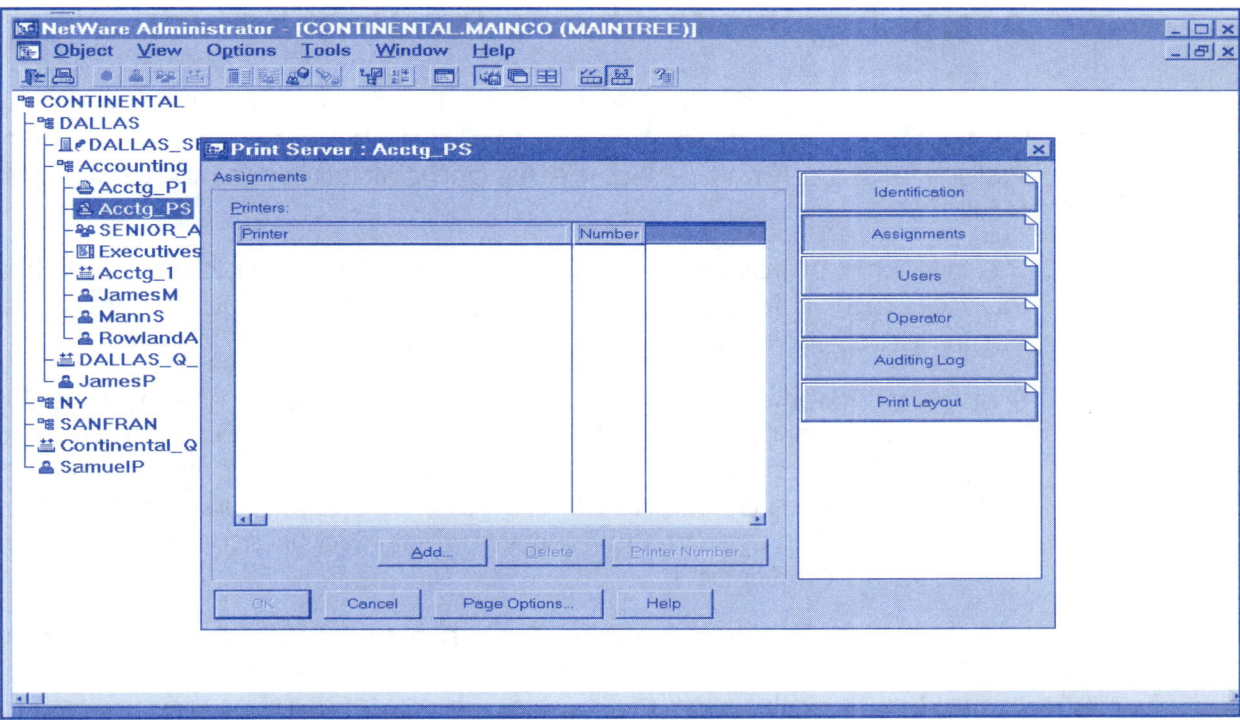

Figure 6-6. Assignments page for a print server.

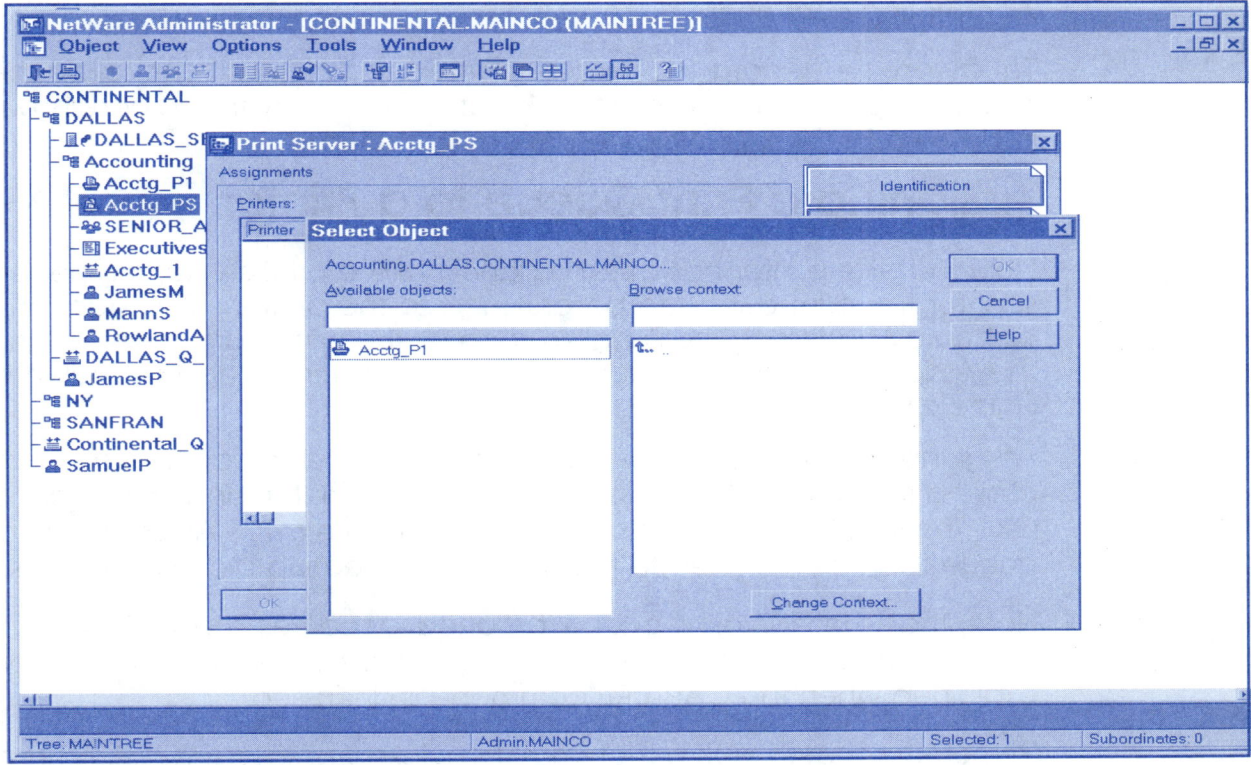

Figure 6-7. Adding a Printer to a Print Server.

151

Assigning the Printer to the Print Server

First, using the details screen for the print server, (double-click on the Print Server object to access the details screen), click on the Assignments button to reveal the Assignments screen as shown in Figure 6-6.

The printers controlled by this print server must be added by clicking the Add button to access the Add dialog box for each printer to be controlled as shown in Figure 6-7.

A single print server can control up to 256 printers, numbered 0 to 255, but only one printer can occupy a given printer port number. For example, it would be wrong to attempt to place two printers at port 1. In fact, if this were done, the print server would return an error condition upon attempting to start, advising you that two or more printers occupy the same printer port.

Further, when adding printers to a given print server, it is simpler and far more effective in the long run to assign printers that exist in the same context as the print server. Figure 6-7, in fact, first gives the opportunity of selecting the Acctg_P1 printer created earlier. Note that the Acctg_P1 printer and the Acctg_PS print server both exist in the Accounting container.

To assign the Acctg_P1 printer to the Acctg_PS printer, click the Acctg_P1 printer, then click the OK button to display the screen shown in Figure 6-8. Click OK to save the configuration.

Assigning a Print Queue to a Printer

Now that the printer has been assigned to the print server, it is necessary for the print queue to be assigned to the printer. This is accomplished by accessing the Details screen for the printer and then clicking the Assignments button to display the Assignments page as shown in Figure 6-9.

Assigning the Acctg_1 print queue to this printer is accomplished by clicking the Add button, clicking the Acctg_1 printer, and then clicking OK. The result of these actions is shown in Figure 6-10. Additional print queues can be assigned to this printer by repeating the Add process.

Note that the first print queue assigned becomes the default print queue for this printer. The default queue's importance will be explained when the CAPTURE command is discussed.

Remember that the OK button must be clicked to save this assignment.

Network Printing

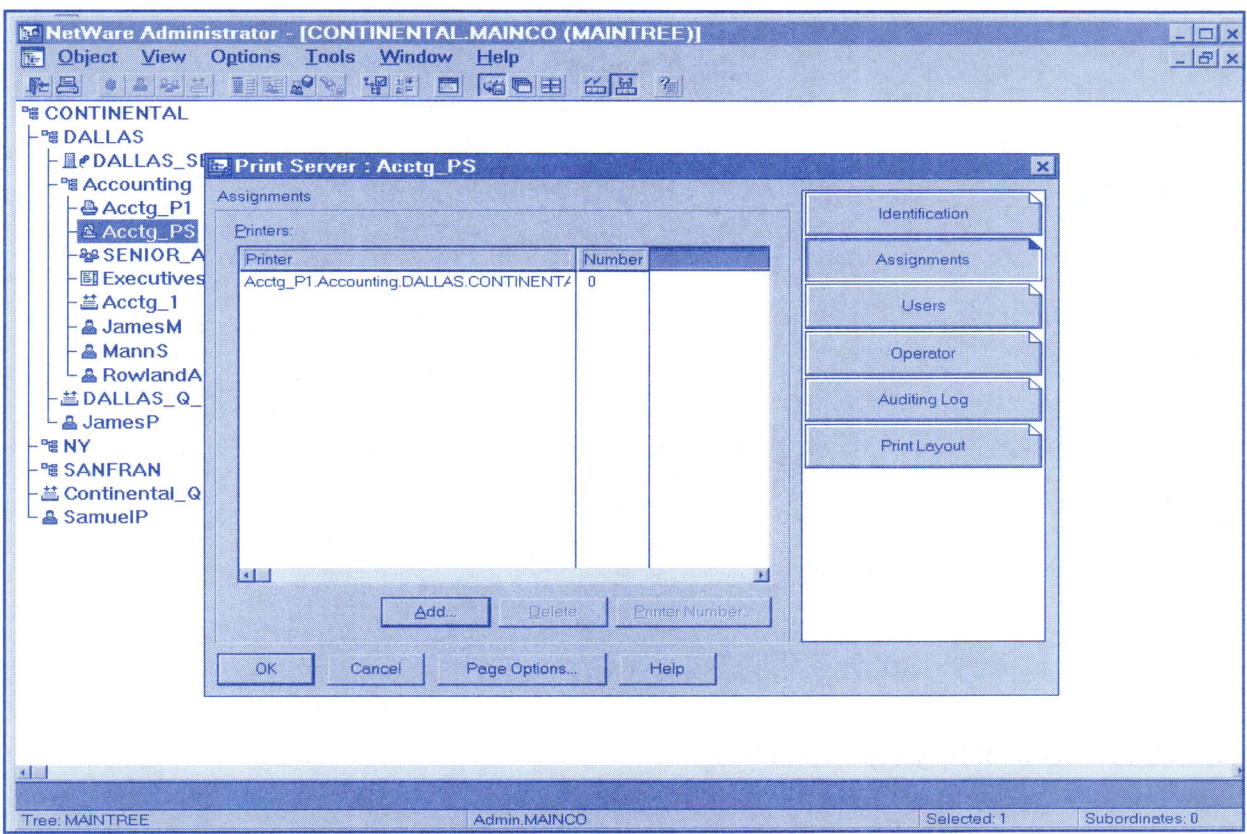

Figure 6-8. Acctg_PS with the Acctg_P1 printer assigned.

At this point, the three printing objects are now linked together. A few more steps are necessary, though, before actual printing can begin.

Configuring the Printer

The printer object itself must be configured to match the physical usage of the printer. This is accomplished by accessing the Configuration button under the Details option for the printer object. To access this screen, double-click the printer object, then click the Configuration button to display the Configuration page as shown in Figure 6-11.

Most of the parameters on this page can be left in their default modes for beginning students. However, it is very important that the printer type match the actual interface of the printer. Usually, the interface is parallel, but this fact must be verified. Also, the communications for the printer must be specified by clicking the Communications button to display the Communications page as shown in Figure 6-12.

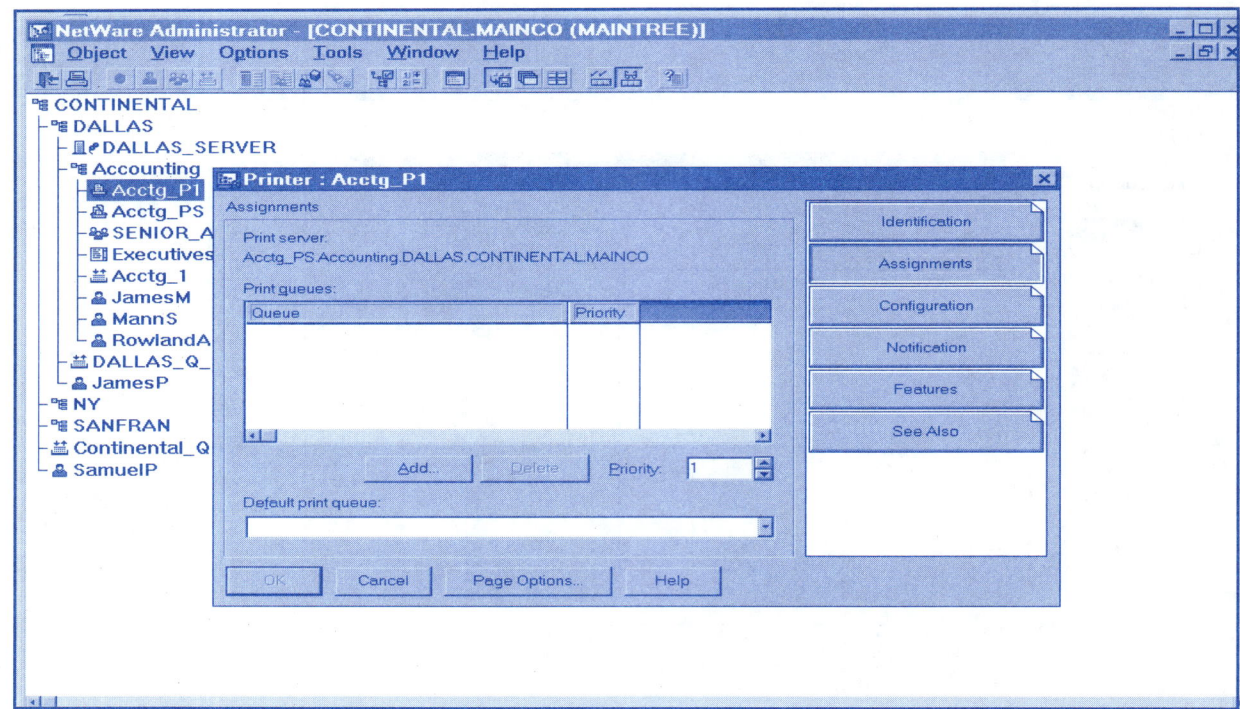

Figure 6-9. The Printer Assignments page.

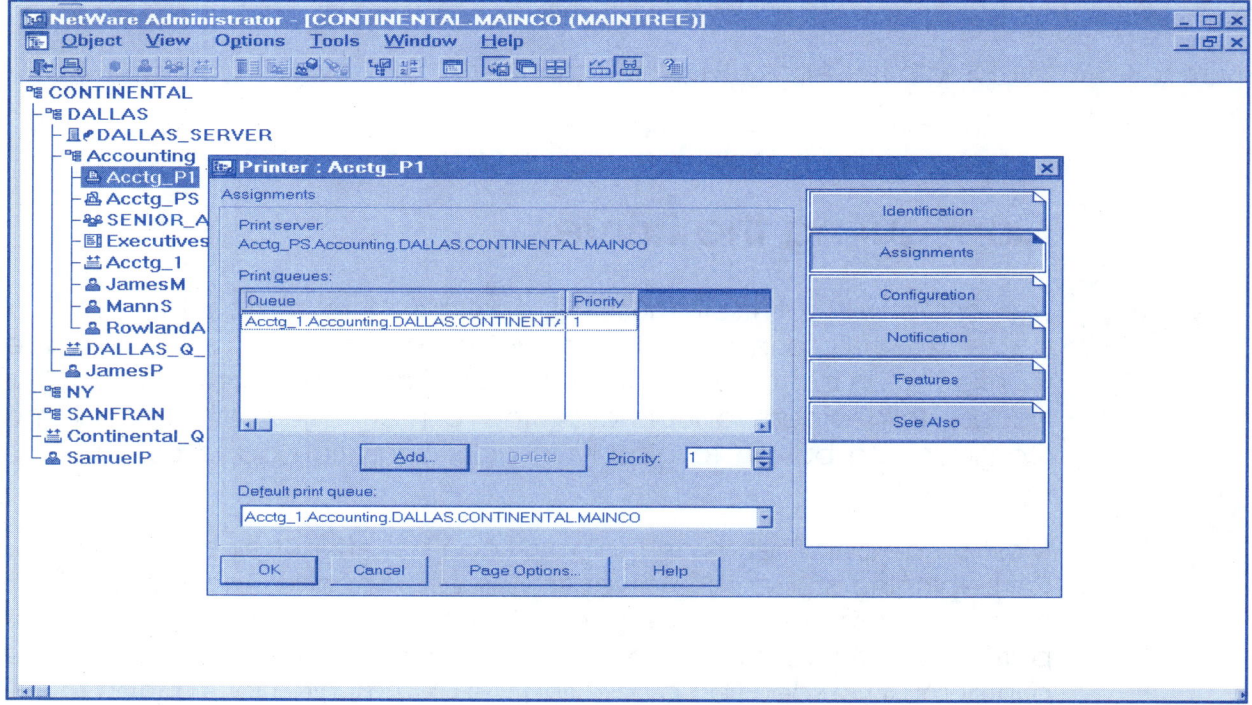

Figure 6-10. Acctg_1 Print Queue assigned to the Acctg_P1 printer.

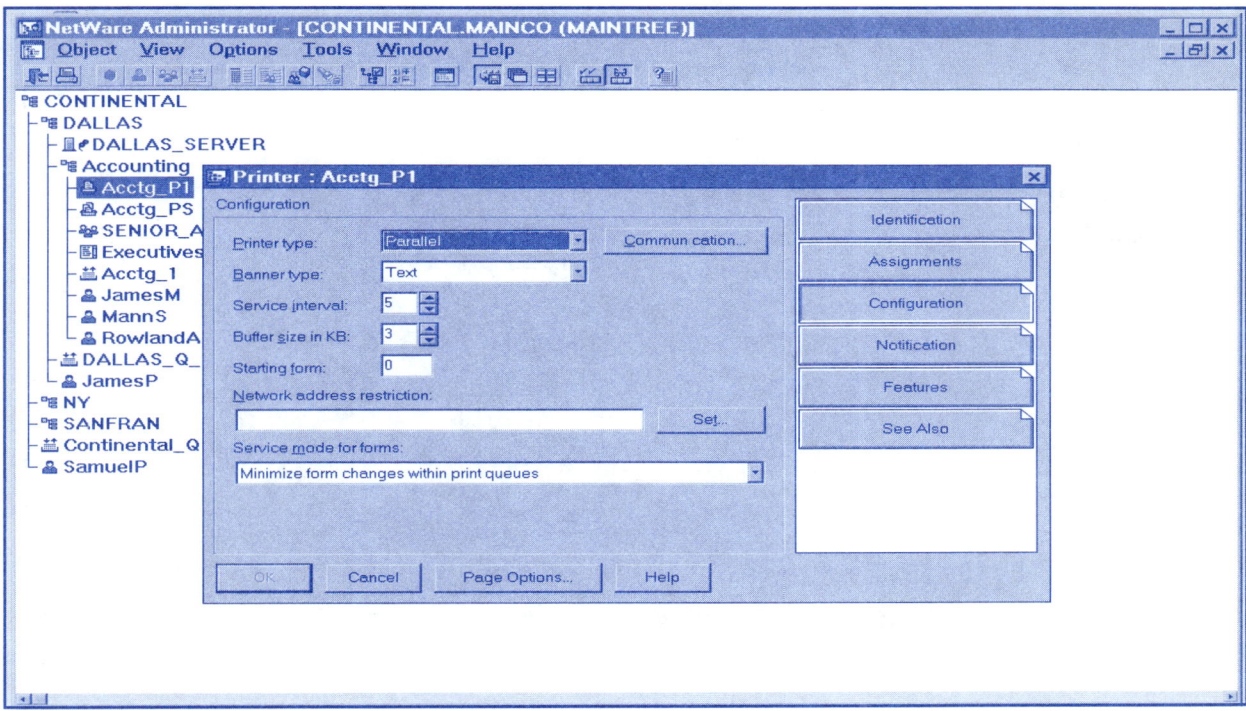

Figure 6-11. Printer Configuration page.

For a printer attached to the computer on LPT1, the normal method of communication is to use interrupt 7, and for LPT2, usually interrupt 5 is used. However, if there is no interrupt available because all interrupts are used for other devices, the printer can be operated in polled mode. Using polling, the computer to which the printer and any other polled devices are attached periodically checks with the devices to see if they need attention. The polled method is slow but it does function when an interrupt is not available. For purposes of discussion, though, interrupt 7 has been chosen.

The next item that must be specified is the connection type for the printer. Very simply, if the printer is to be directly attached to the file server running the PSERVER.NLM software controlling the print server, then the print should be specified as an **Auto Load** printer by clicking the box to the left of the Auto Load selection. If the printer is to be attached to another file server that is not running **PSERVER** or it is attached to a workstation, the printer must be specified as a **Manual Load** printer. Figure 6-13 shows a printer set up on LPT1 of the file server running PSERVER.

Chapter 6

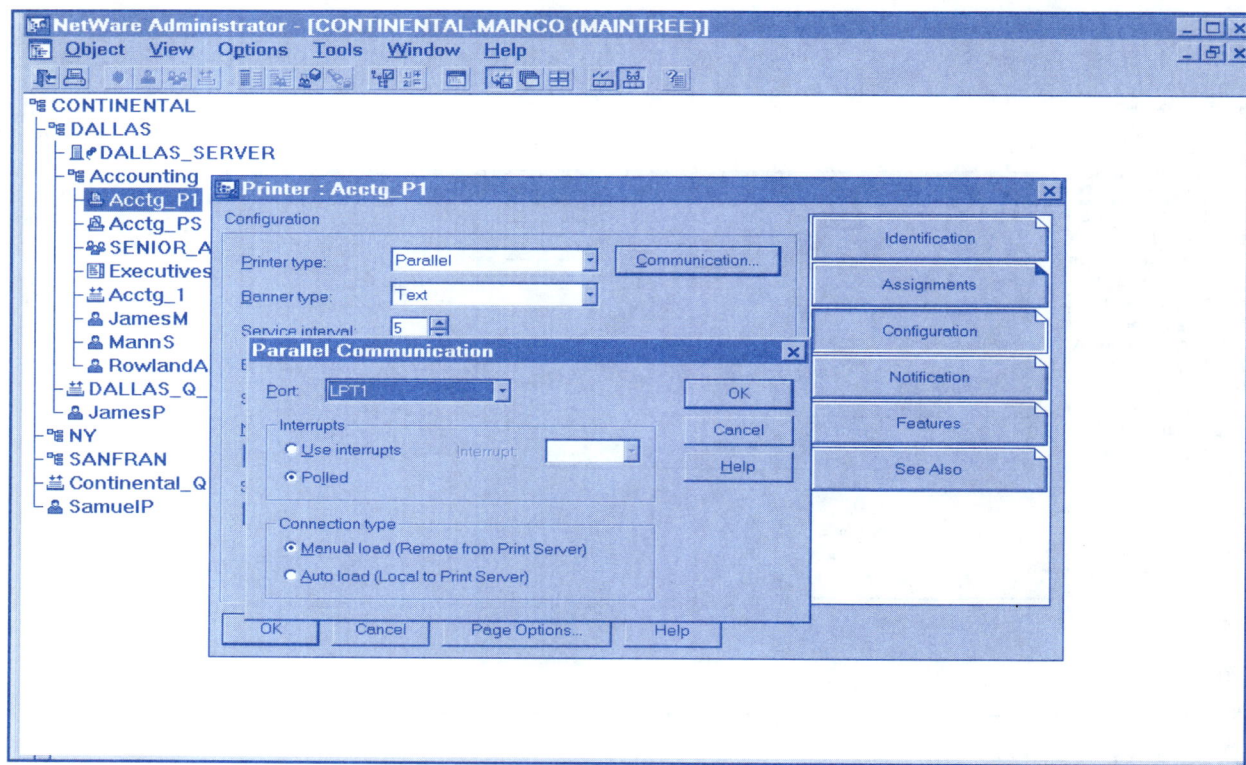

Figure 6-12. Parallel Communication page for printer Acctg_P1.

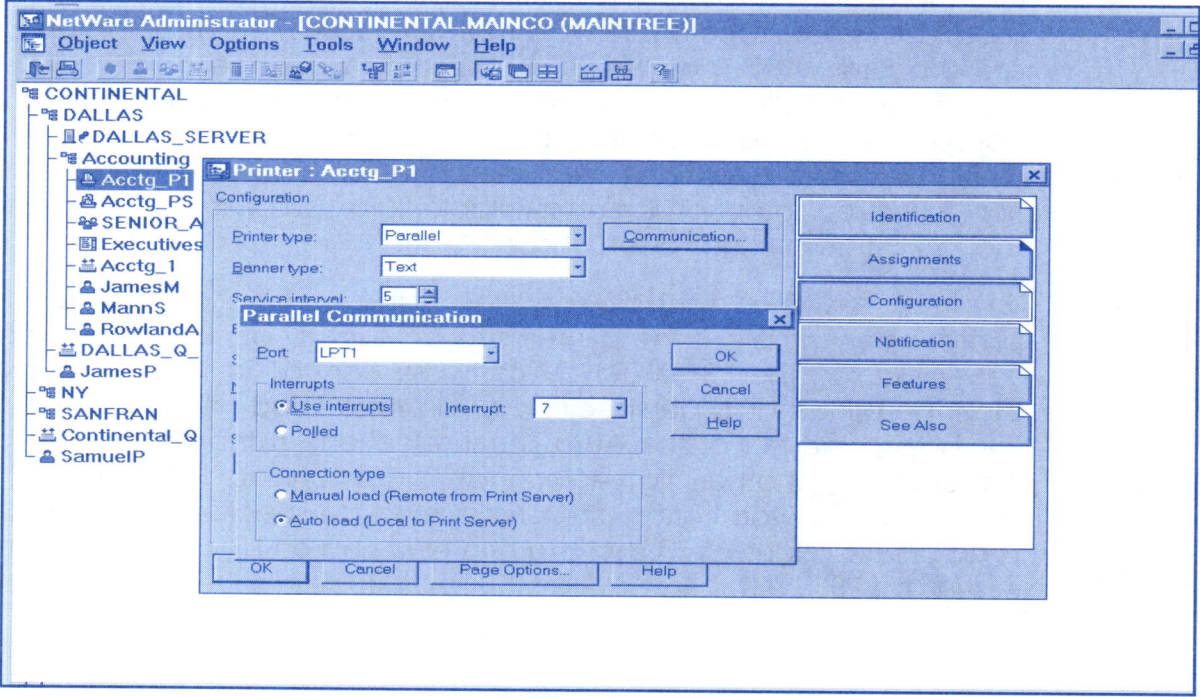

Figure 6-13. Parallel communications for Acctg_P1 attached to the file server running PSERVER.

Network Printing

Checking the Print Queue Assignments

Now that the printer has been assigned to the print server and the print queue has been assigned to the printer, it is time to check the assignments page for the print queue. The assignments for print queue Acctg_1 are shown in Figure 6-14.

Note that by assigning the printer to the print server and the print queue to the printer that the Acctg_1 queue is automatically assigned to the print server Acctg_PS. A further check can be done by examining the print layout button under details of the print server. This screen, shown in Figure 6-15, shows that there is a queue called Acctg_1 that is assigned to a printer called Acctg_P1, which is then serviced by Acctg_PS. The exclamation point by the print server indicates that the print server is not functioning.

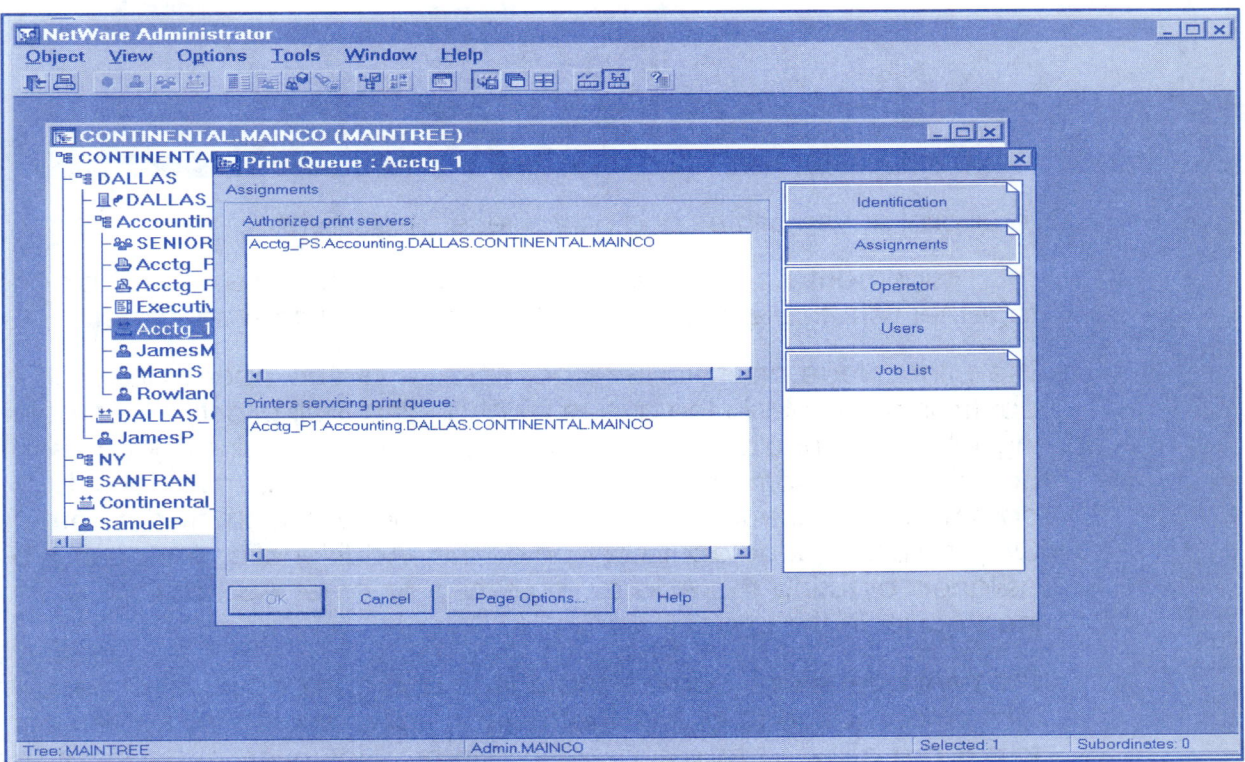

Figure 6-14. Print queue Acctg_1 assignments.

Print Queue Operators and Users

By default, the print queue operator is the user that created the queue, and the print queue users are the users in the container containing the queue and print queue creator as shown in Figures 6-16 and 6-17.

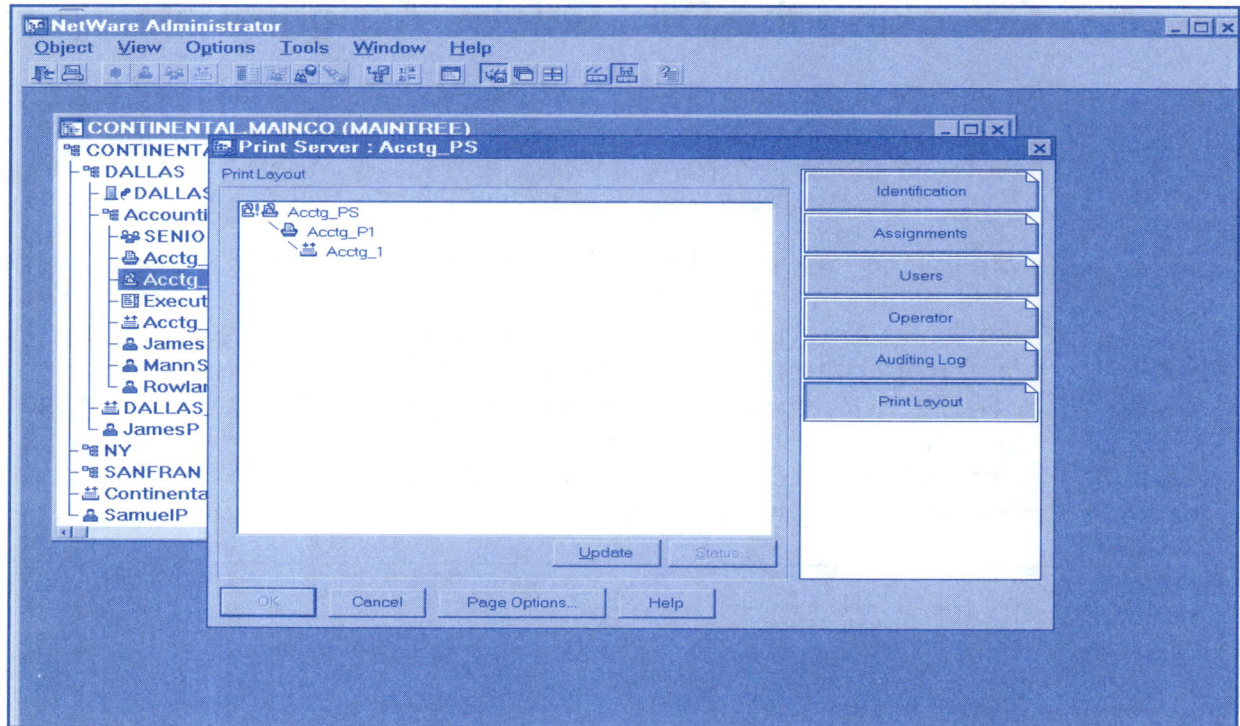

Figure 6-15. Overall print server, printer, and print queue assignments.

This assignment is usually sufficient because users are usually placed together with the resources that they use in the same container.

The print queue operator is responsible for queue operations such as controlling the jobs in the queue by changing their priority order, deleting jobs that should not have been sent, etc. A print queue user is capable of performing these functions on his or her own jobs, but a common print queue user cannot affect the jobs submitted by others. Only the print queue operator can do this. Additional operators can be assigned by using the Add dialog similar to other Add dialogs examined earlier in this chapter.

The print queue user can use the queue and can access his or her own jobs in the queue to delete them. Generally, all users in a given container are allowed to use a given printer. However, if this is not the desired situation, users can be added and deleted using the Add/Delete dialog discussed earlier in the chapter.

Network Printing

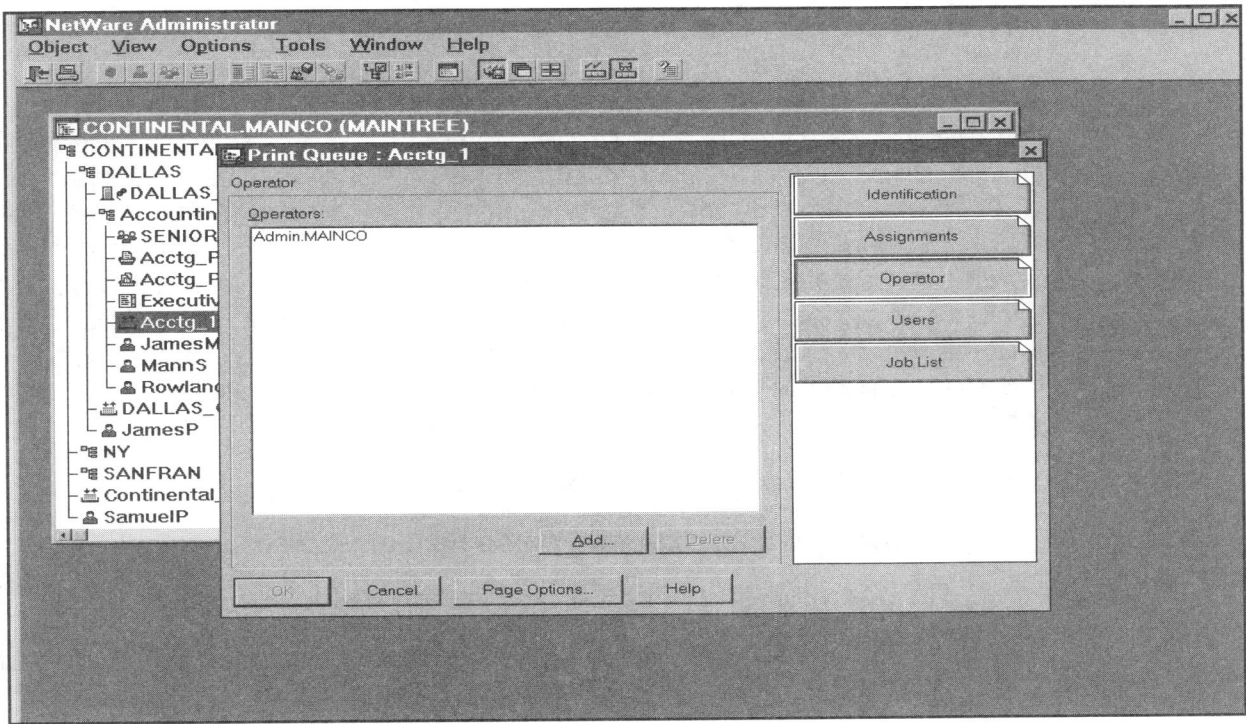

Figure 6-16. Print queue operator for print queue Acctg_1.

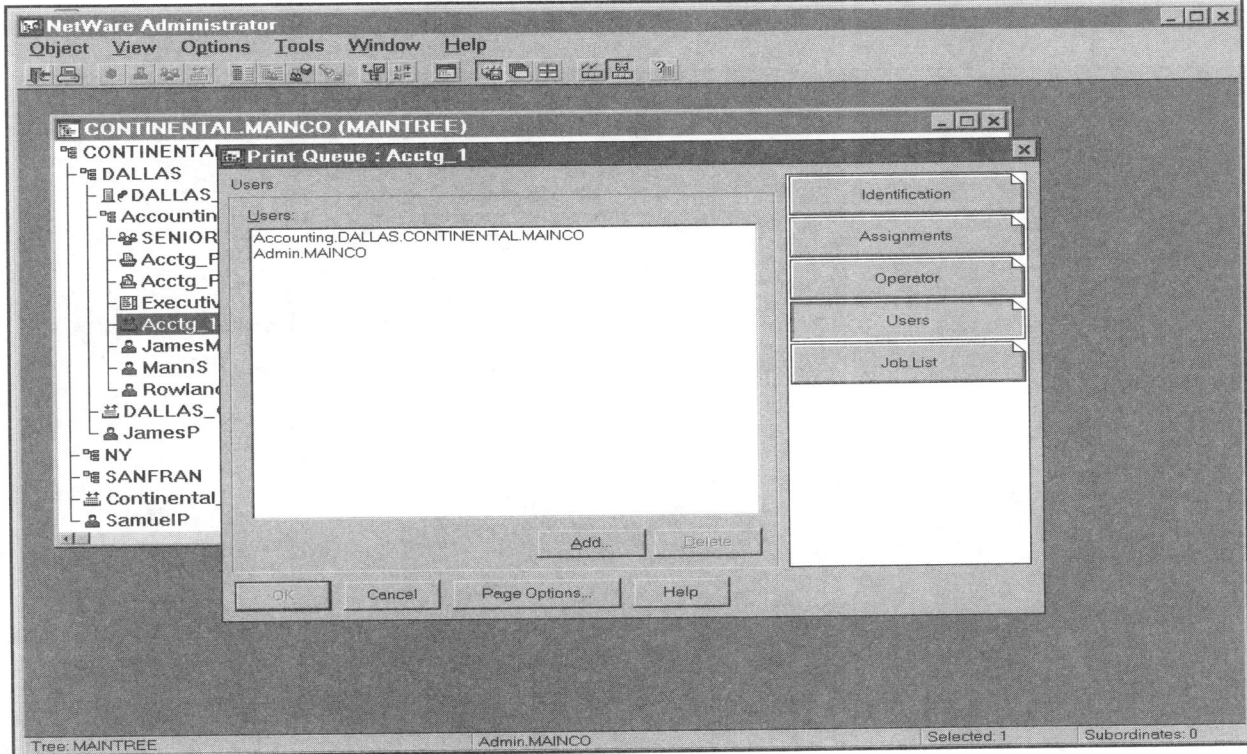

Figure 6-17. Print queue users for print queue Acctg_1.

Chapter 6

Print Queue Jobs

The print queue's job list is accessed under Print Queue Details by clicking the Job List button. This page shows the current status of the print queue and allows the user to affect his or her own jobs and the print queue operator to affect any user's jobs. Figure 6-18 shows the Acctg_1 queue's identification page with the Allow Print Servers to Service Jobs selection deselected so that the jobs will stay in the queue for us to examine. Figure 6-19 shows the queue with three outstanding jobs, all ready to print. A specific print job is selected by clicking on the line containing the job and then clicking on the Job Details button. The job details for job 3 are shown in Figure 6-20.

The features that can be controlled are:

1. **User Hold:** The user can place his or her own job on hold.

2. **Operator Hold:** The user can place any job on hold.

3. **Service Sequence:** The operator can adjust the sequencing of jobs by entering a different number in this box.

4. **Number of copies:** The user or the operator can adjust the number of copies for a job that has not started printing.

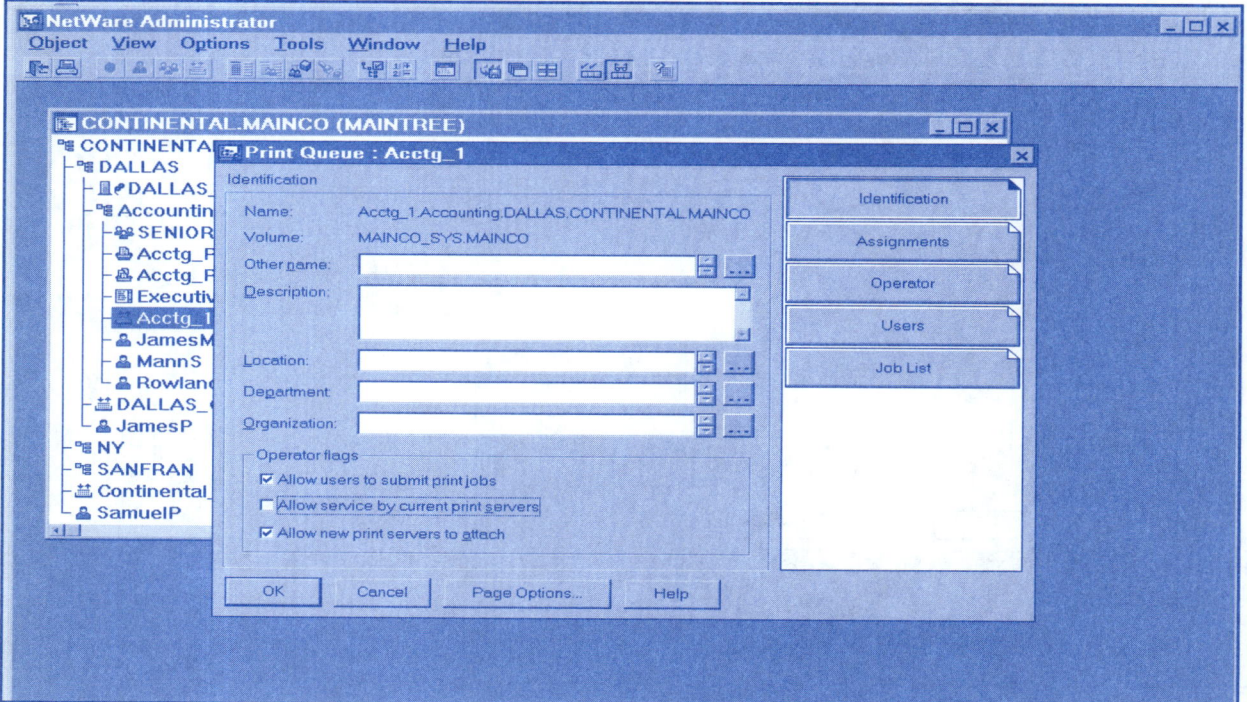

Figure 6-18. Print Queue identification page.

Network Printing

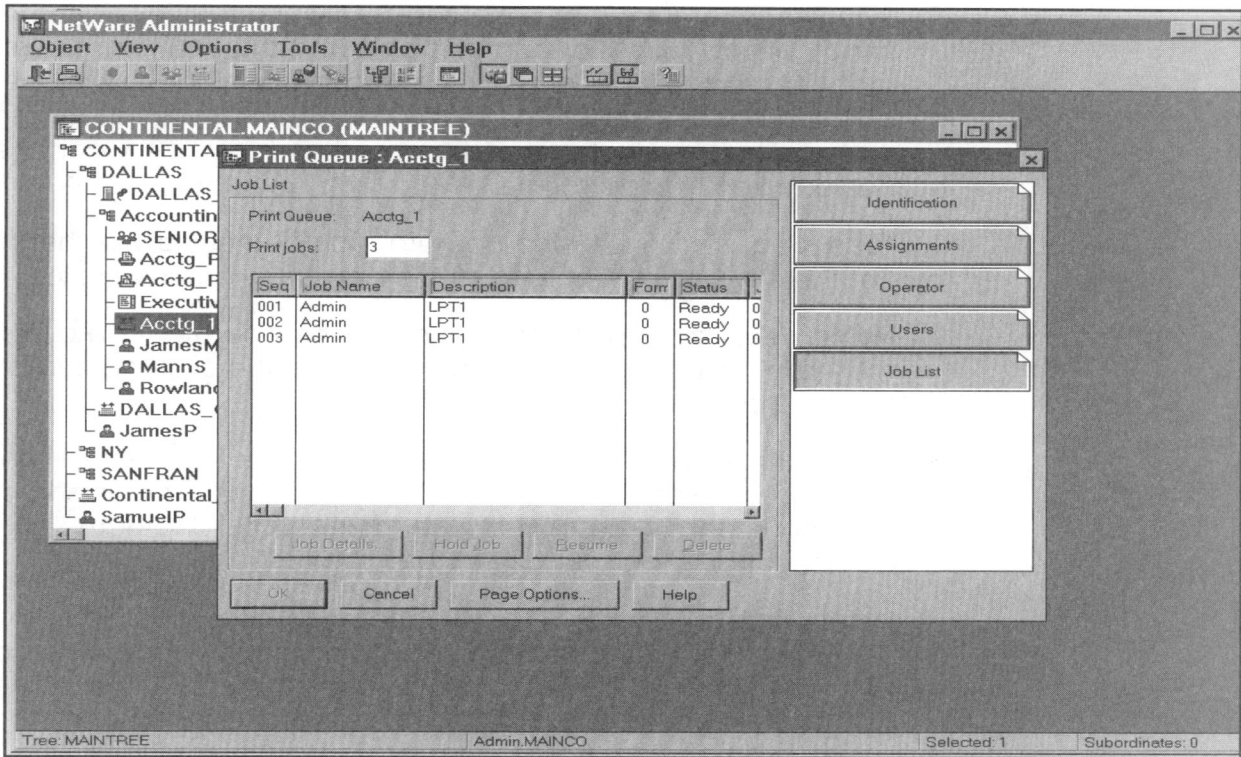

Figure 6-19. Print queue Job List page.

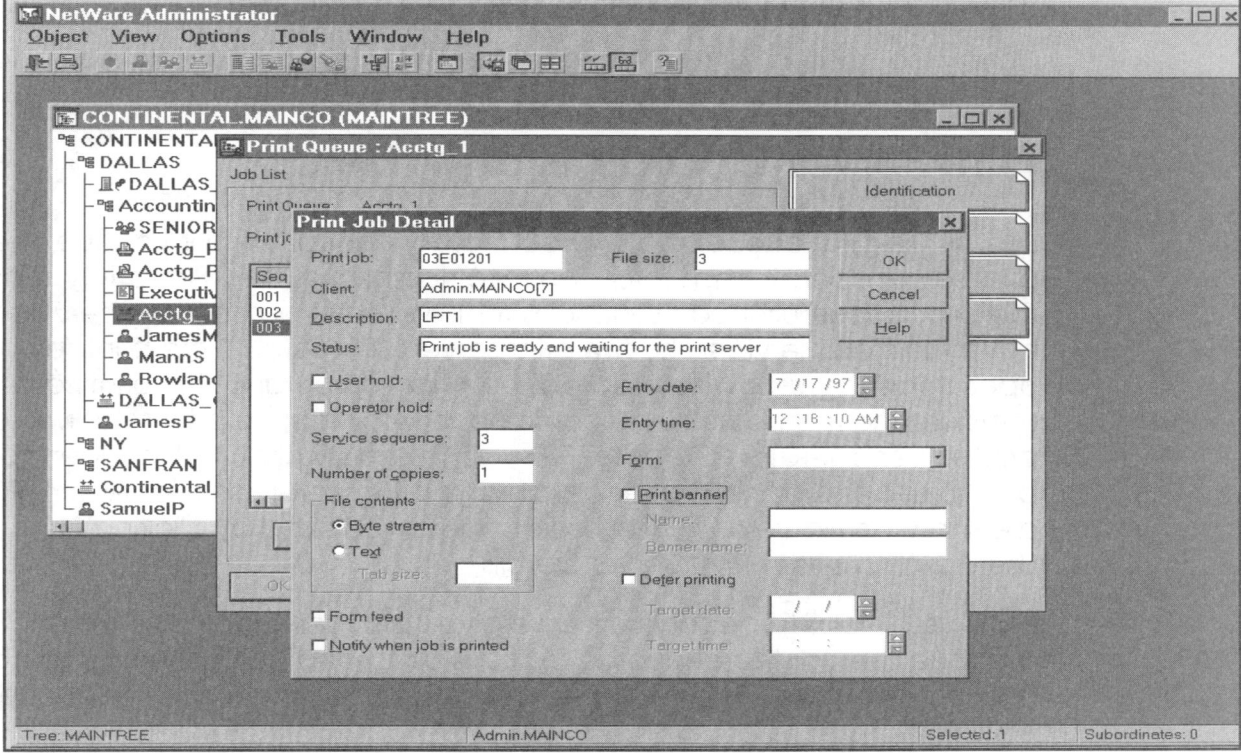

Figure 6-20. Print queue Job Details page.

161

5. **Byte Stream or Text:** The user or the operator can select whether or not the job passes all control characters through to the printer (byte stream) or if each tab character is replaced by a specific number of spaces. The customary choice is byte stream so that control characters inserted by the application can be passed directly to the printer.

6. **Form feed:** The user or the operator can determine whether or not there will be a form feed at the beginning of the print job.

7. **Notify when job is printed:** The user or the operator can adjust the job in the queue to notify the user when the printer begins to service the job.

8. **Print banner:** The user or the operator can determine whether there will be a print banner separator page at the beginning of the document. If the print banner box is marked, a name and a banner name can also be entered.

9. **Defer printing:** The user or the operator can defer printing of this job until a later date and time. This is especially useful when a user has submitted a lengthy job during the busiest hours of the day and the print output needs to be deferred so as not to adversely impact overall printing throughput.

When the desired flags and entries have been made, the changes are saved by clicking the OK button.

Note also that a given job can be held (paused), deleted, and resumed from the Job Details page.

Print Server Operators and Users

Just as the print queue operator can totally control the print queue, the print server operator has total control of the print server. Similarly, just as the print queue user can send jobs to the queue, print server users can have their jobs serviced by the print server. By default, the print server operator is the user who created the print server, and the print server users are the members of the container containing the print server. The print server operator for Acctg_PS is accessed by clicking the Operator button under the Print Server details. The print server users for Acctg_PS are shown in Figure 6-21. The Users page is accessed by clicking on the Users button under Print Server Details.

For a user's jobs to be serviced by a given print server, the user must be a queue user for the queue he or she is using and he or she must be a print server user for the print server that is assigned to service the queue.

Activating the Print Server

To activate the print server, enter

LOAD PSERVER printservername

on the file server console. This action will autoload **NRINTER.NLM** for all printers configured as directly attached to the file server (configured as Auto Load). There can be a maximum of 7 printers directly attached to the file server.

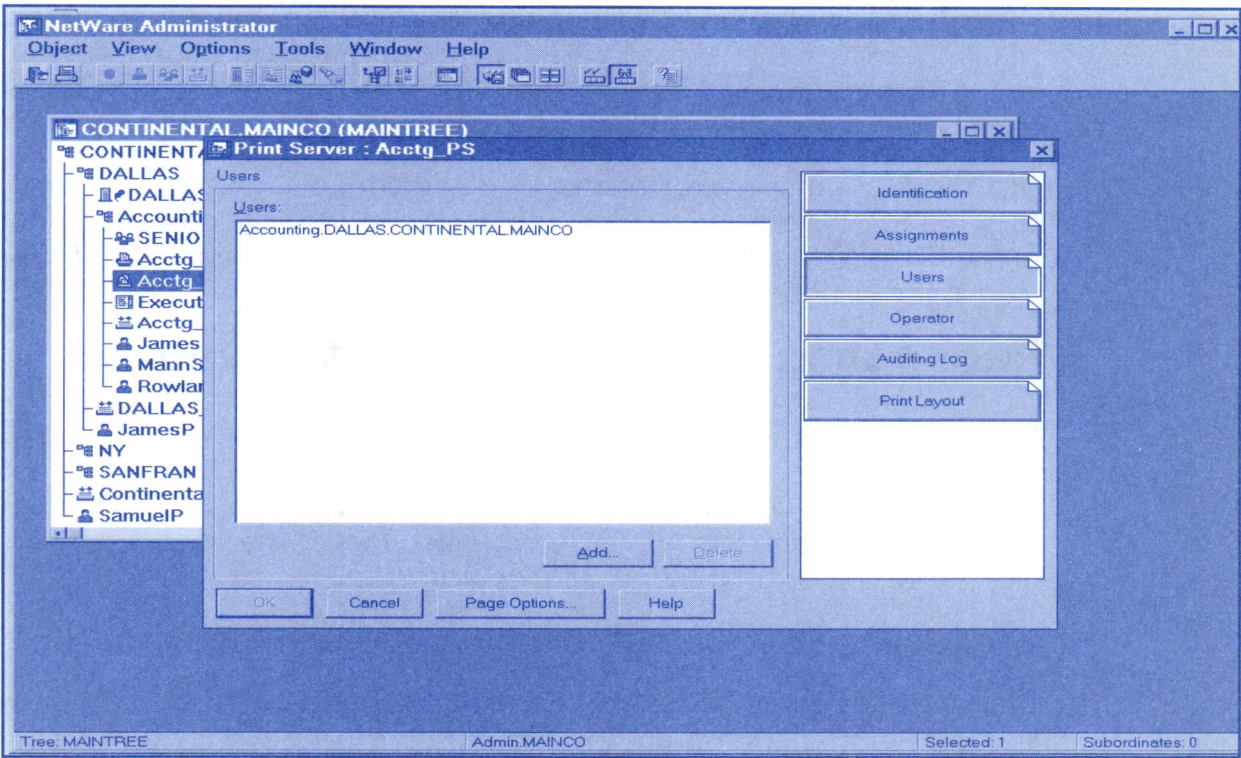

Figure 6-21. Print server users for Acctg_PS.

To activate **remote printing** for a printer attached to another file server that is not the print server, the print server itself must first be running, and then on the remote file server, the following command must be entered:

LOAD NPRINTER printservername printerport

where printservername is the name of the print server that is to control this printer and printerport is the port number assigned to this printer in the port assignments under the print server. The printer that is being configured in this manner must have been set up as a Manual Load printer.

To unload a print server, enter:

UNLOAD PSERVER

To activate remote printing for a printer attached to a workstation, it is easiest to log in and then go to the command prompt and enter

NPRINTER printservername printerport.

The only difference between activating the remote printer on a workstation and activating a remote printer on a file server that is not running PSERVER is that the NPRINTER referred to for the workstation is **NPRINTER.EXE** while the NPRINTER referred to for the remote file server is NPRINTER.NLM. Just like the remote printer attached through a file server that is not running PSERVER, the remote printer for the workstation must have been configured for Manual Load.

The most common error made in activating a remote printer is to attempt to activate the remote printer prior to activating the print server itself. Since the remote printer depends upon the print server to service it, the print server must be running first.

Redirecting Print Output to a Print Queue

From a Windows 3.1 station or from a Windows 95 station, print can be redirected to a NetWare 4.11 print queue through Windows printer settings. From a DOS station, a CAPTURE command can be used. Since the Capture command will also work with either of the Windows clients, this text will focus on the CAPTURE command.

Redirecting Print Output Using the CAPTURE command

The CAPTURE command is a very old DOS-based command that can be entered from the command prompt on a Windows 3.1 or Windows 95 station as well. It has numerous flags that can be displayed by first going to the command prompt and then entering:

CAPTURE /?

This command causes the various options for the CAPTURE command to be displayed as shown in Figure 6-22 through 6-24. Only a few of these flags are customarily used and will therefore be discussed here. Almost any application can be used with network printers using the CAPTURE program. It is a memory-resident program that intercepts data that the workstation sends to its printer ports, and redirects that data to a print queue. The CAPTURE program can be used in three different ways: in conjunction with the CAPTURE /ENDCAP program, with the AUTO ENDCAP feature, or with the TIMEOUT feature.

Network Printing

The CAPTURE /ENDCAP program is used to turn off redirection of the printer data. It essentially unloads the CAPTURE program from memory and places the data in the print queue. Notice that the data is only stored, not put in the queue, until the CAPTURE /ENDCAP program is run. This way a user may send data to the network printer in many separate pieces. When the CAPTURE /ENDCAP command is given, all the data is placed in the queue.

With the AUTO ENDCAP feature of the CAPTURE program enabled, the printer output data is sent on to the print queue when the application that created the print job terminates. For instance, if a user wants to send data to a network printer using a word processor, he or she would first run the CAPTURE program, then start the word processing program. Any printing that is done from the word processing program is stored until the user exits the word processing program. It is only then that the data is placed in the print queue.

Using the TIMEOUT feature (TI=XX) allows the user's data to be sent to the print queue while the user is still in the application program. A timeout period is given in seconds and tells the CAPTURE program when to send the data that it has captured on to the print queue. The CAPTURE program waits the time specified after the last output has been captured before placing the data in the print queue.

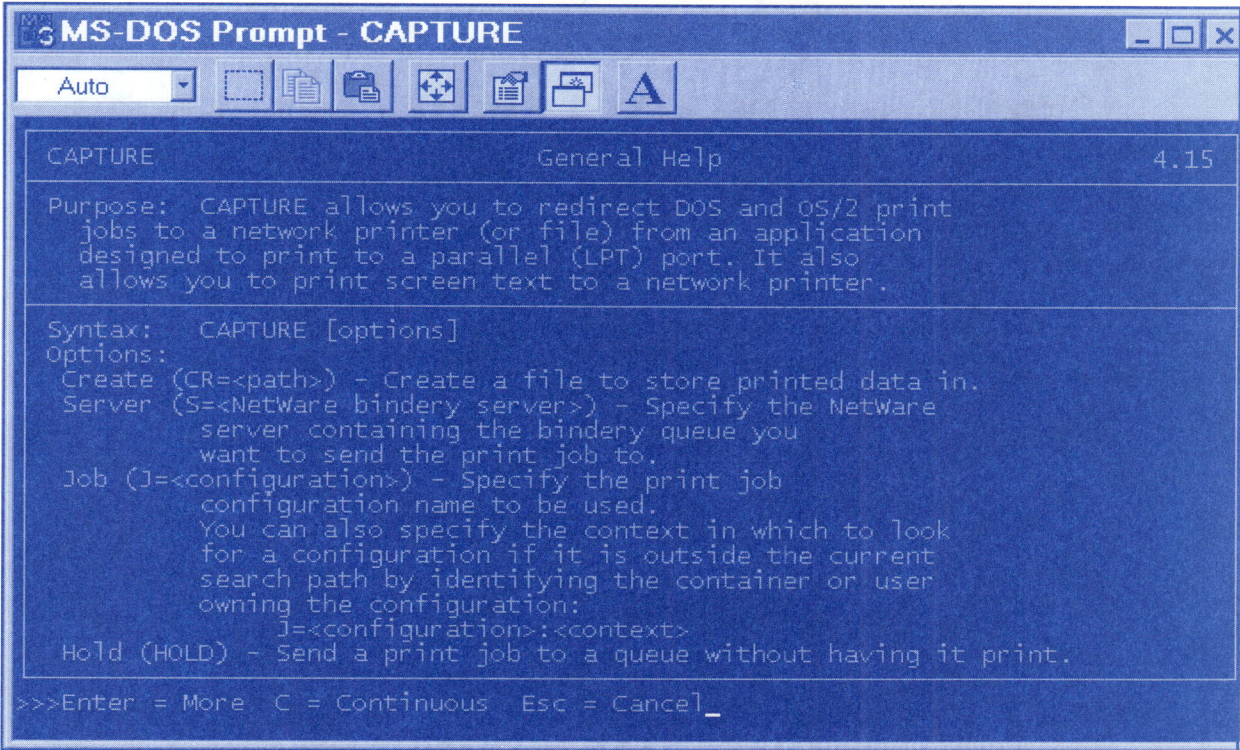

Figure 6-22. CAPTURE command help screens.

Chapter 6

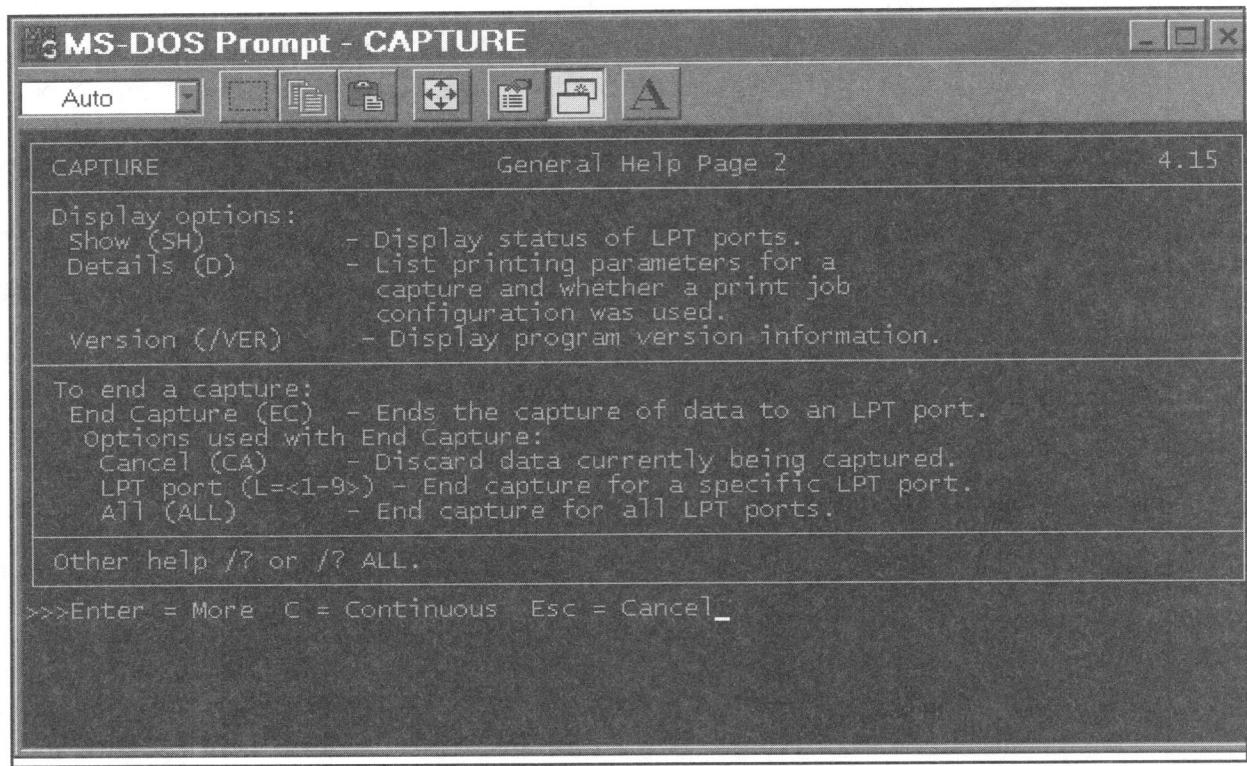

Figure 6-23. CAPTURE command help screens (Cont'd).

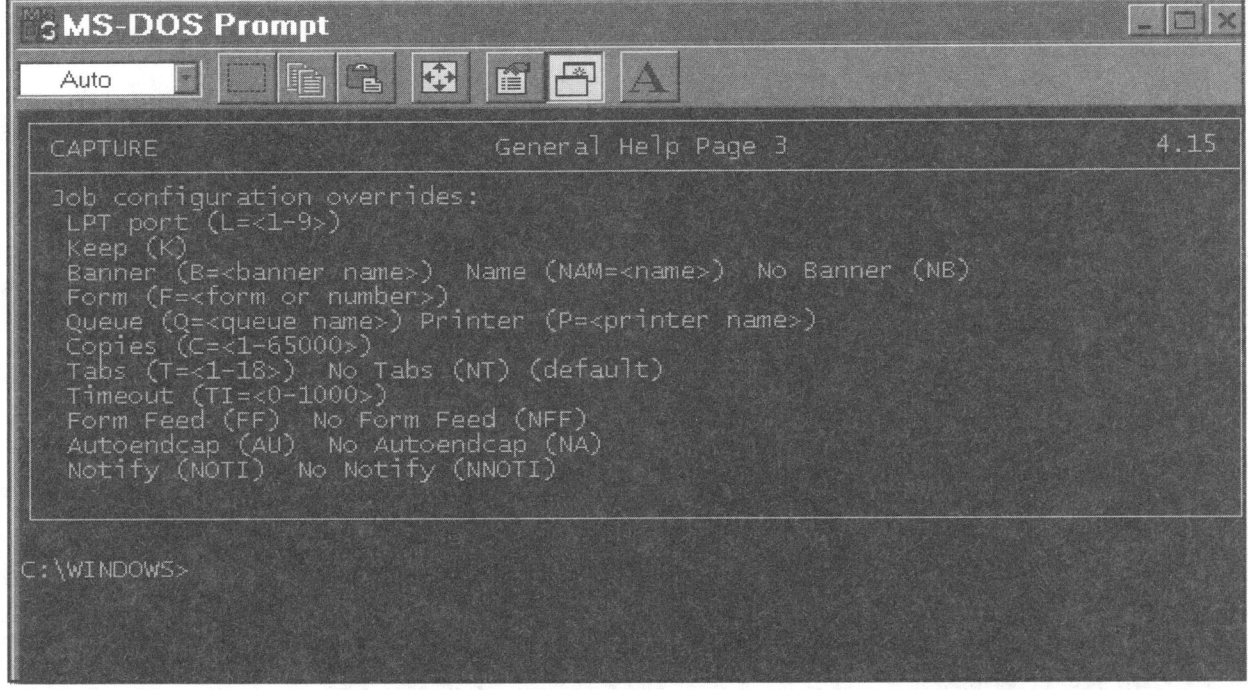

Figure 6-24. CAPTURE command help screens (Cont'd).

Suppose a spreadsheet program is being used with the TIMEOUT feature set to 15 seconds. When the user requests a chart to be printed, the output is stored, and a timer starts counting after the last byte is captured. If the user prints another chart less than 15 seconds later, the data will continue to be stored. The data will be sent to the print queue only when a time longer than 15 seconds passes between print requests.

Making the timeout period too short may break up data that should be printed together. For instance, it may take longer than 15 seconds for the second chart in a single report to be calculated. Someone else's data could be placed in the queue between the first and second charts.

Making the period too long may cause data that the user intended to be printed separately to be printed together instead. If the user wanted the charts to be printed separately, he or she would have to watch the clock until the 15 seconds had passed before printing the second chart. This is not usually a problem since most applications would advance to the next page before printing the second time. A period longer than a few seconds may also be a source of frustration for the user. Even when only one person is sending data to be printed, he or she must wait for the data to be captured, wait the timeout period, then wait for the print server to start processing the data in the queue. These delays can add up to a long enough time that the user may wonder if there is a problem with the printer.

The last and easiest way to send data to a network printer is to use an application program that is designed to send its output to a print queue on a NetWare network. While both Windows 3.1 and Windows 95 can be configured in this manner, the discussion of procedures used to accomplish this type of redirection are too lengthy for an introductory textbook.

A sample CAPTURE command might be:

CAPTURE Q=.Acctg_1.Accounting.DALLAS.CONTINENTAL.MAINCONT NB NFF TI=120

The effect of this capture would be to redirect output normally intended for LPT1 to the Acctg_1 queue in Byte Stream format (NT) with No Banner (NB), No initial Form Feed (NFF), and with printing starting after 120 seconds of inactivity in the print queue.

Chapter 6

Hands-on NetWare

In order to complete the following exercises, the file server and at least two workstations should be ready to use.

1. The file server should be on.

2. Your station must be logged into the server using your ADMINXXX account following procedures previously explained.

3. The accounts and objects created earlier should be available.

Configuring the Print Server and Print Queue

The long list of steps below creates a new print server, new printer, and new print queue. These operations can be carried out at any workstation that is logged into the network using your ADMINXXX user created earlier. Since only one print server can be running on a file server at a time, it might be a good idea for students to work in teams to perform this hands-on exercise and the projects at the end of the chapter.

1. After logging in, start NetWare Administrator and position on the MAINCO container as shown in Figure 6-25.

2. Create a print queue called PQXXX where XXX are your initials. Use the **Browse button** to select the appropriate volume on your classroom server and then click the **Create button**.

3. Create a print server called PSXXX where XXX are your initials. Click the **Create button** after entering the name **PSXXX**.

4. Create a printer called PTRXXX where XXX are your initials. Click the **Create button** after entering the name **PTRXXX**.

5. Double-click **the printer object** just created, and click the **Assignments button**. Click the **Add button**, click **PQXXX**, and then click the **OK button**. This action associates the print queue with a given printer. Note that if you desire, you could add additional printers to the list of queues serviced by this printer. Your screen should look similar to Figure 6-26.

6. Click the **Configuration button** to display the configuration page for the printer, and then click the **Communication button** to set up the physical communications for the printer. Consult your instructor to determine the actual physical setup of the printer attached to your file server. In most cases, it will be running on LPT1 port with Interrupt 7, and the printer will be configured for Auto Load since it is attached to the file server. Click the **OK button** to save the configuration. Your screen should look similar to

Network Printing

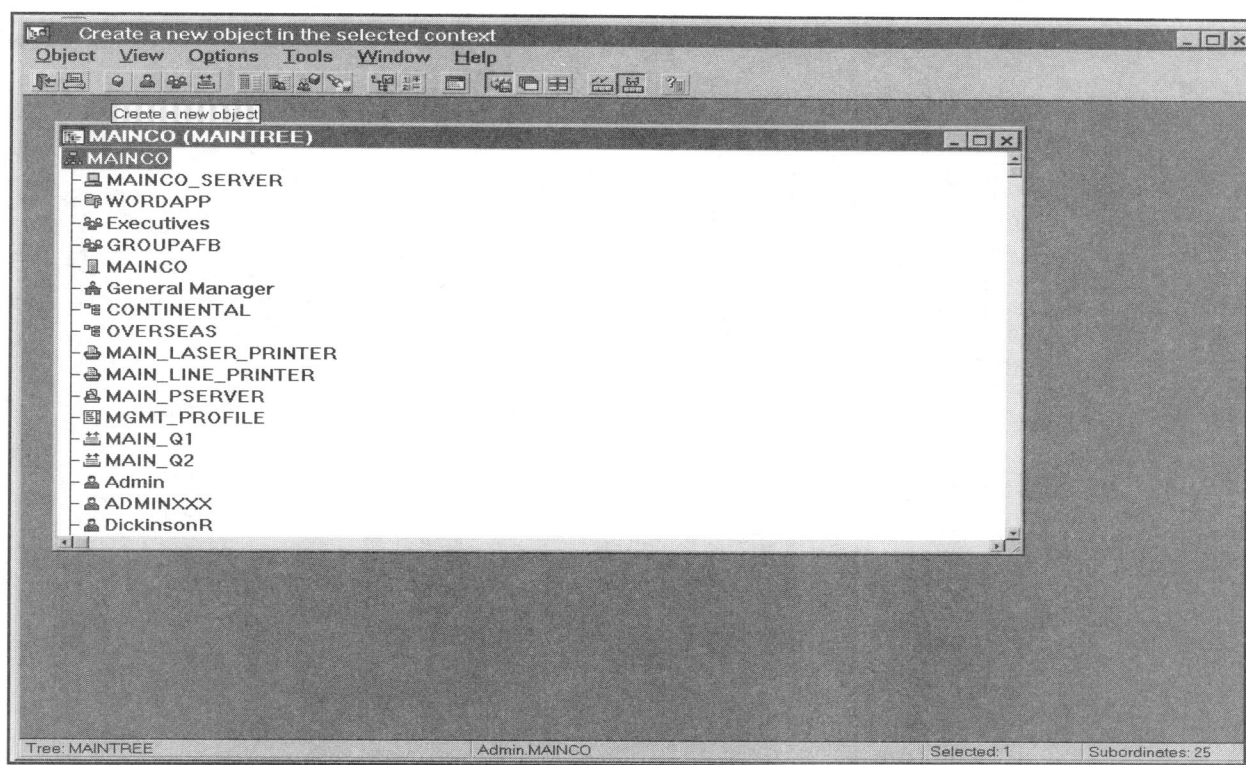

Figure 6-25. Position on MAINCO to create a print queue.

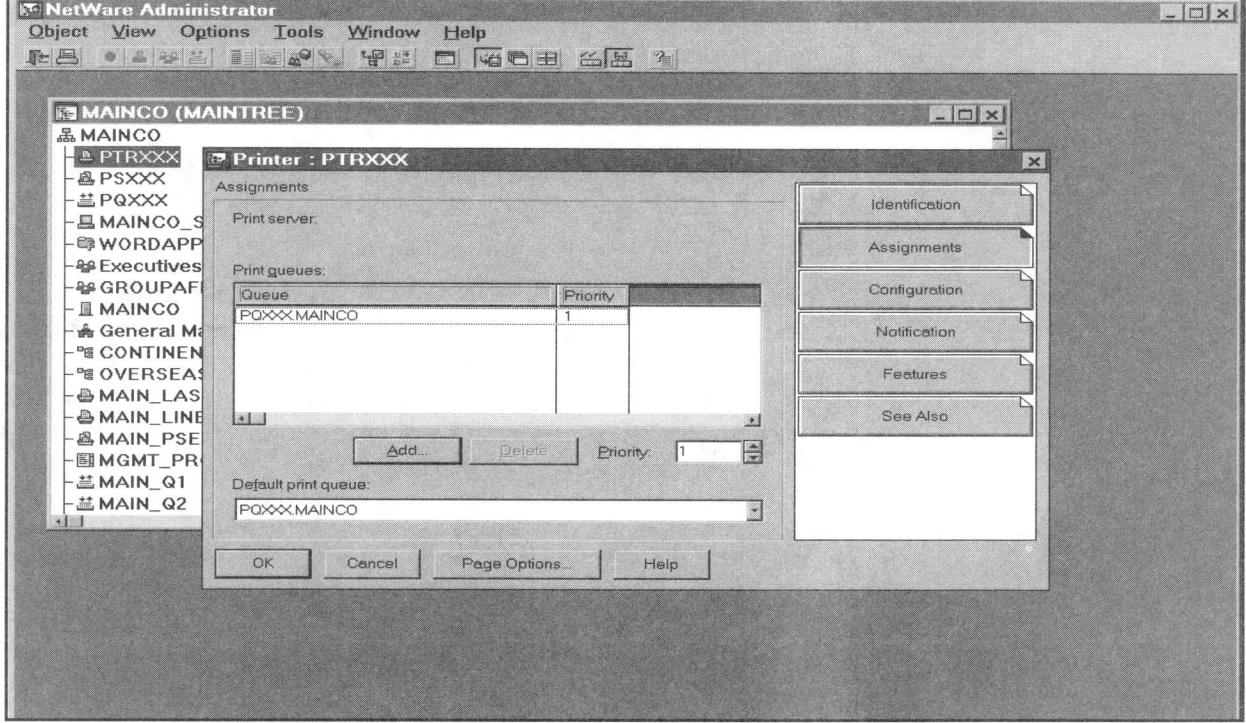

Figure 6-26. PQ_XXX assigned to printer PTRXXX.

Chapter 6

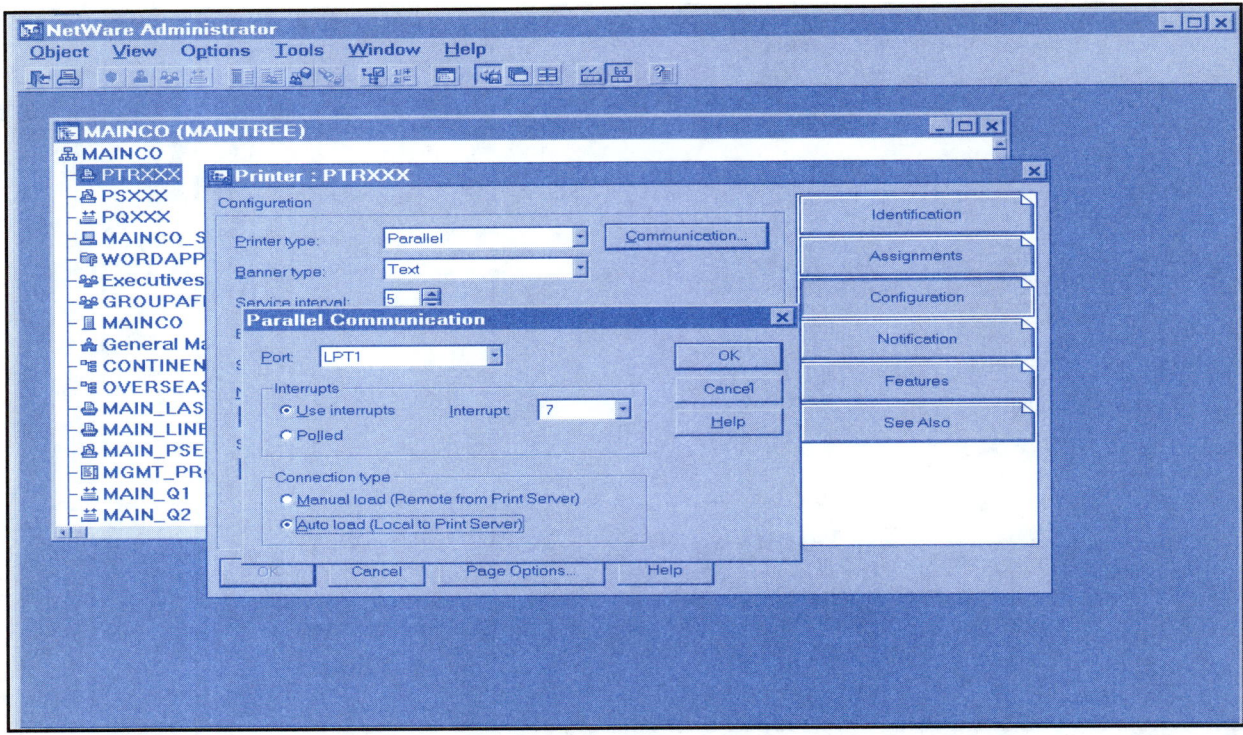

Figure 6-27. Configuration for PTRXXX.

Figure 6-27 unless your printer is physically configured differently than described here. Then click the **OK button** on the Printer Assignments page.

7. Double-click the **PSXXX object** just created.

8. Click the **Assignments button** and then add **PTRXXX**. Click the **OK button** after selecting the printer. Click **OK** to save the assignment.

9. To check that the configuration is entered correctly, double-click **the PQXXX** object and then click the **Assignments button** to display the print server assigned to service the queue and the printer assigned to service the queue. Your screen should be similar to Figure 6-28. Click the Cancel button to return to the MAINCO container.

10. As a further check, double-click **the print server object** and then click the **Print Layout button**. Your screen should be similar to Figure 6-29.

Running PSERVER

With the print server object created and configured and the print server software loaded onto the file server hard disk using the NetWare Administrator program, the print server can be started by loading the

170

Network Printing

PSERVER program on the file server. Note that only one student at a time can load his or her print server and test it; therefore, it might be a good idea for students to work in pairs.

1. On the file server console enter

   LOAD PSERVER PSXXX

2. Wait for the print server to load.

Sending Output to the Print Server

The Print Server is up and running. All that remains is to test it. Leave the print server software running. Use a workstation logged in as your ADMINXXX to perform these operations.

1. Get to the Command Prompt and enter:

   CAPTURE Q=.PQXXX.MAINCO NT NB NFF TI=120

2. Enter

   COPY C:\AUTOEXEC.BAT   LPT1:

   to copy a file to the new print queue.

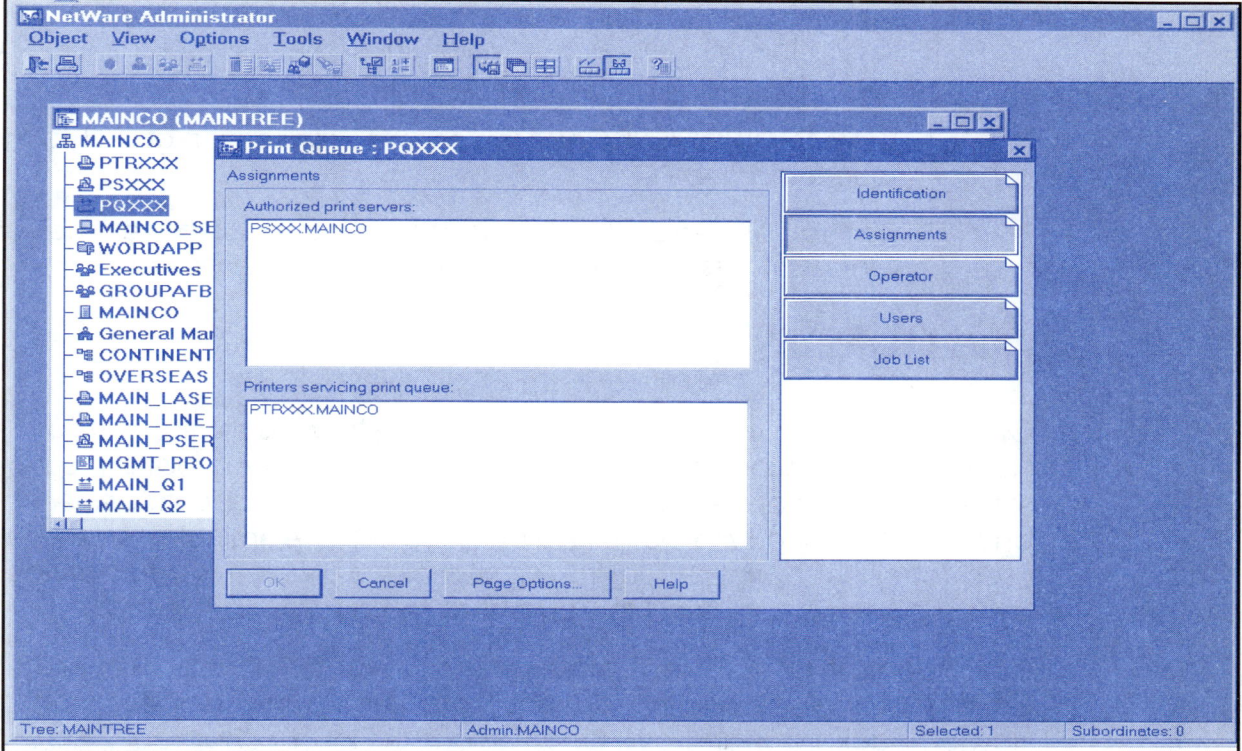

Figure 6-28. Print Queue assignments for print queue PQXXX.

Chapter 6

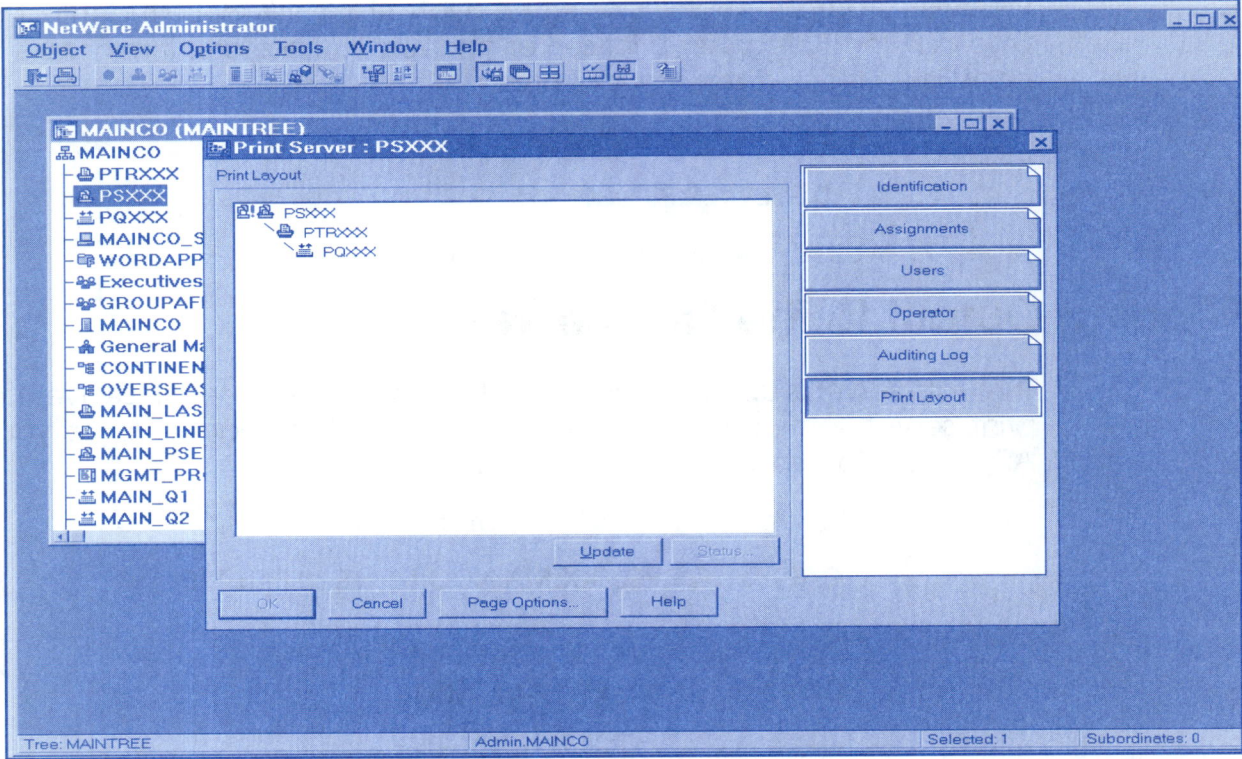

Figure 6-29. Print layout for print server PSXXX.

3. Go to the print server and watch the screens for the print job to get to the printer. Wait for it to print.

4. Enter CAPTURE /ENDCAP. This ends the redirection of LPT1 to the queue named PQXXX.

5. Reattempt step 2. What happened? You should have received an error message since the queue is no longer active.

Summary

One of the most often used features of a network is sharing printers. A Novell network allows printers located on the file server that is the print server, on another file server, or on a workstation to be accessed by any user or group with authorization. NetWare Administrator can be used to redirect print output to a given queue, which is then serviced by the print server to send the output to the appropriate printer.

It is important to note that there are many other Novell printer setup options as well as printing options from third party vendors such as Hewlett-Packard than have been discussed in this chapter. Students are referred to Novell's product documentation and to the various third party printing vendors for further information.

Questions

1. In what ways can a printer be attached to a network using NetWare 4's printer control software?

2. How many printers can be attached to file server that is running the PSERVER software?

3. If a print server has only one printer port, but two printers are attached, where are the two other places the second printer can reside?

4. Can a single print queue feed data to more than one printer?

5. What is the syntax for loading and activating a print server called MYPSERVER on a NetWare 4 file server?

6. What are the steps for creating a print queue, printer, and print server and then tying them together?

7. How can you determine whether or not you have associated the print queue, printer, and print server properly?

8. What is the CAPTURE command to redirect print from LPT1 to a print queue under the MAINCO container named MAIN_Q2?

9. What is the syntax for ending a CAPTURE command redirection?

10. What is the meaning of TI=0 for the CAPTURE command? What is the meaning of TI=120?

Projects

Objective

The following projects provide additional practice with the basic networking printing facilities of NetWare. Additionally, the second project provides more hands-on training in creating print queues and sending print jobs across the network.

Project 1. Basic Network Printing

1. Create another print queue on the print server you created during the Hands-On exercise. This print queue should also be serviced by PSXXX and redirected to PTRXXXNEW.

2. Enter a CAPTURE statement that redirects print from LPT1 to the first PQXXX and print a text file from your C: drive.

3. Enter a CAPTURE statement which redirects print from LPT1 to the second print queue PQXXXNEW.

What happened? Why?

Project 2. Advanced Network Printing

1. Create a print queue with a unique name on an existing print server. Be sure to include your user name as a print queue operator.

2. Set the printer to OFF LINE. Send a file to the print queue. Then use the NetWare Administrator utility to remove the file from the queue. Put the printer back on line.

3. Try the same operation as above, but send your data to a classmate's print queue. You should not be able to remove the print job.

Project 3. Setting Up a Print Server with One Locally Attached Printer and One Remote Printer

1. Following instructions given in the Hands-On section of this chapter, modify your print server to have one remote printer.

2. Assign a new queue to this printer and test its operation. You will need to run NPRINTER on a workstation with a printer attached to fully test this exercise.

7
NDS Security

Objectives

After completing this chapter you will

1. Understand the meaning of NDS object and property rights.
2. Know how to assign NDS object and property rights to trustees to provide access to the tree.
3. Recognize default object and property rights assigned to various users and groups by NetWare 4.11.
4. Be able to list the ways a user obtains NDS rights.
5. Calculate a user's effective rights.
6. Understand the general considerations that must be made in assigning NDS object and property trustee rights.

Key Terms

Selected Property Rights

Inherited Rights

Object Rights

Property Rights

Inherited Rights Filter

Effective Rights

Introduction

NDS object and property rights control access to the NDS tree itself, much as directory and file system rights control access to the file system on the server(s) in the network. NDS rights, though, consist of two sets of rights:

Chapter 7

> **Object Rights** that determine what a user can do with the objects in the tree.
>
> **Property Rights** that determine what a user can do with the properties or characteristics of the objects in the tree.

Just as directory and file system rights are assigned to an object called a trustee, NDS object and property rights are also assigned to an object called a trustee. Only trustees can use objects, and the rights either explicitly granted to or inherited by a trustee determine the kinds of actions the trustee can perform with an object. Except for one very small exception, NDS object and property rights have absolutely nothing to do with directory and file system rights. This one exception will be explained later in the chapter.

The purpose of this chapter is to explain the various NDS object and property rights and their meanings, to show the student how to assign these object and property rights, to explain default object and property rights automatically assigned by NetWare 4.11, to delineate the ways that a user can obtain object and property rights, to explain how to calculate effective rights, and finally to discuss considerations that should be made in designing an NDS rights structure for an NDS tree.

NDS Object and Property Rights

A Broad Overview of NDS Trustee Rights

A user can obtain NDS Object and Property Rights from the same sources the user could obtain file system rights from trustee assignments and inherited rights for:

> The user account.
>
> The group(s) to which the user belongs,
>
> The container(s) to which the user belongs,
>
> The organizational roles that the user occupies,
>
> The users to which this user is security equivalent,
>
> The special object (PUBLIC) that supplies rights to all users connected to a file server in a NetWare 4.11 network whether or not the user is logged in.

For a user or other object to be granted object and property rights to a given NDS object, the user must be placed on that object's Access Control List (ACL). The ACL is a property is available for every object in the NDS tree. Thus, the name of each trustee for an object must be placed in the object's Access Control List.

Like file system rights, NDS object rights can be inherited. NDS property rights are broken into two classifications: All properties, and Selected properties. Rights assigned through All Properties can be inherited just like NDS object rights. Rights assigned through the **Selected Properties** feature cannot be inherited.

Additionally, there are **Inherited Rights Filters** or IRFs that can be assigned to NDS objects and NDS properties. These IRFs work like the file system IRFs except that the Supervisor right for NDS Objects and Properties can be blocked, unlike the Supervisor right for the file system, which cannot be blocked.

NDS Object Rights

Object rights determine what a trustee can do with an object. There are five NDS Object Rights:

1. **Supervisor.** This trustee assignment gives the user all access rights to both the object and to all properties of the object. This right, though, can be blocked with an IRF in NetWare 4.11.

2. **Browse**. This trustee assignment gives the users the right to see the objects in the NDS tree. Without this right, the user cannot even see the objects in the tree.

3. **Create**. This trustee assignments gives the user the right to create another object beneath this object. The Create right applies only to container objects since objects cannot be created beneath a leaf.

4. **Delete.** This trustee assignment gives the user the right to delete this object from the NDS tree.

5. **Rename.** This trustee assignment gives the user the right to rename the object.

Some students find it helpful to utilize a phrase (though not in order) such as Black Cats Do Run Swiftly to assist in remembering these five object rights.

NDS Property Rights

NDS **Property Rights** determine what a trustee can do with the characteristics or properties of an object. NDS Property Rights are:

1. **Supervisor**. This trustee assignment gives the trustee all rights to the property. Remember, though, that the Supervisor property right can be blocked by an IRF.

2. **Compare.** This trustee assignment gives the trustee the right to compare the value of the property with other known values to determine whether the property value is greater than, less than, or equal to the external value in question. A comparison returns a simple true or false. With this property right, the trustee cannot see the value of the property.

3. **Read.** This trustee assignment gives the trustee the right to read the value of a property of an object. This property right also implies that the trustee has the Compare right.

4. **Write.** This trustee assignment gives the trustee the right to change the value of a property of an object. This property right also implies that the trustee has the Add Self right.

5. **Add Self.** This trustee assignment gives the trustee the right to add or remove himself to a property. This property only applies to properties that have lists of values such as group membership, etc. One must be careful with this property, as it allows the trustee to place himself on the Access Control List of the object and therefore grant himself more rights to the object.

A phrase (though again not in order) to help you remember the five property rights is Red Cats Walk Away Slowly.

As mentioned earlier, property rights can be assigned through two ways:

All Properties option

Selected Properties option

The All Properties option allows trustee rights to just what it says - All properties - at the same time. Trustee rights granted through the All Properties option can be inherited.

The Selected Properties option allows trustee rights to be set for specific properties. All assignments through the Selected Properties option override assignments for the same property through the All Properties option, yet trustee assignments through Selected Properties are not inherited.

Default NDS Object and Property Trustee Assignments

Through the normal setup of the system, the following default NDS Object and Property trustee assignments are shown in Figure 7-1.

NDS Security

Trustee	Default Object or Property Right	Purpose of Default Right
(PUBLIC)	Browse Object Right to the (ROOT) object	Lets users see the NDS tree and the objects within it
(PUBLIC)	Read property right to the messaging property of the server object	Lets clients on the network identify the messaging server assigned to this server, if any.
(PUBLIC)	Read property right to the Default Server property for every user	Identifies the default server for each user.
Admin	Supervisor Object Right to the (ROOT)	Lets the Admin (the first user object) administer the NDS tree
Server	Supervisor Object Right to itself	Lets the server change its own parameters. This is needed for normal server operation.
(ROOT)	Read property right to the Network Address and Group Membership Properties for every user	Lets all users in the tree identify the network address and group membership of a user.
User	Read right to All Properties of his own user object	Lets the user see all his properties
User	Read and Write selected property to the Login script Property of his own user object	Allows the user to change and execute his of her own login script
User	Read and Write selected property rights to the Print Job Configuration Property of his own user object	Allows the user to create a print job configuration and use it
Container Object when it is created	Browse Object Right to the (ROOT) object	Lets users in the container read (and execute) the container's login script and read (and use) the container's print job configuration.
Users in a Container	Inherit object and rights assigned through All Properties option from the containers above the user object	Lets object and property rights be assigned more easily
Creator of an object	Receives the Supervisor Object Right to the Object	Creator user can reasonably control the object. Allows for administrators for new container to be given only the Create Object right.

Figure 7-1. Default NDS Object and Property Rights.

Inheritance and Effective Rights

Generally, object and property rights assigned through the All Properties option are **inherited** just like file system rights. Just as with file system rights, unwanted inheritance can be limited by placing an Inherited Rights Filter for Object Rights and/or an Inherited Rights Filter for Property Rights at a lower level in the NDS tree. Only the rights specifically listed in the Inherited Rights Filters can be inherited from above. Remember, though, that the Supervisor right for NDS objects and the Supervisor right for the All Properties option can be filtered out by an IRF. The Supervisor file system right cannot be filtered.

Inheritance can also be limited by the application of another specific trustee assignment for the same user, group, organizational role, etc. at a lower level. Explicit trustee assignments always override inherited rights.

Effective rights are the sum of all the explicit and inherited rights that an object has at a given level in the NDS tree. Remember that rights can be obtained in the six ways listed earlier in the chapter.

In a very simple example, suppose that Sam, a user in the MAINCO container, is given NDS object rights of (BCDR) to the CONTINENTAL container. This means that Sam can see the objects in the tree under the CONTINENTAL container, he can create objects under the CONTINENTAL container, he can delete the CONTINENTAL container, and he can rename the CONTINENTAL container. Assuming there are no IRFs assigned, he will have the same object trustee rights through inheritance to all containers below the CONTINENTAL container.

What happens, though, if there is an IRF at the DALLAS container that allows only (B D)? Simply put, the IRF limits Sam's inherited rights in the DALLAS container to Browse and Delete. Further, the only rights that Sam can inherit in lower containers such as Accounting are Browse and Delete since the rights that can be inherited from above are based on the actual rights that an object has to the container above.

In chart form, the determination of these rights is shown in Figure 7-2.

Now, let's examine a slightly different scenario by granting Sam an additional explicit object trustee assignment at the DALLAS container of (BCD). This additional assignment overrides any inherited rights he may have had. This is shown in Figure 7-3.

NDS Security

	Sam as a user
.CONTINENTAL.MAINCO	
IRF	(SBCDR)
Inherited Rights	--
Trustee Assign.	(BCDR)
Effective Rights	(BCDR)
.DALLAS.CONTINENTAL.MAINCO	
IRF	(B D)
Inherited Rights	(B D)
Trustee Assign.	--
Effective Rights	(B D)
.Accounting.DALLAS.CONTINENTAL.MAINCO	
IRF	(SBCDR)
Inherited Rights	(B D)
Trustee Assign.	--
Effective Rights	(B D)

Figure 7-2. Determining inheritance and effective rights with NDS.

	Sam as a user
.CONTINENTAL.MAINCO	
IRF	(SBCDR)
Inherited Rights	--
Trustee Assign.	(BCDR)
Effective Rights	(BCDR)
.DALLAS.CONTINENTAL.MAINCO	
IRF	(B D)
Inherited Rights	(B D)
Trustee Assign.	(BCD)
Effective Rights	(BCD)
.Accounting.DALLAS.CONTINENTAL.MAINCO	
IRF	(SBCDR)
Inherited Rights	(BCD)
Trustee Assign.	--
Effective Rights	(BCD)

Figure 7-3. Determining effective rights with additional trustee assignments.

Further, let's consider Sam's effective rights assuming that the special object (PUBLIC) had the Browse right to the (ROOT); Sam is a member of a group called .MAINGRP.MAINCO, which has an explicit object trustee assignment to .DALLAS.CONTINENTAL.MAINCO of (BC R); and Sam's container, MAINCO, has (SBCDR) to the Accounting container. To figure Sam's effective rights at each container, each method for obtaining rights must be considered and calculated separately. Then, the effective rights at each container are added together to determine Sam's ultimate effective rights at that container. These calculations are shown in Figure 7-4.

The effective property rights a user obtains from explicit assignments to the All Properties and from inheritance and IRFs for All Properties are calculated the same as the object rights above except that selected property rights at a given level in the tree override All Property rights assignments, and selected property rights are not inherited.

Considerations for Proper Assignment of NDS Object and Property Rights

NDS Object and Property Rights should be assigned sparingly, giving users only the rights necessary for them to do their jobs using the system.

As a rule, the best place to start is to consider what rights are assigned by default. These rights are generally sufficient for users to complete their tasks. Then, as with file system rights, rights should be assigned first to group type objects and then to specific users as appropriate.

(PUBLIC)

Rights needed for all users attached to a NetWare 4.11 server whether they are logged in or not (generally just (B)) should be assigned to (PUBLIC). Care should be taken in assigning any additional rights to this object since these rights are available to users whether or not they are authenticated to NDS.

Container Rights

Rights needed by all users in a given container should be assigned to the container so that they can be inherited by the users in the container. Don't forget that some rights are automatically assigned to the container by default upon creation of objects in the container. Refer to Figure 7-1.

Groups

Groups are objects that contain users for members. All object and property rights assigned to a group also belong to each user of the

NDS Security

	Sam	(PUBLIC)	MAINGRP	MAINCO	Sam as a user
(ROOT)					
IRF	(SBCDR)	(SBCDR)	(SBCDR)	(SBCDR)	(SBCDR)
Inherited Rights	--	--	--	--	
Trustee Assign.	--	(B)	--	--	
Effective Rights	--	(B)	--	--	(B)
.MAINCO					
IRF	(SBCDR)	(SBCDR)	(SBCDR)	(SBCDR)	(SBCDR)
Inherited Rights	--	(B)	--	--	
Trustee Assign.	--	--	--	--	
Effective Rights	--	(B)	--	--	(B)
.CONTINENTAL.MAINCO					
IRF	(SBCDR)	(SBCDR)	(SBCDR)	(SBCDR)	(SBCDR)
Inherited Rights	--	(B)	--	--	
Trustee Assign.	(BCDR)	--	--	--	
Effective Rights	(BCDR)	(B)	--	---	(BCDR)
.DALLAS.CONTINENTAL.MAINCO					
IRF	(B D)	(B D)	(B D)	(B D)	(B D)
Inherited Rights	(B D)	(B)	--	--	
Trustee Assign.	--	--	(BCR)	--	
Effective Rights	(B D)	(B)	(BCR)	(B D)	(BCDR)
.Accounting.DALLAS. CONTINENTAL.MAINCO					
IRF	(SBCDR)	(SBCDR)	(SBCDR)	(SBCDR)	(SBCDR)
Inherited Rights	(B D)	(B)	(BCR)	(B D)	
Trustee Assign.	--	--	--	(SBCDR)	
Effective Rights	(B D)	(B)	(BCR)	(SBCDR)	(SBCDR)

Figure 7-4. Complex calculation of NDS effective rights.

group. Groups should be used to organize users with similar needs so that rights can be granted to the single group object rather than to users individually.

Organizational Role Rights

Many times, object and property rights are needed based on the job function that an individual performs. In this case, it is a good idea to create an organizational role object, assign rights to the organizational role object and then make the subject user an occupant of the organizational role. In this way, the user obtains rights based on his or her function rather than individually. When the user transfers to another job, a new person or persons can be made occupants of the organizational role and the person transferring can be removed as an occupant from the former organizational role.

Security Equivalence

A user can be made security equivalent to another user and thereby obtain the object and All Properties rights assigned to the other user. This method for granting rights should be used on a temporary basis only, perhaps for a user who is visiting a given office and helping out on a project. If the user is to have these rights permanently, they should be assigned by other means. If they are not, when the person to which the user is made security equivalent is deleted from the tree, our user will not have the rights necessary to perform his job.

Pitfalls to Avoid

Because of inheritance and other basic NDS principles, the following cautions should be heeded:

1. Avoid granting NDS rights higher in the tree than necessary.

2. Avoid granting the Supervisor object right to the server object to more than a limited number of users since granting this NDS right also grants the user the Supervisory file system right to all volumes on the given server.

3. Remember that granting the Supervisor object right also grants by default the Supervisor right to All Properties. Most notably, this means that the user has the Supervisory right to the Access Control List property (ACL) and can grant rights to others. One method for avoid the latter situation is to grant a further limited Read and Compare Access Control List property right through the Selected Properties option. Also remember, though, that the Selected Property assignment limits the user only at this level of the tree.

4. Granting the Write right to an object through the All Properties option also grants the user the right to place himself on the Access Control List for the object.

5. Be careful when setting Inherited Rights Filters for an object or for the properties of the object. Generally, if NDS object and property rights are prudently assigned, an IRF is unnecessary. When an IRF is used, the consequences can be more than intended. For example, initially, to remove the S object right from the IRF for a container, there must be at least one user with an explicit object trustee assignment of Supervisor for that container. The problem comes when that user is removed from the tree. Because the Supervisor right is blocked in the IRF and because the user who had the explicit Supervisor object right has been removed from the tree, that portion of the tree can be non-maintainable. The only choice at this state is to consult Novell

NDS Security

Consulting to reestablish a user with the Supervisor object right to the container.

Hands-On Netware

Assigning Object Rights

Assigning object rights is accomplished through NetWare Administrator. The user assigning object rights to another user, group, etc. must have control over the object to which rights are assigned as well as the object receiving the rights. Therefore, the administrative account is usually used.

The steps for assigning your NEWXXX user the (BCDR) rights to the DALLAS container are as follows:

1. Log in as **your ADMINXXX user** where XXX is your initials.

2. Activate **NetWare Administrator**.

3. Right-click on **the USERXXX user**. You should see a small menu as shown in Figure 7-5.

4. Select **Rights to Other Objects**.

5. The Search Context box is displayed as in Figure 7-6.

6. Press the **Delete key** to begin searching from the (ROOT) and select the **Search Entire Subtree option**. Then click **OK**. Note that you could use the Browse button to begin searching from any place in the tree. The Rights to Other Objects box is displayed as in Figure 7-7.

7. Note that the selections for Object and Property Rights are dimmed until you click on **the USERXXX object**. Then the screen will appear as in Figure 7-8 showing that the user has the Read right to all of his or her own properties. Note in this screen that the user indicated on the top is the object having rights and the object to which the user has rights is listed in the Assigned Objects box. This is a little confusing since the user is the same in both cases so far.

Chapter 7

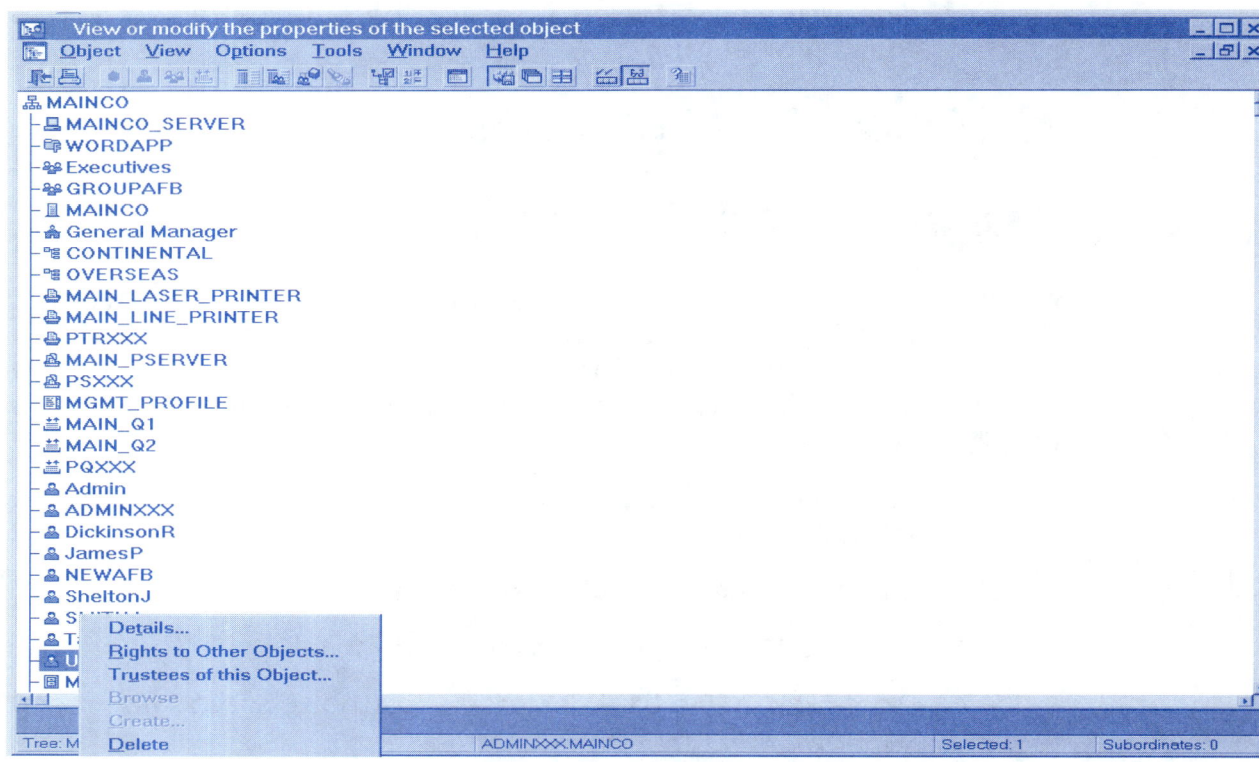

Figure 7-5. Small menu of NWAdmin options.

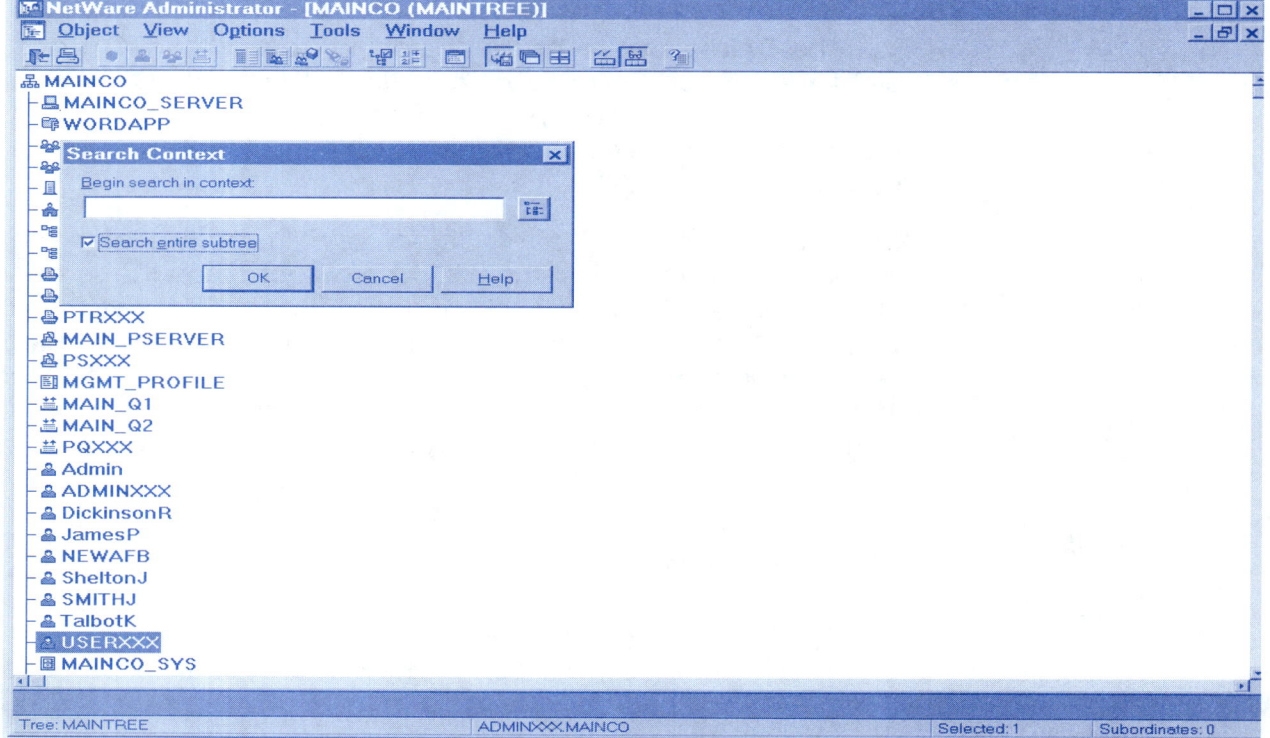

Figure 7-6. Search Context box.

NDS Security

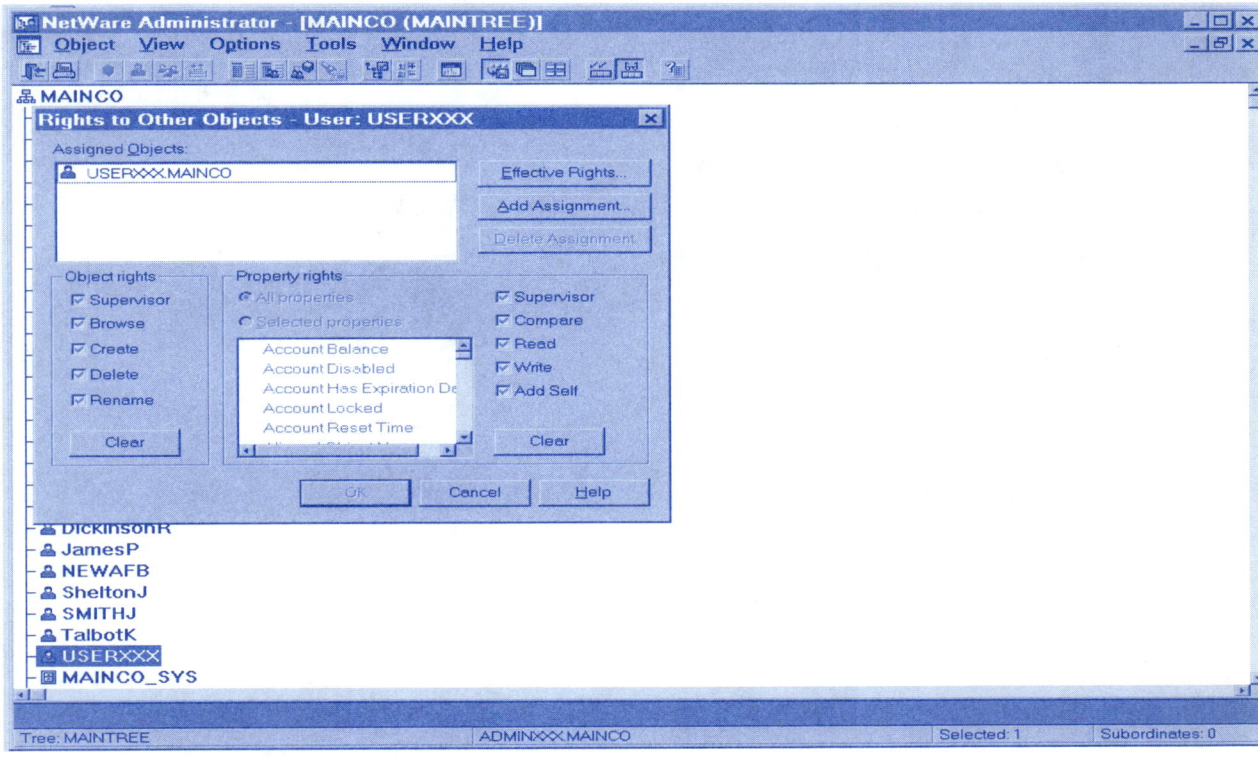

Figure 7-7. Rights to Other Objects box.

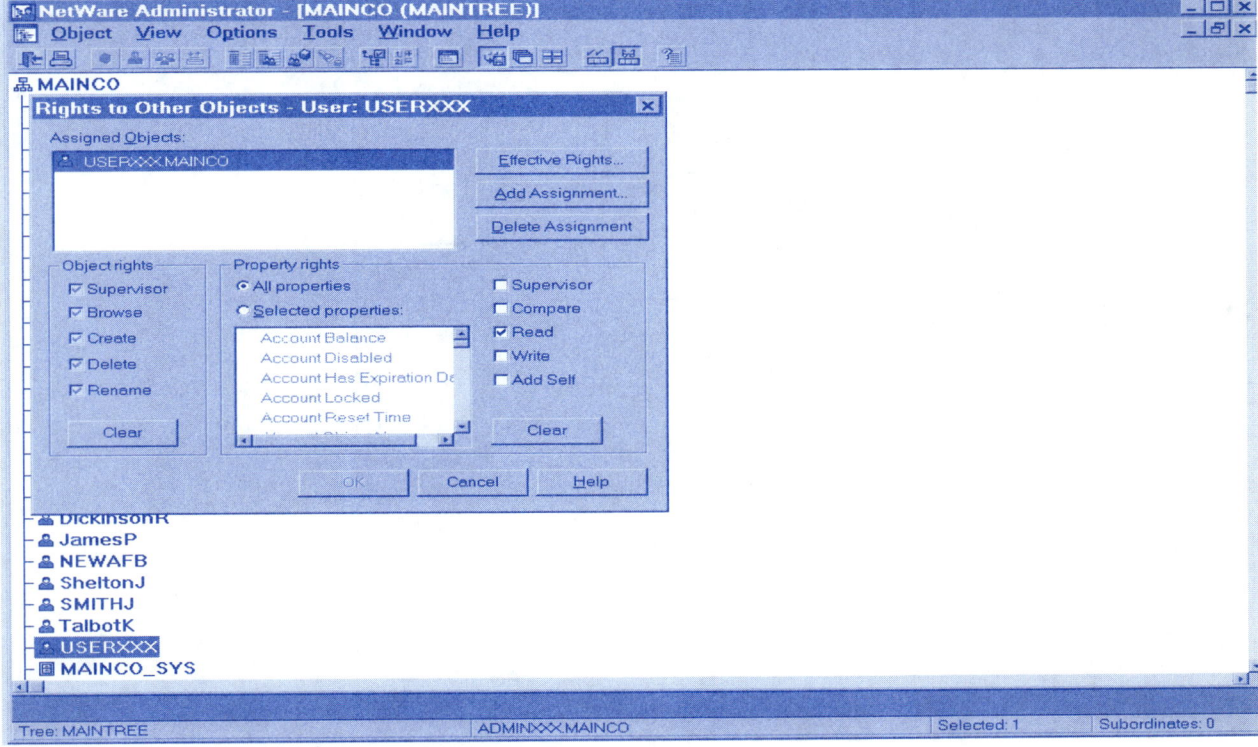

Figure 7-8. USERXXX existing object and property rights.

187

Chapter 7

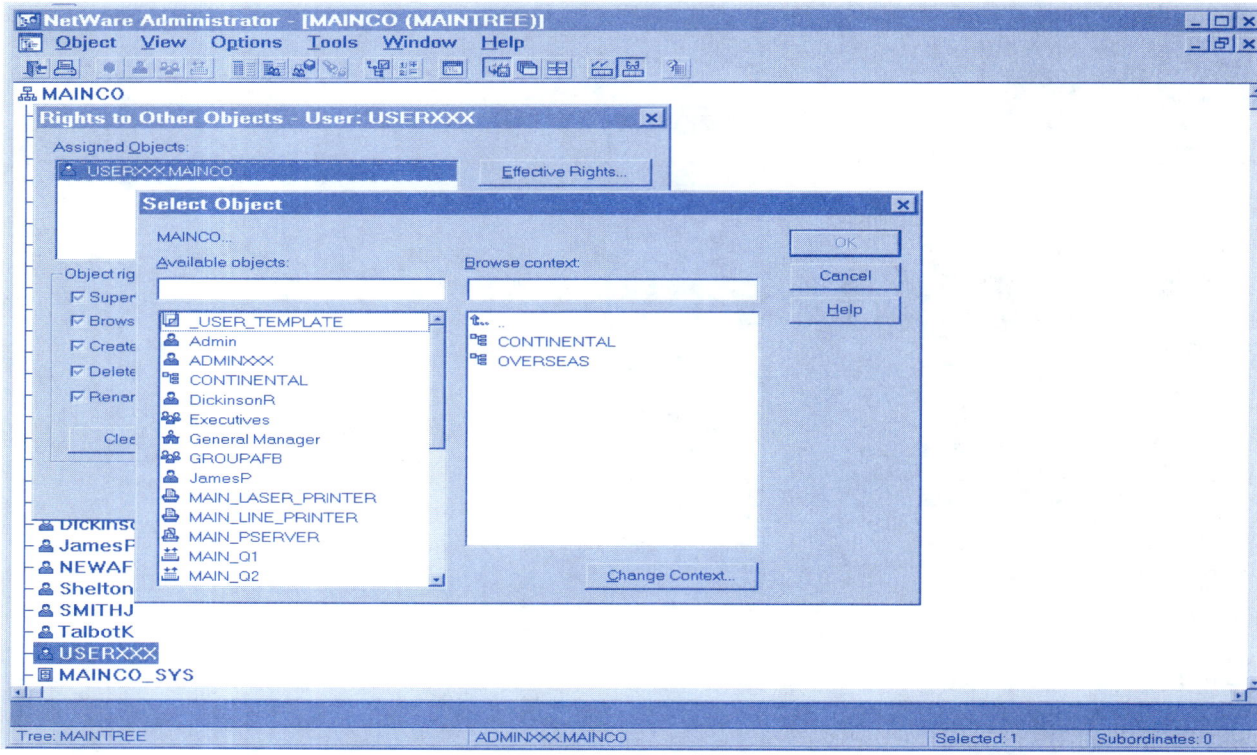

Figure 7-9. Add assignment dialog box.

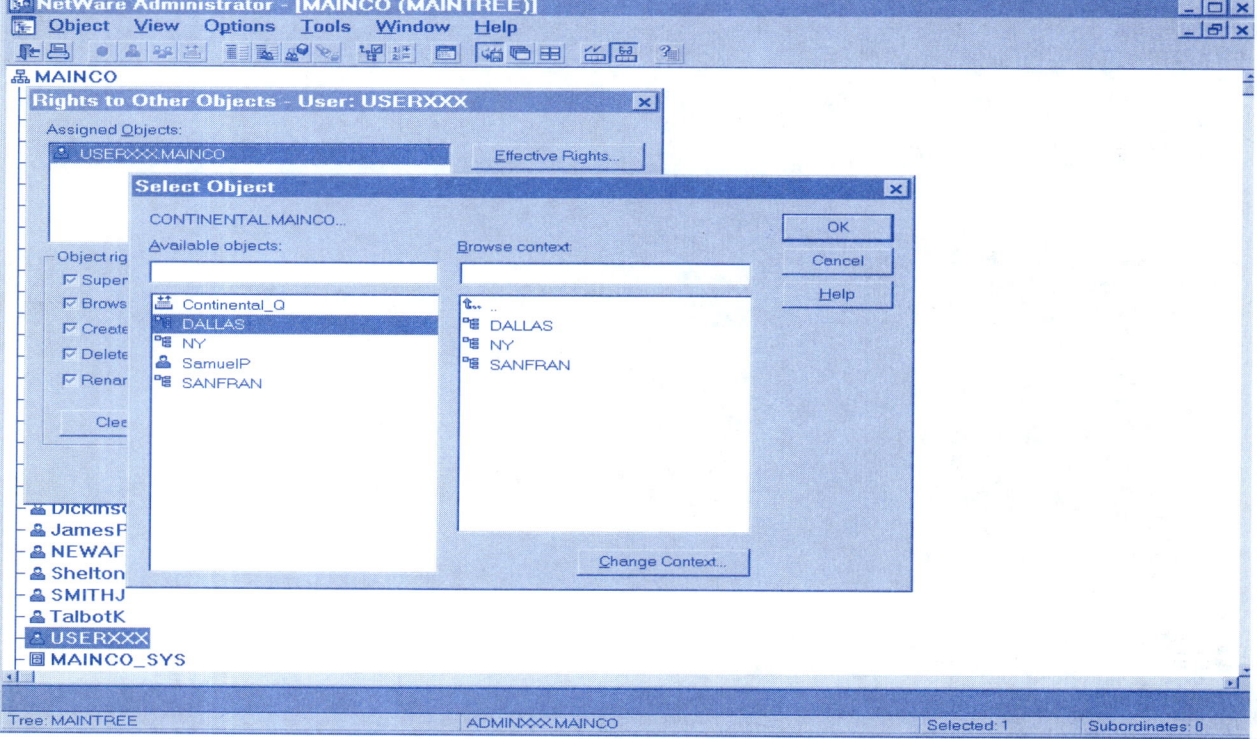

Figure 7-10. Available objects to which rights can be granted.

NDS Security

8. Click the **Add Assignments button** to obtain the screen shown in Figure 7-9.

9. Navigate on the right until the container DALLAS is available as an object to be chosen in the left box. (Double-click **the CONTINENTAL Organizational Unit** to expose the DALLAS container.)

10. Click **the Dallas container** in the Available Objects Box and then click the **OK button** as shown in Figure 7-10.

11. Note that by default USERXXX obtains the Browse Object Right and the Read and Compare property rights to All Properties of the Dallas container object as shown in Figure 7-11.

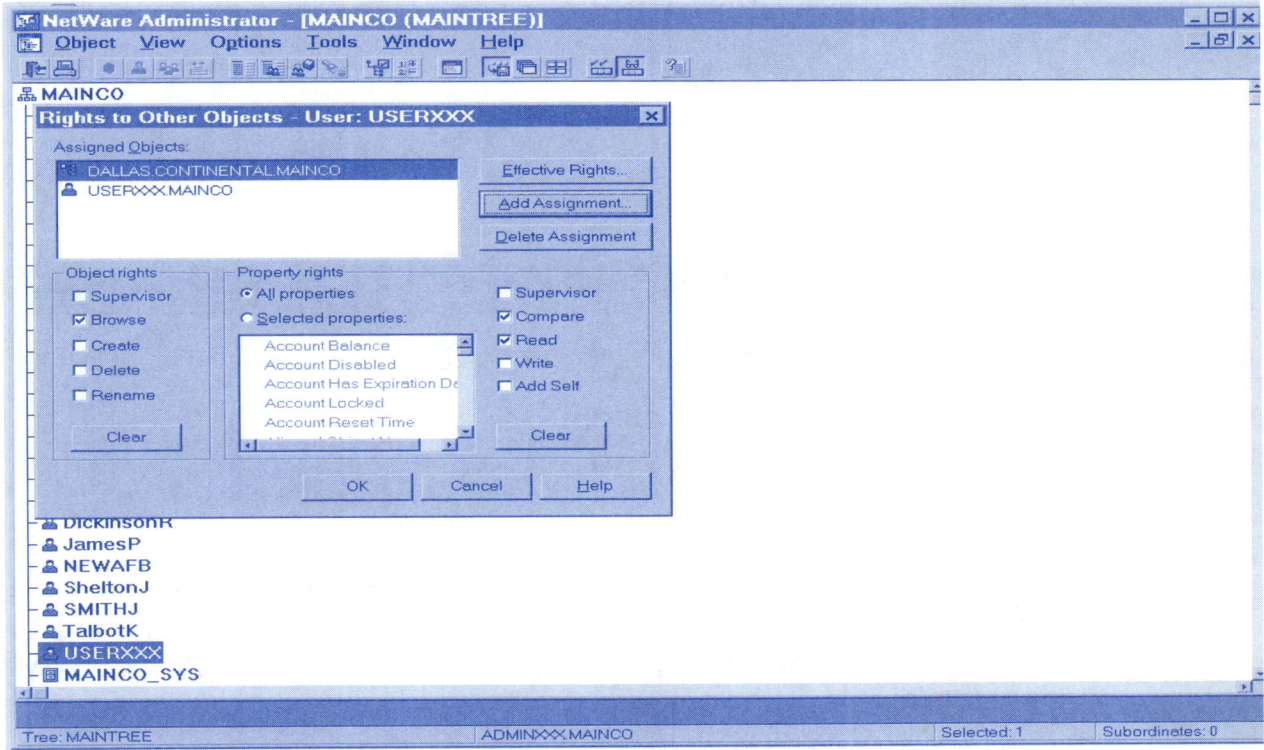

Figure 7-11. Default object rights for Dallas container for USERXXX.

12. Click **the box next to the Create, Delete, and Rename object rights** as shown in Figure 7-12, and then click the **OK button**.

Exercising the NDS Rights Assigned

Log in as USERXXX and create a user object called PETERXXX in the Dallas container to prove that USERXXX has the Create right to the DALLAS container.

Chapter 7

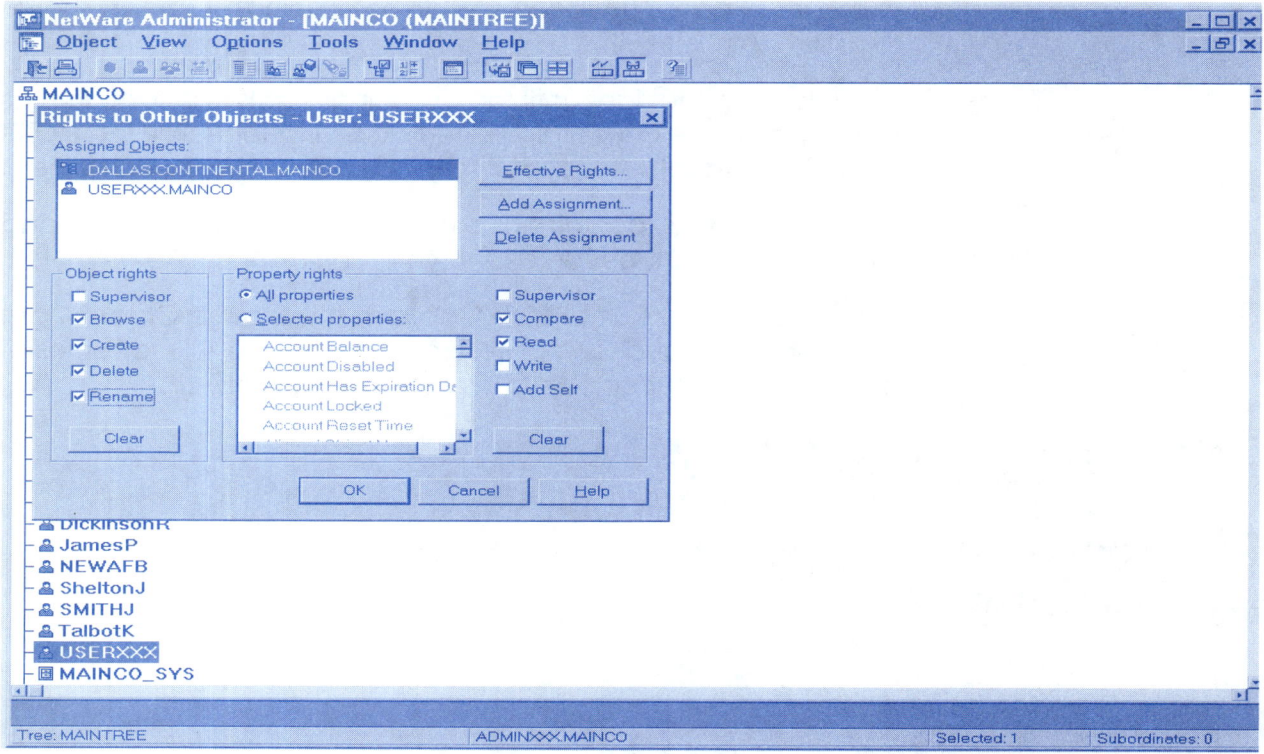

Figure 7-12. Assigning Object Rights of (BCDR) for the DALLAS container to USERXXX.

Now that your USERXXX is created,

1. Log in as **USERXXX**.

2. Activate **NetWare Administrator**.

What happened? USERXXX was unable to access the NetWare Administrator program because he didn't have file system rights on MAINCO\SYS:. This underlines the separation between NDS and file system rights.

Giving USERXXX File System Rights

Log in as ADMINXXX and give USERXXX file system rights to MAINCO\SYS: of (RWCEMF) as follows:

1. Log in as **ADMINXXX.**

2. Activate **NetWare Administrator**.

3. Locate **the USERXXX** and double-click it to display the details about USERXXX.

4. Click the **Rights to Files and Directories button** to display the Rights to Files and Directories page.

NDS Security

5. For good measure, display existing file system rights on MAIN-CO_SYS first by clicking the **Show button**, then clicking **the MAIN-CO_SYS object**, and then clicking the **OK button**. Click the **Files and Directory assignment** shown. The file system rights already assigned to USERXXX are only to his home directory as shown in Figure 7-13.

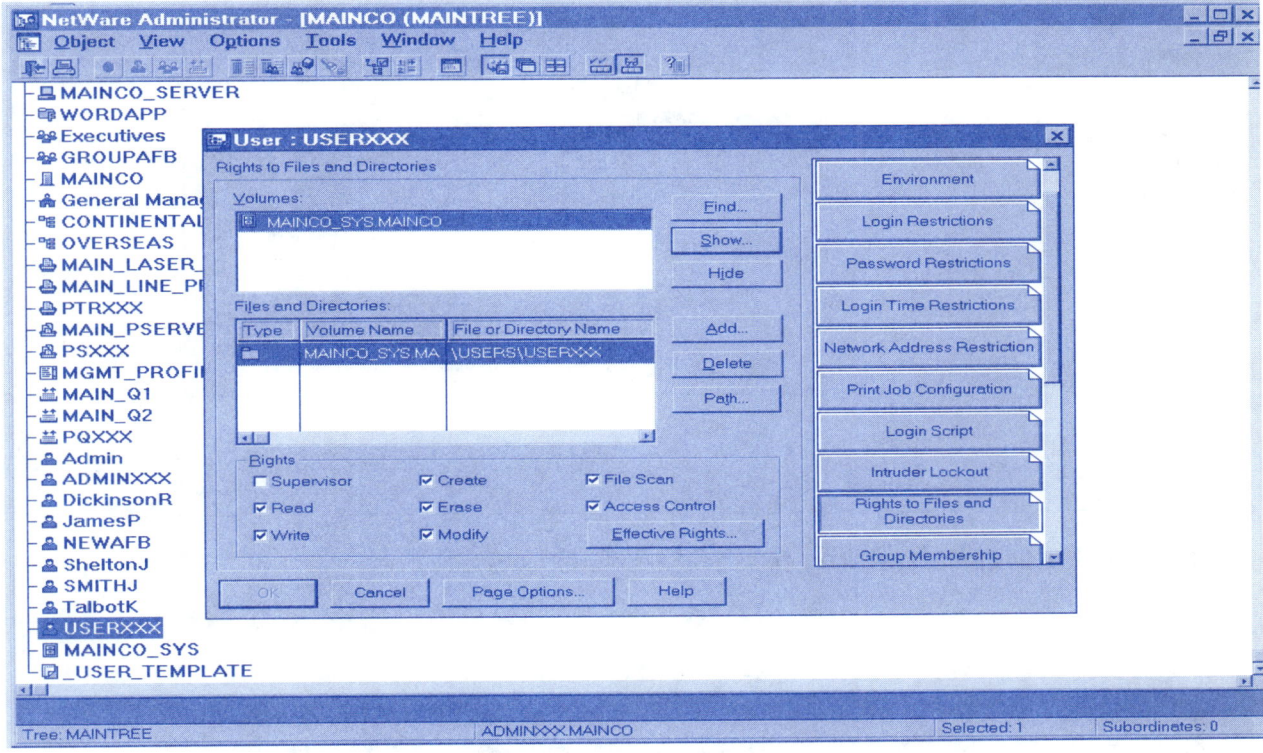

Figure 7-13. Rights granted to files and directories.

6. Click the **Add button** to add file system rights. Select **MAIN-CO_SYS** and click the **OK button** to add rights to the entire volume as shown in Figure 7-14. Note that we might not want the rights at the root of the SYS volume if this were a live system.

7. Note that USERXXX by default receives only the Read and File Scan file system rights as shown in Figure 7-15. Click **the boxes by Write, Create, Erase, and Modify,** and then click the **OK button**.

Reattempt the Hands-On Activity: Exercising NDS Object Rights Assigned

1. Log in as **USERXXX**.

2. Activate **NetWare Administrator**.

Chapter 7

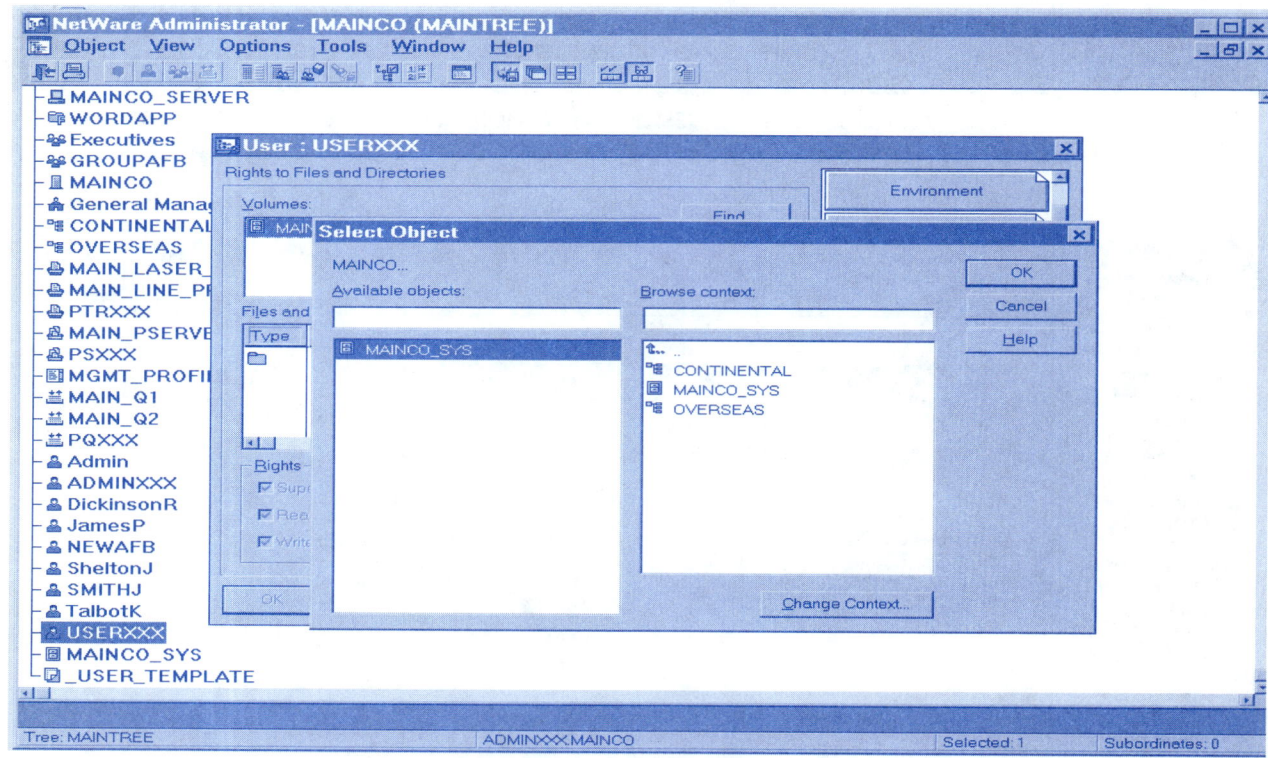

Figure 7-14. Adding file system rights to MAINCO_SYS volume.

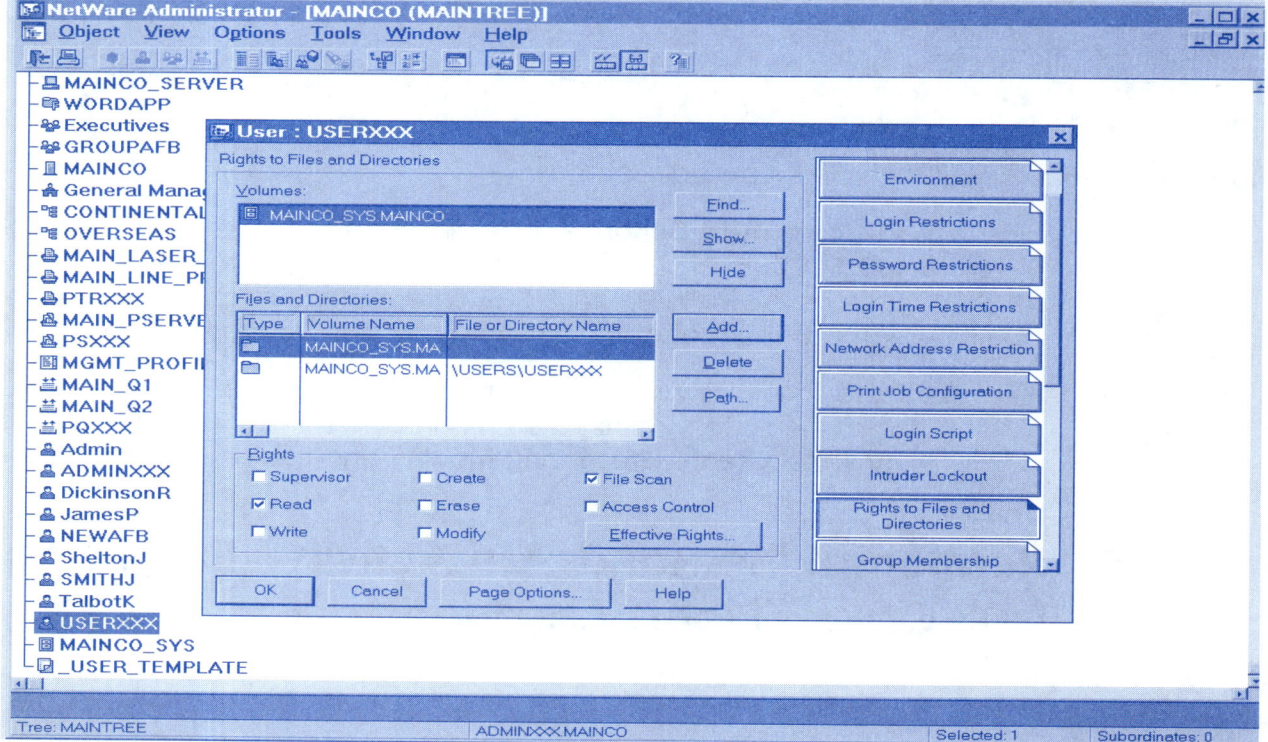

Figure 7-15. Default file system rights for trustee USERXXX.

NDS Security

The process has again failed. Do you have any idea why it has failed? (Hint: Examine the shortcut or the program item for NetWare Administrator, and then examine the Login script for USERXXX. If you completed the login script exercise, USERXXX has a MAP ROOT drive to SYS:\USERS\USERXXX. Therefore, he cannot use the H: drive mapping to get to NetWare Administrator.)

Change the USERXXX login script to MAP ROOT J: to the user's home directory.

1. Log in as **ADMINXXX**.

2. Activate **NetWare Administrator.**

3. Double-click on **USERXXX**.

4. Click on the **Login Script button** to display the current login script.

5. Change the H: drive mapping to a J: drive mapping and click the **OK button.**

6. Close **NetWare Administrator**.

7. Log in as **USERXXX**.

8. Activate **NetWare Administrator**.

9. Double-click **the CONTINENTAL container** to expose the DALLAS container.

10. Right-click **the Dallas container** and select **Create** as shown in Figure 7-16.

11. Create a user called **PETERXXX** with a home directory under SYS:\USERS called PETERXXX. Refer to the details about creating a user in Chapter 11 if you don't remember how to create the home directory. Your screen should look like Figure 7-17 before you click the Create button.

12. Double-click **the DALLAS container** to expose PETERXXX.

13. Right click on **PETERXXX** and select Trustees of this object.

14. Click on the **USERXXX.MAINCO** user, the user you used to create PETERXXX. Notice that USERXXX has the Supervisor right to PETERXXX as shown in Figure 7-18 because USERXXX created PETERXXX.

15. Click **the (PUBLIC)** object and notice that all rights are dimmed.

Chapter 7

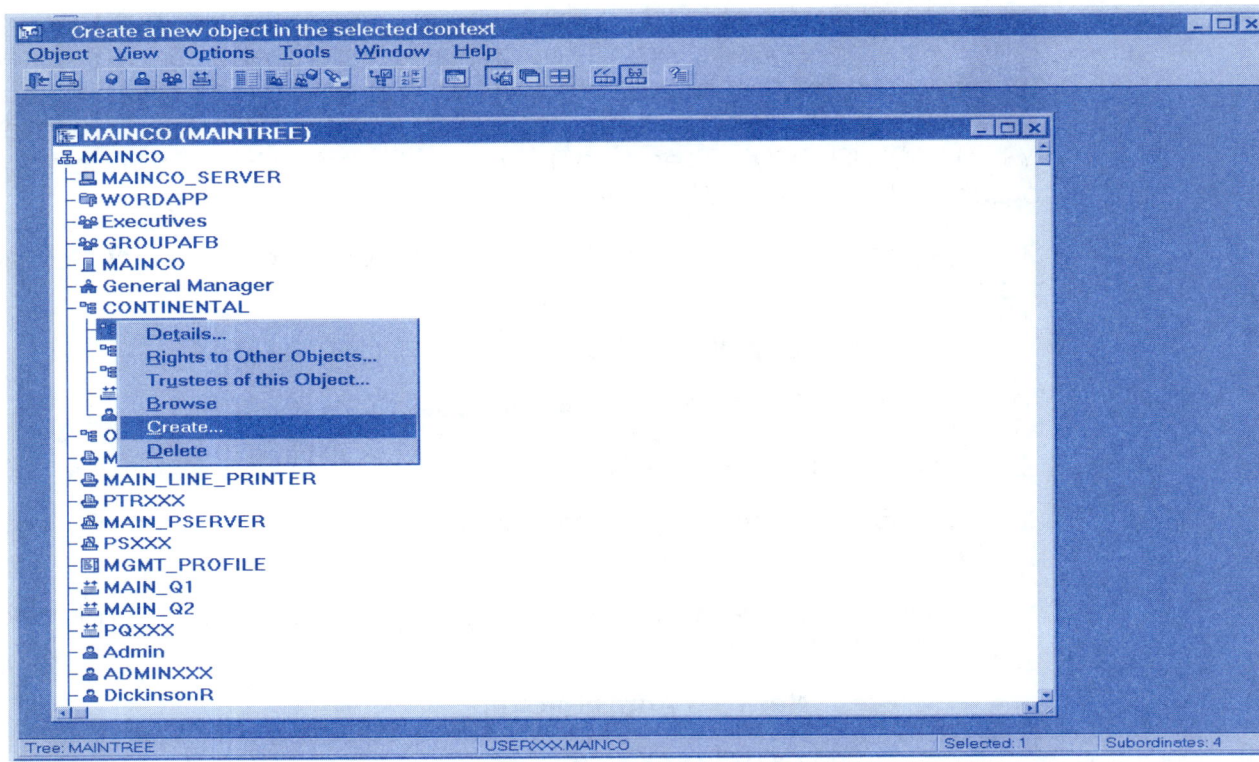

Figure 7-16. Creating an object under the DALLAS container.

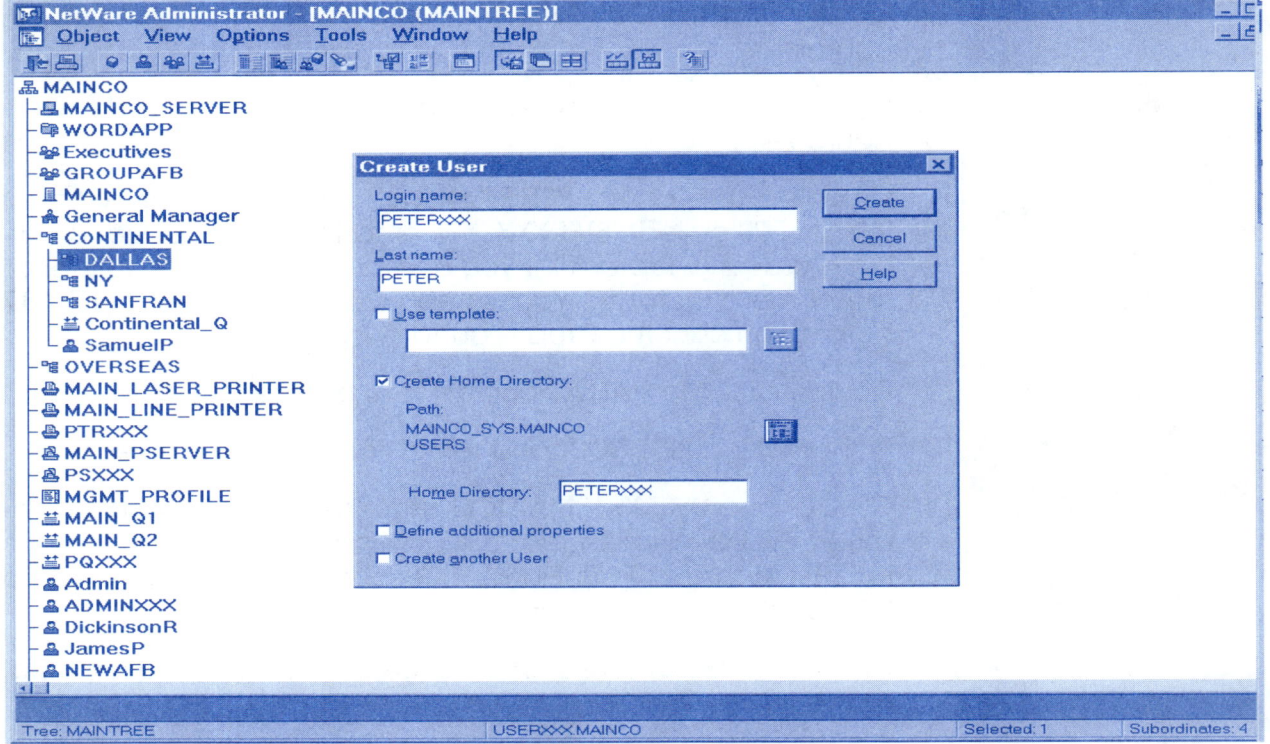

Figure 7-17. Creating user PETERXXX.

NDS Security

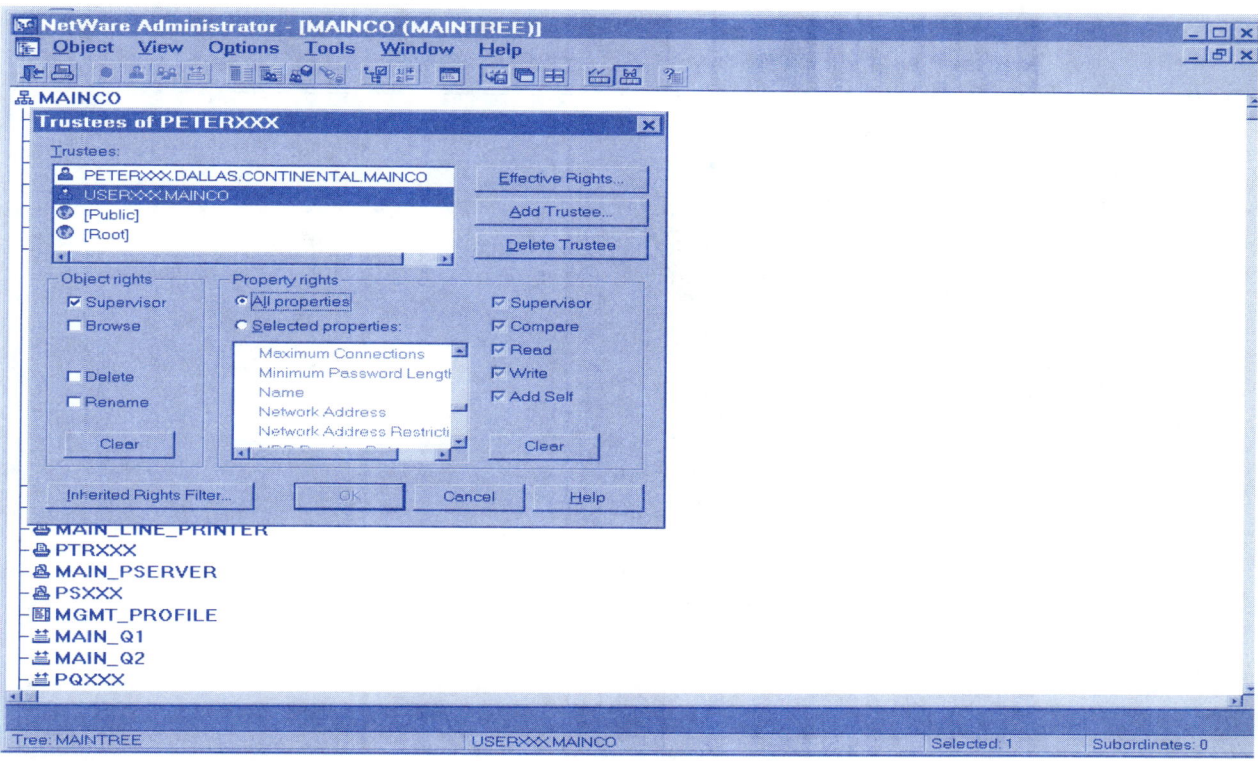

Figure 7-18. USERXXX, the creator, has Supervisor object right to PETERXXX.

16. Click the **Selected Properties button** under Property Rights and then use the up and down arrows to determine what selected properties are assigned to (PUBLIC). Notice that the Default Server property is checked. Click on this property to determine the rights that (PUBLIC) has. This means that all users can read the default server assigned to PETERXXX.

17. Check out the same information for (ROOT). Note that (ROOT) has Read rights to the Network Address property.

18. Do not log out. Continue with the next exercise.

Setting an Inherited Rights Filter and Determining Its Effect

1. Continuing on from the previous exercise, click **the Inherited Rights Filter button** for PETERXXX to display Figure 7-19.

2. Deselect **the Supervisor, Delete, and Rename rights by clicking in the box** to the left of each right. Then click the **OK button**.

3. Close **Netware Administrator**.

4. Log in as your **ADMINXXX** object.

5. Activate **NetWare Administrator**.

Chapter 7

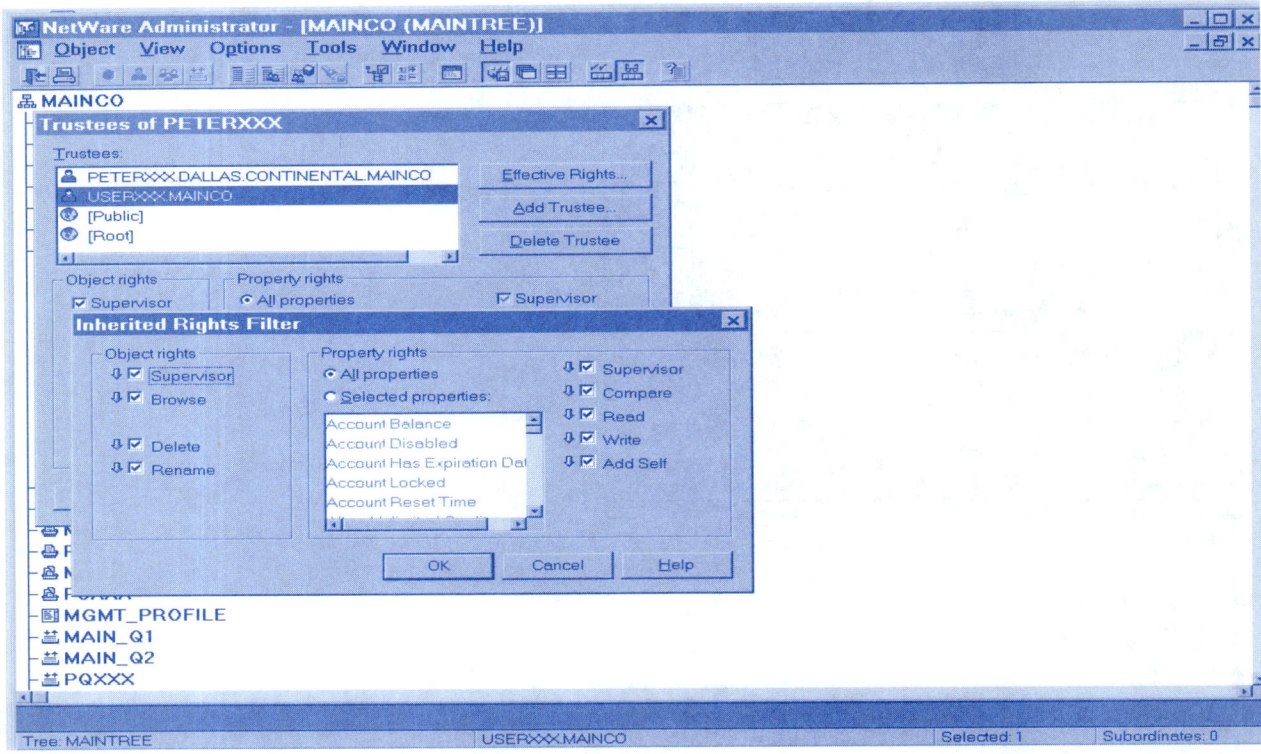

Figure 7-19. Inherited Rights Filter for PETERXXX.

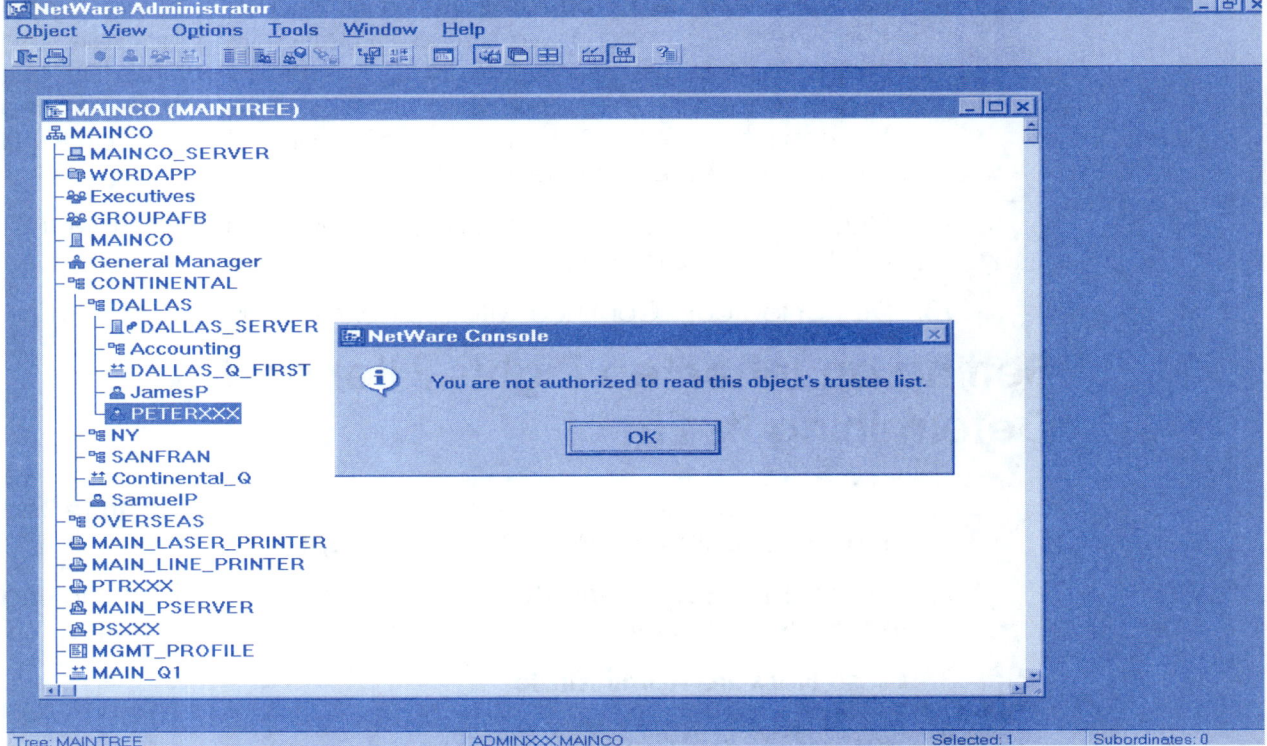

Figure 7-20. Access failure message.

NDS Security

6. Double-click **the CONTINENTAL container** and then double-click **the DALLAS container** to expose PETERXXX.

7. Right-click on **PETERXXX**. A screen like Figure 7-20 is displayed. Why can't ADMINXXX access PETERXXX's object trustee list? ADMINXXX cannot read PETERXXX's object trustee list because the inherited rights filter you set blocked ADMINXXX's Supervisor Object Right from the above containers.

Summary

NetWare 4 provides an additional level of security through NDS Object and Property Rights. NDS Object rights determine what a given object can do with other objects while Property rights determine what a given object can do with the properties of another object. NDS Object and Property Rights granted through the All Properties option are inherited by lower containers in the tree. An explicit trustee assignment overrides inherited rights for both objects and properties.

A user can obtain object and property rights in six ways:

> The user account.
>
> The group(s) to which the user belongs,
>
> The container(s) to which the user belongs,
>
> The organizational roles that the user occupies,
>
> The users to which this user is security equivalent,
>
> The special object (PUBLIC) that supplies rights to all users connected to a file server in a NetWare 4.11 network whether or not the user is logged in.

Inherited Rights Filters exist for both NDS Object rights and NDS Property rights. The IRFs limit rights that can be inherited for an object. A user's effective rights are determined by calculating all six ways that a user can obtain rights, limiting those rights by the appropriate IRFs, and then adding the effective rights together.

Questions

1. What do NDS Object rights control?

2. What are the NDS Object rights, and what is the meaning of each right?

3. What do Property Rights govern?

4. What are the NDS Property Rights and what is the meaning of each right?

5. What is the difference between rights granted using the All Properties option and rights granted using the Selected Properties option?

6. What is an Inherited Rights Filter? How is it used?

7. What are effective rights?

8. In what ways can a given user obtain NDS object and property rights?

9. Can rights granted to selected properties be inherited?

10. Can rights granted to selected properties override rights granted using the All Properties option?

11. What is the problem with giving all users the Supervisor object right to the server? What can they do with the server object, and what rights do they have to the file system on the server?

12. What NDS object and property rights does a user receive for objects he or she created?

13. What is the ACL property? Why is it important?

14. What can a user do with the Add Self property right to all properties?

15. (True/False) The Supervisor NDS Object Right cannot be blocked.

16. What can happen if the Supervisor right is removed from the IRF for a container object?

17. (True/False) NDS object rights control file system rights.

18. Why does special care need to be taken when assigning object and file rights to the (PUBLIC) object?

Projects

Objective

The following projects provide reinforcement for NDS Object and Property Right principles discussed in this chapter.

Project 1:

Using the NDS tree structure for the class and paper and pencil, determine the effective NDS Object rights for your user USERXXX, assuming the following:

    a. USERXXX has an explicit NDS trustee assignment to the OVERSEAS container granting him (SBCDR) rights, and there is an IRF of (BCDR) at the FRANKFURT container. What are USERXXX's effective rights to the FRANKFURT container? Can USERXXX create an Organizational Unit under FRANKFURT called CARS? If so, what object rights would USERXXX have to the CARS container?

    b. Consider that USERXXX is also a member of a group called MAINGROUP which has (B) rights to the MAINCO container. What are USERXXX's effective rights in the MAINCO container, the OVERSEAS Container, and the FRANKFURT container assuming that the rights specified in Project 1-a. are also still in effect?

    c. Discarding all rights granted above, what are USERXXX's effective rights at each container in the tree assuming that USERXXX has the (BC) rights to MAINCO; USERXXX belongs to a group that has the (BCR) rights to the LONDON container; USERXXX is in an organizational role called Managers in the MAINCO container which has the (S) right to the CONTINENTAL container; and the following IRFs exist:

CONTINENTAL	(BCDR)
FRANKFURT	(S)
LONDON	(BC R)
DALLAS	(B)

Project 2:

Repeat each of the exercises in Project 1 on the system, examining the effective rights at each container indicated.

8
Backing Up NetWare 4.11

Objectives

After completing this chapter, the student will

1. Understand the importance of regular backups.

2. Be able to explain common backup methodologies and be able to select the appropriate backup methodology for a given case study company.

3. Understand the components of the SBACKUP backup utility for NetWare 4.11.

4. Understand practical considerations for restoring a server after failure.

Key Terms

Backup

Full Backup

Incremental Backup

Differential Backup

SBACKUP

Introduction

Making regular backups is probably the most important but least glamorous job that befalls a network administrator. It is a thankless job but a very necessary job that must be accomplished and documented on a regular basis so that the server(s) can be restored in the event of failure.

This chapter will explore the reasons for regular backups and will explore several methodologies for backups. It will also give the student the opportunity to design an effective backup strategy for a given business scenario. Finally, it will examine the built-in backup utility for

NetWare 4.11 as an example of a backup system that a network administrator might use for backing up a NetWare 4.11 system. Since many classrooms do not have tape equipment available and since the SBACKUP utility itself is not commonly used, an actual backup will not be performed.

Why Take the Time to Perform Backups?

There are really only two reasons for performing **backups**:

Hardware and software failure

Human error

With that said, it is apparent that neither of these reasons for backup can be successfully eliminated; therefore, regular backups must be performed so that a company can survive hardware and software failures and can recover from human error.

Regardless of the type of hardware utilized in a system, hardware can and does fail or malfunction. Hard drives fail; memory chips fail; other hardware components fail. Software, especially system software, is highly tested before it is released, but even well-tested software programs can have bugs that can adversely affect the data stored on a file server. Although systems may have other, more easily used, methods for data recovery, regular backups are the standard method of recovery from hardware and software failure.

Humans sometimes make mistakes. A user may inadvertently save a new file on top of an older, but still needed, file. A backup of the system gives the network administrator the ability to recover the user's previous file. A user may inadvertently erase a file, and this erasure may not be detected for some time. A consistent backup plan and methodology for archiving backup media can assist in restoring erased files.

Backups are commonly made to tape media although other media such as optical disks are gaining popularity.

Common Backup Methodologies

The most common backup methodologies usually involve doing daily backups. They are:

- **Full Backup:** This method involve making a full system backup of each server, including files, directories, and NDS, on a daily basis. The Archive flag for each file and directory backed up on a full backup is reset.

- **Incremental Backup:** This method involve making a full system backup on the first day of the week and then making a backup daily of only those files, directories, and NDS items that have changed since the last backup, whether incremental or full. Each incremental and each full backup resets the Archive flags for the files backed up.

- **Differential Backup:** This method involve making a full backup on the first day of the week and then backing up all the files, directories, and NDS items that have changed since that backup each day until the next full backup is made. This type of backup does not reset the Archive flag for any file. Only the full backup resets the Archive flag.

Regardless of the method chosen, the backup needs to be set so that it occurs automatically, in an unattended fashion. Historically, a backup that requires human intervention, either to set up the backup or to change tapes during the backup translates to a backup that does not get done on an on-going basis.

Ideally, as long as there is enough time available for a backup to be performed and for the backup to be verified during off-hours for the system, full backups should be performed on a daily basis, and tapes should be retained for a significant period of time. This method provides the best options for recovery should a given backup tape fail. Obviously, in the event of a failure, the latest backup tape would be the preferred restore medium, but if there is a problem with this medium, yesterday's full backup would be available. If there were a problem with yesterday's full backup tape, the previous day's full backup would be available, and so on.

Unfortunately, there may come a time for a business when it is no longer possible to complete a full backup on a daily basis. In this situation, a full backup must still be periodically created, perhaps during "down" hours over a weekend. Then, either incremental or differential backups can be performed during the week.

The trade-off between incremental and differential backups is that incremental backups require less time to create because they include only those files and directories that have changed since the previous day's full or incremental backup, while a differential requires a longer time to create each day. However, in the event of a failure, restoring a system with an incremental backup approach depends on restoring more tapes than the differential approach would require.

	Full Backup	Incremental Backup	Differential Backup
Time to Back Up Daily	Most	Least	Grows daily, medium
Time to Restore	Least	Most	Medium
Archive Bit	Reset	Reset	Not Reset

Figure 8-1. Main characteristics of Full, Incremental, and Differential backups.

Figure 8-1 shows the various characteristics of the three main backup methodologies for an 8 a.m. to 5 p.m., five days per week business that makes its full backup tape on Friday.

Notice that the tradeoff essentially becomes time spent daily versus time and number of tapes that must be used to restore a system.

Now, consider a seven days per week/twenty-four hours per day operation. For a business of this sort, special considerations must be made. Perhaps the system must be made totally unavailable for a period until a full backup can be created on a less than daily basis. Another approach would be to have fault tolerant servers such that a given server is really two servers that are updated simultaneously. Then, on a periodic basis, the link between the servers could be severed with one server continuing to service the company's needs and the other server being backed up. In any event, regular backups must be made.

The Backup Tape Archival Approach

Ideally, for a five days per week operation that can still make full backups, the following is a backup approach that will provide significant fault tolerance. It provides a large number of alternatives for restoration in the event that a given tape cannot be restored due to media malfunction or if something like a natural disaster destroys the servers and the computer room in which these servers are kept.

The process essentially requires 25 backup tapes to be used for daily backup, 5 tapes to be taken off-site for weekly backups in a secure, separate area, and 12 tapes per year that must be taken off-site and retained for a long period or perhaps forever, depending on the type of business the network is supporting.

There are 25 tapes utilized for backing up on a daily basis, perhaps numbered Daily W-D where W is the week number, 1-5, and D is the day number, 1-5. Tape Daily1-1 would be used for the backup on the first day of the first week, Daily 1-2 would be used for the backup of the second day of the first week, and so on.

Then, on a given day during each week, the daily tape would be exchanged with the previous weekly tape (from off-site), thus meaning that one tape per week is taken off-site for extra backup security.

At the end of a month's processing, perhaps the last day of the month or perhaps the day just before the month's accounting close, the daily tape is taken off-site for permanent retention, and a new tape is placed into the rotation.

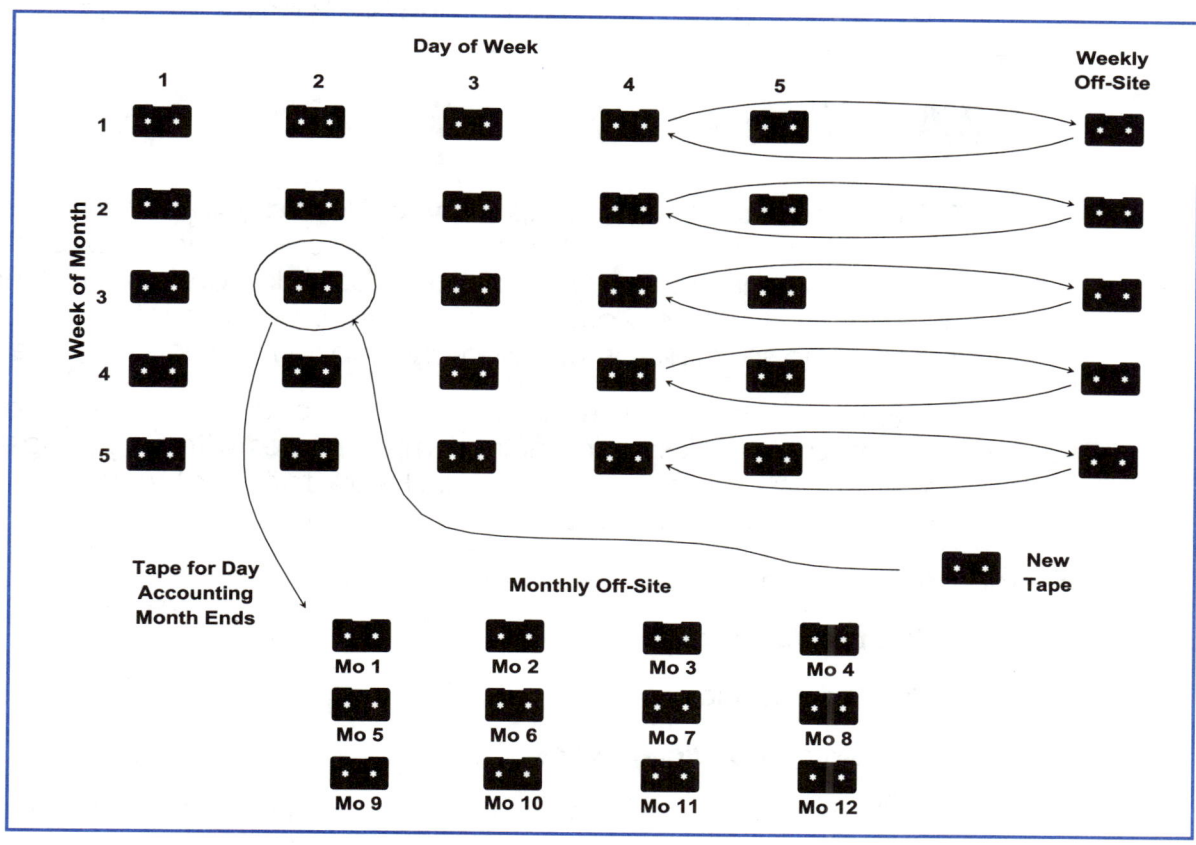

Figure 8-2. A comprehensive backup method.

Figure 8-2 depicts this tape backup method.

The advantage of the above approach is that it provides maximum fallback positions should a single backup tape fail or should the computer site be totally destroyed.

For example, let's say that the backup tape is taken off-site after the fourth day of the week and let's say that a disaster happened during the fourth day of the second week. This disaster occurs before the weekly backup tape was made. The network administrator would first attempt to restore from the backup tape labeled Daily 2-3. If there were some problem with this tape, the Daily 2-2 could be used. If there were some problem with this tape, the Daily 2-1 could be used, and so on. If a total disaster were to occur, the weekly tape from the fourth day of the previous week is kept off-site, and the network administrator would attempt to use it. If that weekly backup tape were bad, the previous week's backup tape could be used, and so on.

Also, let's say that a user uses a specific spreadsheet only once per year and at the end of the year, and let's say that he inadvertently erases the spreadsheet only a month into the new year. The daily and weekly backup tapes containing the file in questions would long ago have been erased, but the off-site monthly tapes would provide a vehicle for restoring the required file.

SBACKUP

SBACKUP is Novell's built-in backup utility for NetWare 4.11. It is a representative backup utility to examine, but because it has few of the simple to use desirable features of good backup software, it is not widely used. Most live network installations utilize backup software from thirdparties who specialize in creating and supporting such software.

SBACKUP, as a representative software package, utilizes host software that runs on a host file server which communicates with target agent software running on other file servers and workstations of various types so that files servers and workstations alike can be backed up.

The Host software is composed of three parts:

> **The backup engine**
>
> **The Data Requester**
>
> **The Storage Device Driver.**

Each of these functions is accomplished through NLMs running on the NetWare 4 file server.

The Target Agent software takes the form of an NLM when running on a target file server or a TSR (Terminate and Stay Resident) program when running on a target workstation. The Target software for SBACKUP is available to back up other NetWare 3.1x and 4 servers and NDS, as well as DOS, Windows 95, OS/2, and Macintosh workstations.

SBACKUP is initiated from the NetWare 4 file server. The network administrator can then select the targets to be backed up. Once the backup has been accomplished, the tape must be recorded and taken off-site as needed.

Practical Considerations for Backups and Restores

Backups must be made so that restores can be done when needed. The method of backup must fit the business hours of operation and the business needs. In general, performing full backups is the safest approach to take although the time available sometimes does not permit this approach. Regardless of the approach taken, though, several things can be done to ensure accuracy of the backup and availability of the backup media when it is needed.

Backup Responsibility

One of the most important people in a business is the person who is responsible for performing and documenting the backup. This person does not necessarily need to be the network administrator, but the person must first and foremost be responsible and meticulous about detail. The backup should be set up by the network administrator such that it initiates automatically on a daily basis; therefore, the person who performs the backup should need only to ensure that the backups actually get made and document which tape contains which backup data. To determine whether or not the backup was successful, the daily backup person must be taught to examine the verification logs for error messages and to notify the network administrator if error messages do occur. Further, the backup person must meticulously document the tape library and must be responsible for seeing that those tapes that should be stored off-site actually do get taken off-site for storage.

How to Determine Whether or Not a Backup Is Good

Every time a backup is made, a verify operation should be performed. This operation compares what is on the tape to what is actually still on the hard disk of the server. As accurate as most verification software is, it is possible that the verify program could malfunction and report that a tape is good when it is not.

The best way to help ensure that backup tapes are actually good is to perform a sample restore on a periodic basis, perhaps monthly, whereby a file in the middle of the tape is actually restored to the file server and examined for accuracy. This extra effort can prove invaluable should a backup tape actually be needed for restoration.

What to Back Up

While it is desirable and easy to back up everything every day, it might be impossible to do given business hours of operation and other needs. It is sometimes, possible, though, to perform a full backup of those volumes of the server that are likely to change on a daily basis and avoid the possible downside of performing incremental backups by segregating programs and data on different volumes of the server. For example, the SYS: volume could be reserved for only NetWare system-specific programs and files. This volume could perhaps be fully backed up only once per week or even less often. Another volume could be reserved for just software programs that do not change frequently. This volume, too, could be fully backed up perhaps once per week or less often. Data, then, could be placed on other volumes, and could perhaps be fully backed up daily. This would be a nice compromise that would take maximum advantage of the time available for backup.

Summary

System backups must be performed to ensure recovery in the event of hardware or software failure and to recover from human error. There are three common methodologies for backups: Full, Incremental, and Differential.

The full backup method requires that NDS and every file be backed up on each server daily. This method provide the most fall-back positions in the event of tape media failure, and it required the fewest tapes and therefore the least amount of time to recover from failure.

The incremental backup method requires that a full backup be performed on a set day of the week. Then, each day after that, only those files that have changed since the last full or incremental backup are backed up. This method requires the least amount of time daily to perform the backup, but it requires the most time to restore and provides little fall-back in the event of tape media failure.

The differential backup method also requires that a full backup be made on a set day of the week. Then, each day thereafter, the differential backup includes those files that have changed since the last full backup. The amount of time needed for daily backup grows daily until the next full backup tape is made, but the time to restore falls between the full and the incremental backup, and this method provides several fall-back tapes that can be used should there be a problem with the media on a given differential backup tape.

SBACKUP, as a representative of backup software, functions via host software that runs on the NetWare 4 server, which communicates with Target software that runs on other NetWare 4 servers and workstations.

Questions

1. Explain the advantages and disadvantages of adopting the Full backup methodology.

2. Explain the advantages and disadvantages of adopting the Incremental backup methodology.

3. Explain the advantages and disadvantages of adopting the Differential backup methodology.

4. Explain the components of SBACKUP, specifically the host software and the Target Agent software.

5. Why should backups be performed?

6. Why should backups periodically be taken off-site?

Projects

Project 1 Objectives:

Design a backup strategy for each of the following business scenarios. Be sure to pay special attention to how your strategy performs in the following three situations:

1. The file server hard disk fails on the day before the next full backup is to be made, and a backup or backups must be restored.

2. A user erased a file almost a year ago, and she absolutely must have the file restored.

3. The computer room has been flooded, and limited operations must be set up off-site.

Business Scenario 1:

The Jefferson Hospital District is supported by a NetWare 4 network that supports patient records and billing. The hospital is open 7 days per week, 24 hours per day, but patients normally do not check out between 12 midnight and 6 a.m., although some patients, mostly emergency cases, do check in.

Business Scenario 2:

The Scamp Radio Company is a radio manufacturing company that runs two shifts, 7 a.m. to 3 p.m., and 3 p.m. to 11p.m. The business is a six days per week operation supported by a NetWare 4.11 network, and the system must be up during normal hours of operation. A full backup and verify takes 10 hours.

Business Scenario 3:

Midway Community College retains all its student records and accounting functions on a NetWare 4.11 network. Business hours are normally 8:30 a.m. until 8 p.m. M-F, and 8:30 a.m. until 2:00 p.m. on Saturdays. A full backup and verification takes 12 hours.

Project 2 Objectives:

Research and document at least three of the most popular backup software packages and devices. Prepare a written report and a short presentation to the class explaining your findings. Which of the three software and hardware solutions would you choose for each of the three business scenarios detailed above?

9
Troubleshooting Methodology and Tidbits

Objectives

After completing this chapter, the student will

1. Be familiar with a solid troubleshooting model for analyzing and resolving many networking-related problems.

2. Know about several sources available for troubleshooting information.

3. Know when to use NetWare 4.11's volume repair utility, VREPAIR.

4. Be familiar with several troubleshooting tips and techniques.

Key Terms

Troubleshooting Model

NetWire

CompuServe

Novell Support Connection/NSEPro

VREPAIR

Introduction

Running a network requires installing, configuring, and managing the network. These tasks are all proactive tasks that focus on performing a particular task correctly. Running a network also includes troubleshooting because neither the network hardware nor the people using the network or configuring portions of the network are perfect.

A full discussion of network troubleshooting is well beyond the scope of this textbook. In fact, the topic of network troubleshooting is itself at least an entire course. However, this textbook will discuss a solid outline for a troubleshooting model that will keep a network support specialist's troubleshooting activities focused and effective, regardless of the type of problem that is being solved. Additionally, two sources for supplemental information for use in troubleshooting are discussed. These are Novell's NetWire through CompuServe and the Internet and Novell Support Connection (formerly called NSEPro), Novell's Support Encyclopedia. Both are available by subscription. Finally, the textbook examines several Troubleshooting Tidbits, focusing on several common network problems and an approach for their solution. Example problems discussed address the following problem statements:

"The application I want to run won't run."

"I can't print."

"The SYS volume won't mount."

While these problems are in no way comprehensive with respect to the types of network problems a network support specialist can expect to encounter, they do provide a framework for explaining and applying the solid troubleshooting model presented earlier in the chapter.

A Solid Troubleshooting Model

Troubleshooting is by the nature of the word a reaction to trouble. The word carries with it a sense of urgency to solve the reported problem so that normal work can continue. Synonyms for the word trouble include annoyance and adversity. Thus it is easy to understand why the word commonly implies a pressured situation, which can cause the network support specialist to react rather than act and therefore sometimes to forget to follow a solid **troubleshooting model** in solving the problem. Often, failure to follow a solid troubleshooting model can cause the troubleshooting process to be even more difficult and lengthy, usually leading to more pressure and more reactionary behavior, which is counterproductive in general. The purpose of this chapter is to fully explore a framework for logical, methodical troubleshooting which, when followed, helps ensure that a given problem can be resolved as efficiently as possible.

For many years, troubleshooting has been considered almost totally art. This is largely due to the reality that many of those using computers and the networks connecting them have little or no technical expertise and stand in awe of those who do. In fact, though, while troubleshooting does rely to some extent on the creative capabilities of the troubleshooter, successful troubleshooting relies mostly on following a logical troubleshooting model and applying the previous experience of the troubleshooter.

There are many renditions of the following troubleshooting model, but most are very similar, relying on logical problem analysis and methodical examination of possible problem solutions until the problem is solved. The troubleshooting model examined here includes the following steps:

1. Begin to document the problem from its onset.
2. Verify that the problem exists.
3. Gather information about the problem.
4. Formulate possible solutions and prioritize these possibilities.
5. Apply possible "quick fixes" one at a time.
6. Apply other possible solutions, in priority order and one at a time.
7. Resolve and document the problem.

Begin to Document the Problem

From problem report to problem resolution, documentation of the problem and the steps used to resolve the problem must be done. Given that the troubleshooting activity is a pressured one, it would be easy to neglect documentation as an unnecessary activity that slows the troubleshooting process. In fact, though, creating troubleshooting documentation has several advantages.

1. Trouble call documentation helps ensure that the problem is clearly stated and the user is efficiently serviced. A possible trouble call report form is shown in Figure 9-1 at the end of this chapter.

2. It gives order to the troubleshooting process itself, reducing the possibility that the troubleshooter will go in circles, repeatedly trying out the same possible fix because he or she cannot remember whether or not the fix has been tried. As ridiculous as this seems, after several hours of trying to solve the same problem, repeating of steps can easily occur if complete documentation is not created throughout the troubleshooting process. Refer to Figure 9-2 at the end of the chapter for a possible troubleshooting form for the troubleshooter's use.

3. It gives a historical perspective on the particular station or user that might assist in problem resolution. Documentation of a problem and its solution gives the troubleshooter a knowledge base from which to draw for future problem resolution.

Many companies, especially the larger ones, utilize what is often called "Help Desk" software, which supports recording and following up on the trouble call and the knowledge base documentation. In any event, whether software is available or not, some procedures for problem documentation and problem resolution documentation must be developed and followed.

Verify That the Problem Exists

Simply put, users sometimes overreact. Sometimes, there isn't really a problem, and sometimes the problem may be caused by the user himself. Before spending a great deal of time troubleshooting a problem it is a good idea to validate that there truly is a problem beyond user error. At this point, the troubleshooter's customer service skills are very important because he or she must work with the user to determine whether or not the problem is a system problem without insulting or offending the user.

The ideal method of determining whether or not the problem is caused by user error is for the troubleshooter to physically go to the user's station and watch as the user repeats the process he or she says is a problem. Unfortunately, physically witnessing the problem is often not practical, and the process must be handled by talking with the user over the phone or by using management software to take over the user's desktop. Regardless of the method used, the purpose of this step is to have the troubleshooter observe the user repeat whatever he or she was doing in an attempt to recreate the problem. The troubleshooter must be very clear in communicating with the user at this stage so that procedural errors can also be observed and pointed out.

If the reported problem is one that could be caused by equipment not being properly connected or turned on, it would be prudent to ask the user questions similar to the following, depending on the stated problem:

1. Is the network cable securely plugged into the network card in the workstation?

2. Is there anything crimping the network cable?

3. Is the power cord for the computer and/or printer plugged into the wall?

4. Is the printer turned on, and is the online button pressed?

Once the troubleshooter is convinced that there is a problem, then he or she is ready for the next phase.

Gather Information About the Problem

Gathering information about the problem actually begins with the trouble call and proceeds through verification of the problem and throughout the entire troubleshooting event. Once the problem is verified as real, the troubleshooter begins to ask more detailed questions in an attempt to characterize the environment that existed when the problem occurred. Some of the questions that might be asked, depending on the type of problem being reported, are:

- When did the user last do what is now causing trouble? If it the answer is never or several months ago, the problem must be handled differently than it would be if the answer were 30 minutes ago or yesterday. The latter indicates that something has recently been done to the system that possibly caused the problem. The former answer actually gives few clues.

- What else was going on in the system while the user was trying to do the function that caused the trouble? Were any of these simultaneous functions new or recently new?

- Who else was using the network when the problem occurred?

- How heavily was the network used at the time the problem was reported? It may be that there really was no error, just slow response time because of heavy traffic.

- What else can the user tell the troubleshooter? Often, the user has additional information that he must be coaxed to provide. For example, when a computer is beeping and/or keyboard keys create different characters from what they should produce, and when the troubleshooter has not been able to physical verify the problem, the troubleshooter may suspect that liquids have gotten into the keyboard. The user, though, may be unwilling to answer questions about spilling liquids because he is afraid of being blamed for causing the problem.

Once the troubleshooter thinks he or she understands the problem and the circumstances surrounding the problem, it is time to formulate possible solutions.

Formulate and Prioritize Possible Solutions

Equipped with a good understanding of the problem and the circumstances surrounding it, the experienced troubleshooter can often pinpoint several possible educated guesses as to the cause of and the solution to the problem. The less experienced troubleshooter may want to consult other resources such as NetWire or Novell Support Connection, discussed later in the chapter, before formulating a list of possible problem causes and solutions. In either case, the purpose of this step is to determine possible solutions and to prioritize these possible solutions.

Prioritization of possible solutions is based on the length of time a possible solution would take to test and the probability that the possible solution will actually result in a solution. Generally, possible solutions that take small amounts of time are called "quick fixes" and are tested first. Possible solutions requiring a longer time to test are prioritized by the likelihood that a given change will result in resolution of the problem. Throughout this process, it is important to separate the possible solutions into the smallest testable change. Otherwise, changing two or more things simultaneously might mask the correct solution.

Apply Possible "Quick Fixes"

"Quick fixes" are those changes that the troubleshooter reasonably thinks might fix the problem while also taking comparatively little time to check. When a solution is obtained in this manner, the troubleshooter is often considered to be an artist, a genius, or a brain. In reality, the troubleshooter is merely applying his or her experience to achieve a quick problem resolution. Even with "quick fixes," though, only one thing should be changed at a time (and put back in the original state if it did not result in problem resolution), and documentation must be maintained.

Apply Other Possible Solutions

When "quick fixes" have been exhausted without problem resolution, each of the other possible solutions must be tested according to the likelihood that each will remedy the problem. Each possible fix must be tested one at a time, changing only one thing at a time, and putting the system back in its original state after trying each unsuccessful change. During this phase, it is very important to maintain detailed documentation in order to eliminate repetitive work. Further, even for the experienced troubleshooter, it may be necessary to access additional outside resources (such as NetWire and Novell Support Connection or contacts with other networking professionals) to obtain other ideas for problem resolution. Finally, when very complicated

NetWare problems arise, it may be necessary to contact Novell's consulting group for assistance.

Resolve and Document the Problem

Once the troubleshooter believes that he or she has solved the original problem, it is imperative that the user reporting the problem be involved in evaluating the solutions. In general, troubleshooting for proper problem resolution is as much a social science as it is a computer science. The user reporting the problem must be convinced that the reported problem is gone and that other problems have not been introduced before the troubleshooter can say the problem is solved. Once the user is convinced that the problem is solved, it is a good idea to fully document the solution and to get the user to sign off on the problem resolution as shown in Figure 9-3 at the end of this chapter.

Troubleshooting Resources

Depending on the type of problem, there are a variety of resource materials available to assist the troubleshooter in more efficient problem resolution. Several of the key resources for use in a NetWare 4.11 network will be discussed here. These are:

- **Hardware and Software Documentation**
- **NetWire on Novell's Internet Site**
- **Novell Support Connection**
- **Other Troubleshooting Resources**

Hardware and Software Documentation

As simple as it seems, the documentation for the various hardware components and software components of a network can often be scattered and not readily available when problems occur. The prudent network manager will recognize that problems will occur and that it is imperative that the documentation be kept in a safe place. He or she will provide for a locked area to contain all hardware and software documentation. This area might perhaps be a bookcase in a locked room such as the file server room or a locking filing cabinet. The important thing is that all documentation, without fail, is placed in this area originally and is checked out and returned to this area when it is used. Many of the hardware and software manuals themselves have error or troubleshooting sections packed with troubleshooting tips and actual problem resolution steps. Referring to this documentation first can save a great deal of time in the troubleshooting process.

If documentation for a given hardware or software component is not available, the troubleshooter can often obtain information by contacting the manufacturer's Web site. A list of current Web sites is found in the appendix.

NetWire on Novell's Internet Site

Novell's main Internet site can be contacted through www.novell.com. From this point, one can access a wealth of information including technical information documents and files containing patches and fixes. Originally, this information service was called NetWire and was available only through CompuServe Information Services through subscription. But, with the growing emphasis on the Internet, Novell has responded by providing most troubleshooting information on its Web site.

Since the Internet is very flexible, the information available through this means can change rapidly in response to customer need. At present, Novell's Web page provides technical information, product support information, file updates, an area regarding "What's New," Novell Program information, New User Information and Information about Sales and Marketing. Most sections have search capabilities that allow the user to perform keyword searches and filtering so that the most helpful information is displayed.

Novell Support Connection

Novell Support Connection, Novell's Support Encyclopedia, is distributed monthly via a yearly subscription in the form of a CD-ROM. This CD-ROM provides a wealth of technical support information ranging from files with patches and fixes to technical information documents explaining particular problems to online copies of Novell's popular magazine, "AppNotes." Since Novell Support Connection is a monthly publication, it cannot contain the very latest information, but it does provide an extensive search engine for locating documents and files of interest for a particular topic. Each issue of "AppNotes" magazine is a wealth of detailed technical information about the latest software available from Novell. Currently, Novell Support Connection is available at a cost of $495 per year. A subscription to "AppNotes" is available for $99 per year. Of course, all prices are subject to change without notice.

Other Troubleshooting Resources

In addition to the sources mentioned, the wise troubleshooter develops a human web of contacts with whom he or she shares technical issues and answers. This web can be developed as a normal course of business, and it can be accelerated by joining user groups, joining professional organizations, and taking Novell courses at local colleges and universities. In our technological world, the successful troubleshooter must keep strong contacts with other network professionals as well.

Troubleshooting Scenarios

As explained earlier in the chapter, an extensive examination of network troubleshooting is beyond the scope of this textbook. This section will apply the troubleshooting model explained earlier and will outline a successful process for resolving the indicated problem. In some cases, additional outside utilities and tools will also be introduced as appropriate. By examining the problem solving techniques illustrated in these three scenarios, you will begin to develop your own troubleshooting skills.

"The application I want to run won't run."

Sam Kinse calls in a trouble report that he cannot run the company's accounting package, specifically the Accounts Payable Vendor update program. The following is the problem verification and a list of questions, answers, and comments leading to an eventual solution:

Problem Verification:

The troubleshooter calls Sam and asks him to go through logging into the network, calling up the accounting package, and attempting to access the desired program. He determines that Sam can access the accounting system and he can access the Account Payable vendor update program, but Sam cannot save any changes he attempts to make. He gets a message, "Access denied."

Question for Sam:

How long has the problem been occurring?

Sam's Response:

I don't know - I can't run the program today.

Question for Sam:

Have you ever been able to run this program?

Sam's Response:

> I've never tried to run it, but I can run the rest of the Accounts Payable programs.

Commentary:

If Sam has never been able to run the program, perhaps it wasn't set up for him to run. It might be a file system rights issue, but it is too early in the analysis to consider this the prime hypothesis. It is also important to verify that Sam is supposed to have the ability to run this program. Management may not want Sam to run this program. Before modifying the system so that he can run the program, appropriate management must be contacted to determine Sam's needs.

Question for Sam:

> What other programs in the Accounts Payable portion of the accounting package can you run?

Sam's Response:

> I'm able to run all the reports, but in actuality, I've never tried to run any of the update programs.

Commentary:

After verifying that Sam is indeed supposed to be able to update vendors, the most plausible solution appears to be:

Checking to see that Sam has the appropriate file system rights to update the Accounts Payable Vendor file. This will likely require examination of the accounting system's documentation or checking out the file system rights for someone who is already able to run this program.

Problem Resolution:

Sam had only the Read and File Scan file system rights to the directory containing the Vendor file. According to the Accounting system documentation, he also needed the Write, Create, Delete, and Modify rights. Once those rights were granted, Sam could run the program and signed the problem report showing that the problem had been resolved.

"I can't print."

This problem is one of the most common and often one of the most complicated to resolve because of the many things that can cause a user not to be able to print. The following scenario gives one problem resolution sequence for a particular reason that a given user cannot print. Be aware that this problem resolution will certainly not resolve all

Troubleshooting Methodology and Tidbits

printing problems. Also be aware that the user may actually have called in a problem that the network is down because he may equate his being able to print with the network's being "up."

Problem Verification:

Katy Kirce calls to say that she cannot print her month-end reports. The troubleshooter in this case can physically go to Katy's desk to help her because her office is just down the hall. Therefore, many of the questions the troubleshooter would have asked Katy can be answered by observation and will be noted as such.

Question for Katy:

> When could you last print? What printer do you use?

Answer from Katy:

> I last printed just before leaving to go home last night. I haven't tried to print today until just now. I use this printer next to my desk.

Question for Katy:

> Would you please show me the message you receive when you try to print?

Answer from Katy:

> There wasn't an error message. My report just didn't print. I'll be happy, though, to show you how I run the report so that you can see for yourself. (She attempts to run the report again, and no message appears.)

Observations and Commentary:

The printer is online and plugged into both power and to Katy's computer. The troubleshooter has Katy turn the printer on and off and reboot her computer just to make sure there isn't some simple problem, but these actions do not seem to fix the problem.

The troubleshooter develops the following educated guesses as to the cause of the problem, knowing that there is no error message:

1. Katy's printer might be redirected to another printer in the building.

2. There might be a problem with the queue/printer/print server hookup that Katy is using.

3. Maybe NPRINTER isn't loaded as a TSR on the computer that is attached to the printer Katy wants to use because the boot configuration files have been changed.

Chapter 9

4. Maybe the print server isn't running.

All these hypotheses require that the troubleshooter verify the queue or printer to which Katy's print is directed. After examining her login scripts and her machine setup, the troubleshooter determines that Katy is redirected to a queue that is serviced by a printer down the hall because Katy had been working on another application earlier in the day. The troubleshooter and Katy find her output on that printer.

"The SYS volume won't mount."

When bringing up a system or when troubleshooting why users can't log in, the troubleshooter determine that the SYS volume on a server won't mount either automatically as the server is brought up or when the troubleshooter issues the MOUNT SYS command at the console prompt on the server. Often when this happens, the system itself advises the operator to run **VREPAIR**, the volume repair utility. This utility is the first line of defense when a volume will not mount. Before running this utility, explained below, the troubleshooter should verify the circumstances surrounding why the volume will not mount. Was there a power failure? Do other volumes mount? Did the SYS volume run out of space because of a large print job, etc.? If the answers are "yes," then running VREPAIR can be a reasonable "quick fix." This option will be examined through the following Hands-On exercise.

Hands-On with NetWare

To simulate the problem indicated, go to the console of the file server and do the following:

1. Dismount the SYS volume by entering:

   DISMOUNT SYS

2. Wait for the file server prompt to reappear.

3. Enter

   LOAD C:\NWSERVER\VREPAIR

4. Note that the VREPAIR NLM must be loaded from the C: drive directory because the SYS volume is dismounted. Fortunately, this utility was copied to the NWSERVER directory when the server was installed.

5. Select Set VREPAIR options and select Repair a Volume. A list of volumes to choose from will appear only if more than one volume is dismounted. In this case, you should not be asked to select a volume because SYS should be the only dismounted volume.

Troubleshooting Methodology and Tidbits

6. Change the current error settings so that the screen does not pause after each error and then choose the option to execute the repair. Wait for the utility to finish and then exit the utility.

7. Run VREPAIR one more time, and then mount the SYS volume.

The problem is usually resolved at this point, but care should be taken to make sure that the server is on a uninterruptible power source so that a power interruption will not cause the problem again and that there is plenty of free space on the SYS volume. When the SYS volume runs out of space, the various tables are corrupted so that the SYS volume cannot mount.

Summary

Troubleshooting activities, while part art, must follow a solid troubleshooting model. This chapter examined the troubleshooting model that consists of the following steps:

Begin to document the problem

Verify that the problem exists

Gather information about the problem

Formulate possible solutions and prioritize these possibilities

Apply possible "quick fixes," one at a time

Apply other possible solutions one at a time

Resolve and document the problem

Special emphasis must be placed on documenting the problem both to eliminate redundant efforts troubleshooting a specific problem and to provide a historical reference for the future.

In addition to the troubleshooter's previous knowledge, several other resources for troubleshooting were examined. These include the hardware and software manuals that came with the system, the Web sites for the hardware and software for the system, NetWire through Novell's Web pages, Novell Support Connection, and the human network of other networking professionals. These resources are ready sources for additional information should the troubleshooter not be able to readily resolve the problem.

Finally, the chapter examined three troubleshooting scenarios as examples of troubleshooting techniques that led to problem resolution.

Questions:

1. Why is documentation required before, during, and after the troubleshooting process?
2. What is a "quick fix"?
3. Why are the hardware and software manuals for the components of the system needed?
4. What types of information are available on Novell's Web page?
5. What is Novell Support Connection?
6. What is "AppNotes"?
7. What is VREPAIR and when is its use indicated? Where must VREPAIR be loaded from?
8. Do you think that troubleshooting is part art and part science? Why or why not? Where does the troubleshooter's experience enter in?
9. Why was it stated that troubleshooting is part social science? Give a troubleshooting scenario where social skills might be very important.
10. How do you verify that a problem is solved?

Projects

Objectives:

The purpose of these projects is to familiarize the student with various resources available for troubleshooting. Project I depends on making hardware and software manuals for the system available to the students for perusal. Project II requires the use of the Internet.

Project I

Locate the hardware and software manuals for the classroom system. Examine each manual and summarize the types of troubleshooting information that is available.

Project II

Access Novell's Web pages (www.novell.com) and do the following:

1. Locate and document how to obtain the latest patches and fixes for NetWare 4.

2. Locate and document information on Novell's Beta program.

3. Locate and document information on the next version of NetWare.

Chapter 9

User Name/Extension:	Trouble Report Number:	Report Date:
	Person Taking Report:	Report Time:
Assigned to:	Date:	Time:
Problem resolution:		Resolution Date:
		Resolution Time:
User Signature indicating problem is resolved:		
Problem Description:		
When Was Problem First Noticed?		
Other information about the problem:		
User estimate of criticality of the problem		
Intake person's estimate of criticality of the problem:		

Figure 9-1. Trouble Report form.

User Name/Extension:	Trouble Report Number:	Report Date:
	Person Taking Report:	Report Time:
Assigned to:	Date:	Time:

Questions Asked/Answers Given to Verify Problem Existence:

Likelihood of Solution	Possible Solution	Results:

Figure 9-2. Troubleshooting Documentation form1.

Chapter 9

User Name/Extension: Sam Kinse	Trouble Report Number: A209	Report Date: 10/26
	Person Taking Report: JRB	Report Time: 9:30 am
Assigned to: KRC	Date: 10/26	Time: 10:00 am
Problem resolution: Gave Sam Write, Create, Erase, and Modify File System rights to the SYS:\ACCTG\AP\DATA directory on file server ACCT_MAIN		Resolution Date: 10/26 Resolution Time: 11:30 am
User Signature indicating problem is resolved: Verbal approval by Phone, KRC		
Problem Description: Cannot run the Vendor Update Program in the Accounting System		
When Was Problem First Noticed? Today, but Sam hasn't ever run this program		
Other information about the problem: Can run Accounts Payable reports		
User estimate of criticality of the problem Moderate		
Intake person's estimate of criticality of the problem: Moderate		

Figure 9-3. Sample troubleshooting documentation with user signoff.

Appendix

Where to Get Product Information and Technical Support

Usually, the best way of getting technical support or product information for a data communications or networking product is to access it through the Internet. Typically, a vendor will have a home page identified by www.vendorname.com. This home page usually will have links to various products and technical support for these products.

If you are unable to locate a given product's Web site, you might want to try using an Internet search engine. Through a search engine, you can search for information about a product by typing in key words. Two of the most popular search engines can be accessed through www.yahoo.com and www.lycos.com.

If you still need help, there are several technical support indices. These indices have search engines to locate technical support information via key words. Using these indices, you can obtain freeware and free technical support information not tied to a specific vendor.

Three of the current technical support indices may be accessed by:

CMPnet's Tech Helper at www.techweb.com/helper/

PC-Help Online at www.pchelponline.com/

Software.Net's Vendor Support Directory at www.software.net/directory.htm

Appendix

Vendor Listing

Vendors of Communications-Related Hardware and Software

3Com Corp.

5400 Bayfront Plaza, Santa Clara, CA 95052

Telephone: 408-764-5000

Fax: 408-764-5001

Toll Free: 800-NET-3COM

E-mail: 3com@3mail.3com.com

Adaptec, Inc.

691 South Milpitas Blvd., Milpitas, CA 95035

Telephone: 408-945-8600

Fax: 408-262-2533

Toll Free: 800-655-3977

Alcatel Network Systems, Inc.

1225 North Alma Rd., Richardson, TX 75081

Telephone: 972-996-5000

Fax: 972-996-5409

Toll Free: 800-ALCATEL

Apple Computer, Inc.

1 Infinite Loop, Cupertino, CA 95014

Telephone: 408-996-1010

Fax: 408-974-5200

Appendix

Cabletron Systems, Inc.

35 Industrial Way, PO Box 5005, Rochester, NH 03866

Telephone: 603-332-9400

Fax: 603-337-2211

E-mail: sales@ctron.com

Cheyenne Software, Inc.

3 Expressway Plaza, Roslyn Heights, NY 11577

Telephone: 516-465-4000

Fax: 516-484-3446

Toll Free: 800-CHEYINC

Cisco Systems, Inc.

170 West Tasman Dr., San Jose, CA 95134

Telephone: 408-526-4000

Fax: 408-526-4100

Compaq Computer Corp.

PO Box 69200, Houston, TX 77269

Telephone: 281-370-0670

Fax: 281-514-1740

Dell Computer Corp.

2214 West Braker Ln., Austin, TX 78758

Telephone: 512-338-4400

Fax: 512-728-3653

Toll Free: 800-289-3355

Appendix

Digital Equipment Corporation

111 Powdermill Rd., Maynard, MA 01754

Telephone: 508-493-5111

Fax: 508-493-8780

Fujitsu Computer Products of America

2904 Orchard Pkwy., San Jose, CA 95134

Telephone: 408-432-6333

Fax: 408-894-1706

Toll Free: 800-626-4686

E-mail: info@fcpa.fujitsu.com

Hewlett-Packard Company

3000 Hanover St., Palo Alto, CA 94304

Telephone: 650-857-1501

Fax: 650-857-5518

Toll Free: 800-752-0900

Hitachi America, Ltd. / Computer Division

110 Summit Ave., Montvale, NJ 07645

Telephone: 201-573-0774

Toll Free: 800-225-1370

International Business Machines Corp.

New Orchard Rd., Armonk, NY 10504

Telephone: 914-499-1900

Fax: 914-499-6021

Appendix

Intel Corp.

PO Box 58119, Santa Clara, CA 95051

Telephone: 408-765-8080

Fax: 408-765-1402

Iomega Corp.

1821 West Iomega Way, Roy, UT 84067

Telephone: 801-778-1000

Fax: 801-778-3450

Logitech Inc.

6505 Kaiser Dr., Fremont, CA 94555

Telephone: 510-795-8500

Fax: 510-792-8901

Toll Free: 800-231-7717

Lotus Development Corp.

55 Cambridge Pkwy., Cambridge, MA 02142

Telephone: 617-577-8500

Fax: 617-693-1197

MCI Communications Corp.

1801 Pennsylvania Ave. N.W., Washington, DC 20006

Telephone: 202-872-1600

Fax: 202-887-2023

Toll Free: 800-289-0073

Appendix

Micron Electronics, Inc.

900 East Karcher Rd., Nampa, ID 83687

Telephone: 208-893-3434

Fax: 208-893-7395

Toll Free: 800-438-3343

Microsoft Corp.

One Microsoft Way, Redmond, WA 98052

Telephone: 425-882-8080

Fax: 425-936-7329

NEC America, Inc.

Corporate Center Dr., Suite 8, Melville, NY 11747

Telephone: 516-753-7000

Fax: 516-753-7041

Toll Free: 800-333-9549

E-mail: webmaster@nec.com

Netscape Communications Corp.

501 East Middlefield Rd., Mountain View, CA 94043

Telephone: 650-254-1900

Fax: 650-428-4091

E-mail: info@netscape.com

Network General Corp.

4200 Bohannon Dr., Menlo Park, CA 94025

Telephone: 650-473-2000

Fax: 650-327-2145

Toll Free: 800-SNIFFER

Appendix

NORTEL Broadband Networks

5555 Windward Pkwy. East, Bldg. B, Alpharetta, GA 30201

Telephone: 770-661-4000

Fax: 770-661-4784

Novell, Inc.

122 East 1700 South

Provo, UT 84606

800-453-1267

www.novell.com

Oracle Corp.

500 Oracle Pkwy., Redwood Shores, CA 94065

Telephone: 650-506-7000

Fax: 650-506-7200

Toll Free: 800-345-DBMS

Packard Bell NEC, Inc.

1 Packard Bell Way, Sacramento, CA 95826

Telephone: 916-388-0101

Fax: 916-388-1109

Raytheon E-Systems / Richardson

1301 East Collins Blvd., PO Box 831359

Richardson, TX 75081

Telephone: 972-470-2000

Fax: 972-470-2466

Toll Free: 800-933-5359

Appendix

Rockwell International Corp.

600 Anton Blvd., Suite 700, PO Box 5090

Costa Mesa, CA 92628

Telephone: 714-424-4546

Seagate Software, Inc. / Information Group

& Network Management Group

920 Disc Dr., Scotts Valley, CA 95066

Telephone: 408-439-2881

Fax: 408-342-4600

Storage Dimensions, Inc.

1656 McCarthy Blvd., Milpitas, CA 95035

Telephone: 408-954-0710

Fax: 408-944-1200

Sun Microsystems, Inc.

2550 Garcia Ave., Mountain View, CA 94043

Telephone: 650-960-1300

Fax: 650-969-9131

U.S. Robotice/3Com Corp. / Network Systems Division

1800 West Central Rd., Mount Prospect, IL 60056

Telephone: 847-797-6010

Toll Free: 800-USRCORP

Western Digital Corp.

8105 Irvine Center Dr., Irvine, CA 92718

Telephone: 714-932-5000

Fax: 714-932-6498

Toll Free: 800-832-4778

WorldCom, Inc.

515 East Amite St., Jackson, MS 39201

Telephone: 601-360-8600

Toll Free: 800-844-1009

E-mail: info@wcom.com

Xerox Corp.

PO Box 1600, Stamford, CT 06904

Telephone: 203-968-3000

Fax: 203-968-4566

Toll Free: 800-334-6200

Glossary

ASCII. The acronym for American Standard Code for Information Interchange. This is a standard code for the transmission of data within the U.S. Standard ASCII is composed of 128 characters in a 7-bit format.

Asynchronous. A communication that places data in discrete blocks that are surrounded by framing bits. These bits show the beginning and end of a block of data. These framing bits are sometimes called start and stop bits.

AUTOEXEC.BAT. The batch file on a DOS workstation that is used to automatically run various programs when the DOS workstation is activated.

AUTOEXEC.NCF. The server file that functions similarly to the AUTOEXEC.BAT file when a file server is activated.

Auto Load. A printer that is designated as an auto load printer is physically attached to a file server running PSERVER and is automatically activated when PSERVER is run.

Backup. A copy of the files, directories, and NDS Directory structure of a network.

Bandwidth. The capacity of a media (often a cable) to carry data.

Baseband. A network cable that has only one channel for carrying data signals.

Baud. The rate of data transmission. Specifically, baud refers to state changes per second onto which data can be encoded.

Bit. An abbreviation for binary digit. A bit is the smallest unit of data for the computer.

Bootable Partition. The partition of the hard drive that is designated for use in loading the computer's operating system into the computer when it is turned on.

Boot Disk. A disk used to load the computer's operating system into the computer when it is turned on.

Bridge. A device that divides a "too busy" LAN segment into two different collision domains.

Broadband. A network cable with several simultaneous channels of communication.

Glossary

Brouter. Hybrid devices that incorporate bridge and router technology. Brouters make decisions on whether a data packet uses a protocol that is routable. Then they route those that can be routed and bridge the rest.

Bulletin Board. The electronic bulletin board system consists of a computer that is used to store, retrieve, and catalog messages sent in by the general public through their modems.

Bus Topology. A physical layout of a LAN where all nodes are connected to a single cable.

Byte. A combination of 8 bits.

CAD. Computer-aided design.

CAPTURE. A NetWare utility program used to redirect output from a printer port on the workstation to a network printer.

CD-ROM. A compact disk reader that is used to read digitally recorded compact disks.

CD-ROM driver. The software that controls the functioning of a CD-ROM reader.

Cellular Radio. A form of high-frequency radio transmission where the signals are relayed from antennas that are spaced in strategic locations throughout metropolitan areas.

Channel Extender. A device that links remote stations directly to a host system and operates at high speeds. It functions like a small front end processor to connect remote work stations and computers to a host. It can support auxiliary devices, including printers, disk drives, and microcomputers.

Client 32. Novell's latest 32-bit client communications software. Versions exist for DOS/Windows, Windows 95, and Windows NT.

Client Computer. The computer that functions as a workstation requesting information from one or more file servers.

Cluster Controller. A cluster controller is a device that supports several terminals and the functions required to manage those terminals.

Coaxial Cable. A cable consisting of a single metal wire surrounded by insulation which is itself surrounded by a braided or foil outer shield.

CompuServe. A public, subscription-only information service. NetWire has traditionally been housed on CompuServe.

Concentrator. An intelligent line-sharing device that allows multiple devices to share communication circuits.

Glossary

Common Name. This is simply the name of the object without the names of any containers containing the object.

Computer. A electronic system that can store and process information under program control.

CONSOLE. The file server. Typically used to refer to the monitor and keyboard and console input and output devices.

Container. An NDS object that contains other objects.

Container Login Script. The login script associated with a container. This login script runs first for all users in a container.

Control Code. Special nonprinting codes that cause electronic equipment to perform specific actions.

Country Object. The object at the highest level in a Novell Directory Services Tree. This object represents a country and must be identified with a legal country code.

CPU. Central processing unit. The processor portion of the computer where the logic and control functions are performed.

CSMA/CD. Carrier Sense Multiple Access/Collision Detection. The method for media access for Ethernet networks. When a station wants to send data, it senses the line. If the line is open, it transmits. If a collision occurs, the stations waits a random amount of time and then reattempts transmission.

CX. Change context.

Data Communication. The transmission and receipt of data.

Device Driver. A software program that enables a network operating system and/or the workstation operating system to work with devices such as network adapters, disk controllers, and other devices.

Differential Backup. A backup that backs up all files that have changed since the last full backup.

Digital Line Expander. A device that allows users to concentrate a larger number of voice and data channels into the bandwidth of a standard communication channel by using hardware and software techniques that make use of the entire bandwidth capability of a standard voice circuit.

Directory Attributes. Access rights attached to each directory.

Directory Trustee Rights. Trustee assignments made at a directory level.

Disk Drivers. The software that controls the functioning of the hard disk on a file server

Glossary

Distinguished Name. The full name of an NDS object without regard for current context. The name begins with a period and contains the common name of the object and all containers back to the (ROOT) object, each name separated by a period.

DOS. Disk operating system. This term is usually a shortened notation for MS-DOS by Microsoft and PC-DOS by IBM.

Drive Mapping. An association of a virtual drive letter to a volume and directory location on a file server.

Driver. A memory resident program usually used to control a hardware device.

Effective Rights. The combination of directly assigned and inherited rights that determine what a user can do at a particular location in the file system or at a particular location in the NDS directory tree.

Encryption. The transformation of data from meaningful code into a meaningless stream of bits. To make this transformation, the data is sent through an encrypting algorithm with the result being the set of meaningless bits. To see the data in its original format, the scrambled data is sent back through the algorithm which in essence now works in "reverse," restoring the original message.

Enterprise Network. A network larger than a single file server type network that addresses the needs of a large business, often referred to as an enterprise.

Feasibility Study. The study performed in order to define the existing problem clearly and to determine whether a network is operationally feasible for the type of organization that it plans to serve.

Fiber-Optic Cable. A data transmitting cable that consists of plastic or glass fibers, surrounded by cladding. Data is transmitted over these fibers via light.

File Attributes. Access rights attached to each file.

Full Backup. A backup that backs up everything on a file server.

File Server. A computer running a network operating system that enables other computers to access its files.

File Trustee Rights. Trustee assignments assigned at the file level.

Full Duplex. In full duplex communication, data is transmitted and received over the same cable simultaneously.

Gateway. A device that acts as a translator between totally different systems.

Group. A collection of users.

Glossary

Group Rights. Rights given to a collection of users via the group object.

Half Duplex. In half duplex communication, the terminal transmits and receives data over the same cable, but only one way at a time.

Handshaking. A set of commands recognized by the sending and receiving stations that control the flow of data transmission.

Host. In terminal/mainframe or terminal/minicomputer types of communication, a host is the mainframe computer or minicomputer. When the term host is used in a TCP/IP network, a host is any device, computer or otherwise, that has an IP address.

Incremental Backup. A backup that backs up only those files that have changed since the last full or incremental backup.

Inherited Rights. Rights inherited from a container or directory above.

Inherited Rights Filter. A filter attached to a directory or file that determines which rights can be inherited from above.

Interface. A communication channel that is used to connect a computer to an external device.

Internetwork Packet Exchange (IPX). One of the data transmission protocols used by NetWare.

Interrupt. An IBM PC or PC compatible central processing unit utilizes interrupt numbers for communication with the various devices attached to the PC. Only one device can utilize a given interrupt number, 0 to 15.

Intruder Lockout. A method for locking out a person who repetitively attempts to log in with a known user identification and an illegal password.

IPX Internal Network Number. The 8-digit hexadecimal number that uniquely identifies a file server.

LAN. Local area network. A network that typically encompasses a small geographical area. (This distinction is blurring as the quality and cost of worldwide communications improves.)

LAN Drivers. The software that controls the functioning of the network interface card.

Leaf Object. A object that represents an actual resource in a network. A leaf object can be contained in an Organization object or in an Organization Unit object. A leaf object cannot contain another object.

Glossary

Life Cycle. The life cycle of a network is a representation of the phase through which a network proceeds before it becomes obsolete and ready for replacement.

Line Monitor. A device used to diagnose problems on a communication line or link. It attaches to a communication circuit, and a digital format of the data flowing through the circuit is displayed on a screen, printed to paper, or stored on an auxiliary device for further analysis.

Line Splitter. A device, similar to a port-sharing device, normally found at the remote end of a communication line, where the terminal or workstation is located while port-sharing devices are normally located at the host end of the communication line.

Login Restrictions. Restrictions covering such things as number of concurrent logins, account expiration date, and account disabled flag. Restrictions are stored per user in NDS.

Login Script. A login script contains commands that are executed when a user logs in. These commands set up the environment for the user usually through drive mappings and printer capture statements.

Mainframe. A computer that is the central computer systems that perform data processing functions for a business or industry.

MAN. A metropolitan area network is a network within a metropolitan area.

Manual Load. A printer that is designated as manual load must be activated by running NPRINTER.EXE if the printer is attached to a workstation or by running NPRINTER.NLM if the printer is attached to a remote file server.

Memory Address. Each network interface card usually uses at least some portion of the RAM memory of the PC itself for normal operation.

Microcomputer. A microcomputer is a general-purpose computer with a central processing unit. Microcomputers are computers like mainframes, but they are usually smaller and utilize a microprocessor for their central processing units.

Microwave. A line of sight communication that utilizes radio wave for communication between a sending and receiving station. Sending and receiving stations may either be physically on the earth or satellites orbiting the earth.

Modem. An electronic device that converts (modulates) digital data from a computer into analog signals that the phone equipment can understand. Additionally, the modem converts (demodulates) analog data into digital data.

Glossary

Multiplexer. A device that supports the transmission of multiple signals over a single medium by replacing multiple low-speed transmission lines with a single high-speed transmission line or by combining several frequencies that do not overlap into one transmission.

NDS. Novell Directory Services. A tree-structured Directory of objects with properties that allows for a single log on to a Novell NetWare 4.11 system.

NetAdmin. The DOS-based text program that is used to administer NDS.

NetWire. Novell's support forum on CompuServe. Similar information is available on Novell's Internet Web site.

NetWare. A network operating system produced by Novell, Inc.

NetWare Administrator. NW Admin. The graphical version of a program that is used to administer the NDS tree.

Network. A data communications system connecting multiple devices such as computers, printers, etc.

Network Address. A hexadecimal number used to identify a network cabling system.

Network Address Restrictions. These restrictions control which stations can be used by a given user to log in.

NIC. The network interface card. A circuit board that is installed in the file servers and the workstations that make up the network. It allows the hardware in the network to send and receive data over the transmission media connecting workstations and servers.

Network Management. A plan to prevent network problems where possible and to prepare for network problems that will most likely occur. The plan must address monitoring and controlling hard disk space, monitoring network workload and performance, maintaining user login information and workstation information, monitoring and resetting network devices, performing regular maintenance on software and data files stored in the servers, and making regular backups of data and programs stored in the servers.

Network Modeling. The process of simulating a network prior to creating it to determine its expected operating parameters such as response time.

Network Operating System. A network operating system is the grouping of software programs that are used to control a file server and a client computer and the communications between them.

Network Security. Network security maintains control over the data stored and transmitted by the network with the major goals of preventing computer crime and data loss.

Novell. A company based in Provo, Utah, that produces the NetWare network operating system.

Novell Support Connection/NSEPro. Novell's subscription support CD-ROM service.

NPRINTER. The program that allows other workstations to print to a workstation's printer or to a printer attached to a file server not running PSERVER. NPRINTER.EXE runs on a workstation with a remote printer attached, and NPRINTER.NLM runs on a file server with a remote printer attached.

Object. An item in the NDS tree such as a container or a leaf object like a user.

Object Rights. Trustee rights assigned to an NDS object.

Optical Fiber. Optical fiber consists of thin glass fibers that can carry information at frequencies in the visible light spectrum.

Organization Object. The Organization object falls under the Country object and above the Organizational Unit object in a Novell Directory Services tree. An Organization object can contain leaf objects and Organizational Unit objects and aliases to these objects. It cannot contain another Organization object.

Organizational Unit Object. An Organizational Unit Object must be contained in either an Organization object or another Organizational Unit object. It can also contain leaf objects.

OSI Model. A 7 layer networking communications model created by the International Standards Organization with the purpose of making communication between heterogeneous devices easier.

Packet. A discrete unit of data bits transmitted over a network.

Parallel Port. A port, normally located on the back or a computer or a Centronics interface on a printer or other device, that transmits parallel communication. Using parallel communication, 8 bits of data are transmitted simultaneously.

Password. A secret word used to authenticate a user.

Password Restrictions. These restrictions cover password requirements and what a user can and cannot do with his or her own password.

PBX. A private telephone branch exchange (PBX), normally leased or owned by a company, to connect telephones, terminals and computers within the company.

Glossary

PCONSOLE. A NetWare utility program used to configure and operate print servers. Its name stands for Print Server Console.

PDN. A network using packet-switching techniques for communication. Packet switching is a store-and-forward data transmission technique in which messages are split into small segments called packets.

Port Address. The memory address in the local PCs utilized for communication with the central processing unit.

Printer. The NDS object representing the printer itself. It is connected to a print server and to one or more print queues.

Print Queues. Definitions of the order and location in which a file is to be printed on the network.

Print Server. A computer program, PSERVER.NLM, that periodically checks the print queues to service completed print jobs by sending them to the appropriate printer.

Profile Login Script. The login script associated with a profile object. This object is normally associated with various users to form a group login script.

Property. A characteristic of an object in NDS.

Property Rights. Trustee rights assigned to one or more properties of an NDS object.

Protocol. A set of rules to be followed for two electronic devices to communicate.

Protocol Converter. A device that connects electronic devices with differing protocols so they can communicate with each other.

PSERVER. The print server program.

Public Network. Public networks have standard interfaces that allow almost any type of computer or terminal to connect to other computers or terminals.

RAM. Random access memory.

Relative Distinguished Name. The partial NDS name of an object relative to current context.

Remote Printing. Printing to a printer that is not attached to the file server running PSERVER.NLM.

Response Time. The time that expires between sending an inquiry from a workstation or terminal and receiving the response back at the workstation.

Glossary

Ring Topology. A network configuration that connects all nodes into a logical ring-like structure.

ROM. Read-only memory.

Router. A device, working at the network layer of the OSI model, that determines the most efficient data path between two networks.

RS-232 Interface. A serial communications standard commonly used for modem and other serial communication.

Satellite. A device which orbits the earth and is used to relay microwave transmission.

SBACKUP. Novell's backup utility.

Search Drive. A network drive mapping that functions similar to a directory listed in a path statement on a DOS workstation.

Security Equal To. A user may be made security equal to another uses. This means that the user has the security assigned to the other use as well as the security assigned to the user himself.

Selected Property Rights. Rights assigned to specific properties of an NDS object rather than to all properties of the object.

Serial Port. A port, normally located on the back or a computer that transmits serial communication. Using serial communication, 1 bit of data is transmitted at a time.

Server Computer. The computer that functions as the file server for a network.

Single Login. Single login allows a user to have access to resources throughout an enterprise network through NDS.

SNA. IBM's proprietary Systems Network Architecture.

Software. Programs used to control the functioning of a computer or other device.

Star Topology. A network configuration where each node is connected by a single cable link to a central location, called a hub.

STARTUP.NCF. The server boot file that functions similarly to the CONFIG.SYS file on a DOS workstation when a server is activated. The STARTUP.NCF file must, at minimum, contain the drivers for the hard drive(s) in the file server.

Synchronous. A method of communication using a time interval and a limited number of control characters to distinguish between transmitted blocks of data.

Glossary

TCP/IP. A set of networking standards that grew from the Department of Defense initiatives in the early 1970s to interconnect systems made by different vendors. TCP/IP is now the underlying communications protocol for the Internet.

Telecommuting. The process of working from home via use of a telecommunications connection to an employer's computer systems.

Terminal. A term usually used to describe an electronic input station with no processing power that provides input to a central computer. The word terminal has become recently become more generic, often referring to input stations such as PCs that do have processing power.

The Internet. The worldwide network interconnecting computer systems and devices such that global communication can occur. The underlying protocol for the Internet is TCP/IP.

Token. The data packet used to carry information on LANs using the ring topology.

Topology. The manner in which nodes are connected on a LAN.

Transmission Medium. The physical means for communication between a sender and a receiver.

Troubleshooting Model. An organized methodology for troubleshooting a problem.

Trustee. A user or group that is given rights to the file system or to NDS.

Trustee Rights. Rights given to users or groups to access file system directories or NDS on the file servers.

Twisted Pair. Wire encased in plastic covering and twisted together to minimize interference and crosstalk. The cables are twisted in pairs because the electrical effect of one current is canceled by the electrical effect of the other, thereby reducing the amount of interference that the signal is subjected to. The signals from one pair of cables are prevented from interfering with the signals of another pair, a type of interference that is sometimes called crosstalk.

Uninterruptible Power Supply. A device that keeps computers running after a power failure, providing power from batteries for a short period of time.

User Login Script. Login script information specific to a user's requirements.

Value. A value is the current meaning of a property of an NDS object.

Video Conferencing. Conferencing that occurs through simultaneous, realtime video and audio transmission between two physically separate locations.

Virus. A computer virus is an executable computer program that propagates itself, using other programs as carriers, and sometimes modifies itself during or after replication. It is intended to perform some unwanted function on the computer system attached to the network.

VREPAIR. Novell's utility for repairing a volume that is structurally corrupt.

Volume. The highest level of the directory structure on a Novell file server. This level is often considered equivalent to a drive letter on a local computer.

Wide Area Network. A network that encompasses a large geographical area.

Workstation. A computer attached to a network.

X.25. A communication protocol used on public data networks.

Index

A
Auto Load 155
AUTOEXEC.NCF 27

B
backups 202
bootable 24

C
capture 164-166
client 22
client32 22, 40-45, 52
common name 56
CompuServe 211
container 152
container login script 79
context 54
country object 52
current context 55
CX 58

D
default login script 81
differential backup 205
directory attributes 118-120, 131
directory trustee rights 112
disk drivers 27
distinguished name 56

E
effective rights 133, 180
enterprise network 50
environment 70

F
file attributes 117
file server 116
file trustee rights 112
full backup 203

G
groups 77, 121, 137-139

I
incremental backup 203
identification 70
inherited rights 115. 180
inherited rights filter 115
installation 30
interrupt number 28
intruder lockout 77
IPX internal network number 26

L
LAN Drivers 28
leaf object 53
login restrictions 73
login time restrictions 73
login script 75, 77-93

M
Manual Load 155
mappings 9-11, 89
memory address 29

N
NETADMIN 58
NetWare Administrator 58-59
NetWare DOS Requester 38
NetWire 208
network address restrictions 75
network interface card 4
NIC see network interface card
Novell Directory Services 13
Novell Support Connection 218
nprinter 163-164
NSEPro, see Novell Support Connection

O
object 50
object rights 13, 176-177
open data-link interface 5
Organization 53
Organizational Unit Object 53

P
partition 24
password 110, 124-125
password restrictions 73, 111
print queue 146-148
print queue operator 157
print queue user 157
print server 149
print server operator 162
print server user 162
profile login script 80
Properties 50
property rights 13-14, 176-177
pserver 155, 163, 170

R
Relative distinguished name 56-57
[ROOT] 52

S
SBACKUP 206
Search drive 10
security equal to 77, 184
server 2, 12, 22
STARTUP.NCF 27

T
Troubleshooting Model 460
trustee 259-260
trustee rights 11-13, 112-114

U
user login script 81

V
volume 7
VREPAIR 222